A COMMENTARY

ON THE

New Testament Epistles

BY

DAVID LIPSCOMB

EDITED, WITH ADDITIONAL NOTES,

BY

J. W. SHEPHERD

VOLUME III

Second Corinthians
AND
Galatians

GOSPEL ADVOCATE CO.

Nashville, Tenn. 37202

1989

Complete Set ISBN 0-89225-000-3
This Volume ISBN 0-89225-008-9

COMMENTARY ON THE SECOND
EPISTLE TO THE CORINTHIANS

PREFACE.

The reception of the volumes on Romans and First Corinthians by thoughtful and competent Bible students is very gratifying, and has encouraged the publishers to make arrangements with competent brethren to write on the Gospels and Revelation, with the hope of publishing a commentary on the whole of the New Testament. The volume on Matthew is now ready for the printer, and that on Mark is nearing completion, and the other volumes will be pushed forward with as much rapidity as consistent with accuracy and good work.

Just here I deem it necessary to call attention to the fact that this commentary is intended for the *people,* and only secondarily for scholars. It, therefore, avoids, so far as consistent with the demands of exegesis, the use of Greek words and of elaborate criticisms on the original. Pains have been taken to make prominent such points in the epistle, and such lessons as promised to make a deep impression on the religious sentiments and daily life of the reader.

While the matter of the work is arranged with a view to its being used as a work of reference, much pain has been taken to adapt it to consecutive reading. To those who may attempt to read it consecutively, and such readers are especially desired, I suggest the propriety of uniformly reading the text of each paragraph before reading the comments which belong to it. By so doing the thought will be more easily grasped.

I especially call attention to the fact that the American Standard Revised Version is the text used. It is recognized as the best by men who are entitled to speak with authority —by the leaders of the foremost universities, colleges, theological seminaries, Bible training schools, and publishers of Sunday school literature. It embodies the knowledge of all scientific discoveries in Bible lands up to the time it was made. It is recognized as the best version of the scriptures in any language, because it was made by the greatest Biblical scholars in the world at the time it was produced, and since that time none greater have arisen.

A proper presentation of any subject, according to the methods of common thought, requires a formal designation of its natural divisions. Such designation was not made by the ancient writers, but is an invention of modern times. The division of the Bible into chapters and verses was intended merely to facilitate references, and in many instances quite arbitrary. These divisions have become indispensable, but they should be so printed as to make them only a convenience; and the natural divisions of each book should be restored. In order to this end, the text in this commentary has been distributed into paragraphs. The larger divisions called sections, each including a group of closely-related paragraphs, are also indicated in the notes by proper headings. In addition to these smaller divisions there is a more general division of the matter in nearly every book of the Bible into what is called "Parts." It is necessary to observe these divisions in order to get an intelligible appreciation of the epistle studied and, therefore, they are used in these volumes.

As I stated in the preface to the *Commentary on Romans,* I have added the notes inclosed in brackets []. They neither are nor claim to be original. They have been accumulated from sermons, lectures, commentaries, editorials—in fact, from every source available. These notes I have freely used, the object being to get the thought into the mind and life of the reader.

If life and strength of body and mind permit, I hope to have the next volume—Ephesians, Philippians, and Colossians—ready for publication at an early date.

                                                    J. W. SHEPHERD.

Nashville, Tennessee, April 15, 1936.

CONTENTS

INTRODUCTION TO SECOND CORINTHIANS.

I. OCCASION OF WRITING.

It is generally agreed among scholars that Paul wrote the first epistle to the Corinthians while at Ephesus, about the time of the Passover, 57 A.D. He proposed to remain there till Pentecost, and then go to Corinth. But the tumult precipitated by Demetrius forced him to flee to Troas. In the meantime Titus had been sent to Corinth to learn the state of things and adjust, if possible, the difficulties that disturbed the church and even threatened its existence, and to further the collection for the poor saints in Judæa. Amid great anxiety and restless apprehension (5: 6), Paul awaited at Troas for the return of Titus. His devotion to the cause of Christ would not suffer him to remain idle. He says: "A door was opened unto me in the Lord." (2: 12.) It is probable that at this time the church was planted there. How long he remained is not known, but obviously for some time. Weeks passed, and Titus did not arrive, and Paul suffered all the pangs of hope deferred. (2: 13.) He passed on to Macedonia, but even there the deep depression felt at Troas continued. He says: "When we were come into Macedonia our flesh had no relief, but we were afflicted on every side; without were fightings, within were fears." (7: 5.) The final arrival of Titus served in a great measure to lift the burden and calm his anxiety.

The occasion of writing this epistle was the reception of the tidings from Corinth. He was very solicitous touching the reception that had been accorded his epistle. (2: 3, 4, 9; 7: 8.) If we thoughtfully ponder the stern force with which he wrote (1 Cor. 4: 8-21; 5: 1-8; 11: 17-22; 15: 35-36), we will find little difficulty in accounting for his uneasiness and dejection. His emphatic rebuke of the factional spirit prevailing in the church was enough in itself to excite his deep solicitude for the issue. For aught he knew, the effect might serve to intensify party feeling instead of allaying it. He was now well aware that his apostolic authority was denied, that his motives were impugned, and that his character for candor was assailed by the faction. With these thoughts in his mind, is it any wonder that he awaited the outcome with the utmost apprehension?

The report brought by Titus was in the main favorable. The majority of the church had bowed submissively to his exhortations and admonitions, and had earnestly set about correcting the excesses and abuses he had so faithfully exposed. (1: 13, 14; 7: 9, 15, 16.) The Judaizing faction, however, whose animosity was aroused by his solemn rebuke, were doing all in their power to destroy his influence in the church. They were deprecating his authority, misrepresenting his motives, and conduct: even using his epistle to bring charges against him as having failed to keep his promise to visit them, and of having adopted an authoritative style of writing little in unison, as they alleged, with the contemptibleness of his personable appearance and speech. (10: 10.)

II. PLACE OF WRITING.

There is no ground for supposing that the epistle was written at Philippi as commonly imagined. Such a supposition is itself very improbable. He announces to the Corinthians the generosity which had been the result of God's grace given among the churches of Macedonia. (8: 1.) It is not at all likely that he would have made such announcement, if he had not already visited those churches. All that can certainly be said is that the epistle was written at one of the Macedonian churches; more probably at the last visited than at the first. The principal of those churches were Philippi, Thessalonica, and Berea. We learn from 1 Thess. 2: 17, 18 how anxious Paul was to visit the Thessalonian church, and in the absence of all details respecting this journey (Acts 20: 1, 2), we may conclude that he would spend some time in Thessalonica, where he would have time to write the epistle.

III. TIME OF WRITING.

The date may be thus ascertained: It was written after the riot of Demetrius at Ephesus, which occurred in the spring of 57 A.D. (1: 8.) Paul then traces his passage from Ephesus, through Troas, to Macedonia (2: 12, 13; 7: 5), where he was engaged in making a collection for the saints in Judæa (8: 1);

and the collection was still proceeding at the time of writing (9: 1, 2). Titus returned to Corinth to continue the collection among the Corinthians, and prepare them for the reception of Paul himself. (8: 6, 17; 9: 3-5.) Paul alludes to a revelation made to him fourteen years before (12: 2); and as the vision occurred when he was at Jerusalem at the Passover, 44 A.D., the date of the epistle, under all the circumstances, must be referred to the latter part of the year 57.

IV. SALIENT POINTS IN THE LIFE OF PAUL IN THE EPISTLE.

The Judaizers, who occupy a prominent place in the epistle were those who dealt with the word of God in the spirit of dishonest tradesmen (2: 17), it was they who came to Corinth with letters of commendation (3: 1), and Paul's charges against them show that some of their methods were as odious as their gospel was false. It was another gospel, different from Paul's, a gospel with another spirit, that they preached (11: 4); and with a different gospel went a different and lower moral standard—they had no standard beyond themselves, and so were guilty of ridiculous and immoderate boasting. (10: 12.) After Paul had done the pioneer work, they came upon the scene like evil spirits (11: 15), at once appropriating and perverting the results of his labors (10: 16), but taking good care to break no new ground for the gospel on their own account. As he advanced the indictment took a form of great severity calling them "false apostles, deceitful workers, fashioning themselves into apostles of Christ. And no marvel; for even Satan fashioneth himself into an angel of light. It is no great thing therefore if his ministers also fashion themselves as ministers of righteousness; whose end shall be according to their works." (11: 13-15.)

What had they said or done to call forth such a vehement retort? They accused him of determining his life and conduct by unspiritual motives of walking "according to the flesh." (10: 2.) They admitted that "his letters are weighty and strong," but used this very circumstance to disparage him, saying, "His bodily presence is weak, and his speech of no account." (10: 10.) His escape from Damascus over the wall was apparently used to make him ridiculous. (11: 31-33.)

Yet, coward as he was, he liked to play the tyrant. (1: 24.) They taunted him with his lack of rhetorical skill of which the Greeks made so much. (11: 6.) They argued that he could be no apostle, for he refused to accept support in return for his services. (11: 7.) Did not this refusal betray an uneasy conscience that he was no apostle? Nay, worse—they were mean enough to insinuate that he knew how to compensate himself for any lack he might suffer through self-denying policy; he was not alone helping himself to the collection—if not directly, at any rate, through his agents. (12: 16-18.) Ineffective, avaricious, cunning, a tyrant, a coward, a cheat— as such did his opponents choose to picture Paul; and when we see how venomous was their caricature, we can hardly be surprised at the indignant vehemence of his reply.

How very different is the real Paul! It is a dishonor to the human family that such a man as he should have been accused of crooked dealing. Every one feels that his words palpitate with sincerity—they are spoken in the sight of God (2: 17; 12: 19), and he expects them to appeal to a good conscience (4: 2; 5: 11). If he modifies or reverses his plan which he has formed, there is, we may be sure, deep and satisfactory reason for the change—however his conduct may be of misconstruction, however liable to the charge of vacillation, his life, like his Master's, is marked by an unswerving inner consistency. He was not a man who had "yes" and "no" upon his lips or in his heart at the same time; he was a man of honor and decision. (1: 15-19.) And of courage, too, in spite of the mean insinuations of his detractors. In spite of his manifold sufferings and sorrows, he does not lose heart, his sense of the glory of the dispensation of which he was a minister and of the yet brighter glory that awaited him bore him up. He claimed to be always of good courage (5: 6, 8), and the varied and terrible that he faced without flinching for the gospel's sake would more than justify the most extravagant claims—dangers on land, on rivers, and on the seas (11: 25, 26). Only a man of unbounded devotion to the cause which he embraced would have voluntarily suffered for it hardships so numerous and terrible—hunger, thirst, cold, imprisonment, stripes, stoning, shipwreck (11: 20-26), to say nothing of continual exposure to

misunderstanding, treachery, and cruel forms of persecution
(6: 4-9). He truthfully describes his life as continual "bearing about in the body the dying of Jesus." (4: 10, 11.) In another aspect it is a warfare, with the mighty weapons of the
Spirit he fearlessly faces those high things, in which Judaism
abounded, that are exalted against the knowledge of God, and
leads them captive. (10: 4-6.)

In all this high enterprise, he was sustained by a profound
sense of his mission as "an apostle of Christ Jesus through the
will of God." (1: 1.) His God-given commission was to carry
the gospel to the Gentiles, to Syria, to Greece, and beyond
Greece (10: 16), and to the farthest western confines of the
world (Rom. 15: 24). He moved from place to place on his
triumphant missionary career (2: 14), conscious that he had
been enabled by the grace of God to be a competent minister
of Christ (3: 5, 6), and he sees the success of his work with a
deep and humble satisfaction. To the Corinthians he says:
"Ye are our epistle, written in our hearts, known and read of
all men" (3: 2); he needs and asks for no higher commendation than that. He gloried in them (7: 14; 9: 3), and is over-
joyed when, by their exhibition of true Christian conduct on a
critical occasion, they have shown to the world that he but
spoke the truth (7: 4, 14).

He was a man of the intensest sympathy. He shared the
weakness of the weak, and burned with indignant shame
when a brother was caught in the snare of sin. (11: 2, 9.) He
loved those whom he had brought to Christ (11: 11), and was
ever ready to spend and be spent for their souls (12: 15); and
never was there a baser slander than which it was hinted that
he had helped himself to money which they had collected for
the poor (12: 16-18)—"I seek not yours, but you" (12: 14).
The wonderful delicacy of his mind came out in the plea
which he made for a liberal collection for the poor saints in
Judæa. Money is never once mentioned. The contribution
he solicited was set in the light of Christian privilege (chs. 8,
9), its spiritual value was glorified as a bond of union between
the Gentile and Jewish Christians (9: 12-14), and the Corinthian liberality was stimulated by being brought into comparison with the infinite condescension of Christ in exchanging

for their sakes the heavenly riches for the poverty of an
earthly career (8:9).

He spoke to his brethren out of the fullness of his warm
open heart (6: 11); but when the occasion demanded it, he
was a master of irony. Disappointed at the ease with which
the Corinthians had allowed themselves to be imposed upon
by their opponents, he ironically bespeaks an indulgent hearing for himself as, like a foolish one, he recounts his claims;
their patience with his opponents showed that they tolerated
foolish ones with pleasure and well they might, as they were
so wise themselves. (11: 16-19.) He was a brave man, he admits elsewhere, but he did not have the courage to compare
himself with his opponents; in boasting he knew well that he
was no match for them. (10: 12-16.) He sarcastically suggests that he was perhaps guilty of a sin in accepting no re-
muneration from the Corinthians for his services in proclaiming the gospel to them (11: 7), and asked them to forgive him
this wrong (12: 13).

It is clear from these expressions that the tension between
Paul and the Judaizing faction was tense. Any resentment of
his authority that may have been created by his peremptory
order regarding the incestuous man (1 Cor. 5: 1-8) must have
been deeply intensified by the Judaizers, and this accounts, in
part, for the large space devoted to them (chs. 10-13). He
had, as with the Galatians, to assert vigorously and unambig-
uously that apostolic authority which had been conferred
upon him by the Lord himself, and whose ultimate object was
the building up of the church. (10: 8; 13: 10.) He had no alternative but to deal severely with his opponents, for the
honor and the safety were at stake. They were preaching another gospel (11: 4) which was no gospel (Gal. 1: 6, 7); and
the deep contrast between the two dispensations represented
respectively by himself and them was present to his mind, and
stung him into an assault upon all who would wantonly rob
the gospel of its freedom and glory (3: 1-18). He spoke with
plainness, with fearlessness, and with power, as a minister of
the new covenant (3: 6) and an ambassador on behalf of
Christ (5: 20). The love of Christ constrained him (5: 14)—
Christ who is the great realization of the promises of God (1:

20), Christ who, though he was rich, yet for our sakes became poor (8: 9), Christ, in whom the old things are passed away, and behold! they are become new (5: 17), Christ, the Emancipator, the Redeemer, the glorious Lord (3: 18). It was this sublime conception of Christ that explains the earnestness of Paul's propaganda, his solicitude for the churches that were threatened by the insidious sophistries of the Judaizers, and his uncompromising assault upon them.

The contrast certainly was very remarkable between the physical weakness and the spiritual power of Paul. The precious treasure, as he said, was contained in an earthen vessel. (4: 7.) Beaten and bruised as he had been by land and on the sea, worn down by his ceaseless anxiety for the churches he had founded (11: 28), suffering from an incurable infirmity which impeded the progress of his work (12: 7-9), he literally was dying daily, and even may have looked like a dying man. Yet what a superb impression the epistle leaves upon us of spiritual power. He could accept with joy the refusal of an answer to the most deeply earnest prayers of his life, because his unremoved infirmity gave the most abundant scope to the operation of the grace of Christ within him. (12: 8-10.)

He enjoyed unique spiritual experiences, in which the other world was as close and real to him as this, and the glories of Paradise were as vivid as the thorn that tormented his flesh (12: 1-10); but he was fully conscious of the special temptations to pride that accompanied special gifts and experiences, and he had the grace to interpret his infirmity sent to prevent his being "exalted overmuch" (12: 7). He felt that though the outward man was decaying, the inward man was being renewed day by day (4: 16), and he learned to face the prospects of his own death with quietness and confidence. In the face of death, then, as of danger, he was always of good courage. (5: 6-8.) He saw beyond the light affliction to the eternal weight of glory. (4: 17.)

COMMENTARY ON THE SECOND EPISTLE TO THE CORINTHIANS.

SECTION ONE.

PAUL'S VINDICATION OF HIS APOSTOLIC CHARACTER AND COURSE OF LIFE ACCOMPANIED WITH EARNEST APPEALS AND ADMONITIONS.

1: 1 to 7: 16.

1. THE APOSTOLIC GREETING.
1: 1, 2.

1 Paul, an apostle of Christ Jesus through the will of God, and Timothy
¹our brother, unto the church of God which is at Corinth, with all the saints

¹Gr. *the brother.*

---

1 **Paul, an apostle of Christ Jesus**—This is Paul's title of authority, and in all his epistles but five he uses it. To the Philippians he uses only the "servants of Christ Jesus" for himself and Timothy. To the Thessalonians there is no title of authority given. To Philemon he calls himself "a prisoner of Christ Jesus." If there is any question of his authority he lays strong emphasis on his apostleship. Jesus chose "twelve, whom also he named apostles." (Luke 6: 13.) They were sent forth by Jesus on the business of the kingdom. Though not one of the twelve, Paul was chosen and sent by Jesus Christ no less than they. (Acts 9: 15, 16; 22: 14, 15; 26: 16-18; Gal. 1: 1.) On this he insists with great emphasis. In the Corinthian church certain evil workers had been opposing. He calls them "false apostles, deceitful workers, fashioning themselves into apostles of Christ." (11: 13.)

through the will of God,—Because of these "false apostles" he lays great stress on his credentials. He is an apostle of Christ, not self-appointed, but under God's appointment.

and Timothy our brother,—In these introductory phrases Paul unites with his own name that of Timothy. [Of all Paul's fellow laborers Timothy was the most precious to his heart. It was under the preaching of Paul that he became a

that are in the whole of Achaia: 2 Grace to you and peace from God our
Father and the Lord Jesus Christ.

Christian and soon became active in the Lord's work, so that
a few years later when Paul was on his second missionary
journey and again visited Lystra he found him "well reported
of by the brethren." (Acts 16: 2.) Already the voice of prophecy had indicated that he was destined to special service.
(1 Tim. 1: 18; 4: 14.) Paul therefore determined to take him
with him, and since then he had been Paul's closest companion. By his own presence and preaching he had aided in es-
tablishing the church at Corinth. He was with Paul at Ephesus, whence he was sent to Corinth to correct abuses there (1
Cor. 4: 17), yet for some reason there was a possibility that he
might not reach there (1 Cor. 16: 10); but in any event he
was with Paul in Macedonia when this epistle was written.
He had ability, vigor, and moral courage. His sincerity and
sympathy won the affection of Paul, who calls him "my true
child in faith" (1 Tim. 1: 2); and testifies that his service had
been "as a child serveth a father, so he served with me in fur-
therance of the gospel" (Phil. 2: 22).]

unto the church of God which is at Corinth,—The church as
God ordained it is a company of obedient believers bound together by faith in Jesus Christ to encourage and strengthen
each other, and spread the gospel through the world. A common faith in Christ is the strongest and most permanent bond
of union among men. The mission of the church on earth is
to unite the believers in Christ in one body, each member
seeking his own highest good in promoting the good of others,
and the crowning glory of God in saving sinners.

with all the saints—All Christians are called saints, or sanctified ones, in that they are all set apart to the service of God.
The church at Corinth were all addressed as saints, although
some of them were unworthy. There are degrees of sanctification, just as there are degrees of Christian knowledge and
fidelity to Christ. The growth in sanctification and holiness is
to be attained by a study of, and obedience to, the word of
God. An increase in knowledge and fidelity is to be gained by

a constant and persistent study of God's will and a daily effort
to bring oneself into obedience to that will.

that are in the whole of Achaia:—[One of Paul's methods
in his evangelistic work was to reach the surrounding country
from some city as a strategic center. As early as A.D. 48, at
Antioch in Pisidia, on his first missionary tour, it is said:
"The word of the Lord was spread abroad throughout all the
region." (Acts 13: 49.) Doubtless all Achaia in a similar way
heard the word of the Lord, resulting in many becoming
Christians. There were Christians at Athens (Acts 17: 34),
and at Cenchreae (Rom. 16: 1). Although the epistle is addressed to the church at Corinth, Paul includes in the salutation all the Christians in the province of which Corinth was
the capital. They were certainly associated with the brethren
in Corinth in some intimate way and must have known something of the difficulties that had arisen there.]

2 **Grace to you and peace from God our Father and the
Lord Jesus Christ.**—This is the usual prayer to God for grace
to be with them, and the peace that God our Father and the
Lord Jesus Christ bestows on them that serve him. [Grace
and peace are comprehensive words. They are rich in historical associations. The priestly benedictions (Num. 6: 22-26)
were similar in thought; but they have been wonderfully enriched in the dispensation of God's love through Christ. In
him grace is included in all God's gracious giving. It is his
consummation of the unspeakable gift (9: 15), and of all the
blessings that come to man through him. On the other hand,
peace is the harmony and satisfaction which come into a life
that has accepted God's grace, is reconciled to God, and rests
in the assurance of the forgiveness of sin. In this sense Jesus
Christ is the peacemaker. Grace and peace sum up all the
blessings in Christ, the wealth of God's gracious giving, the results of man's full acceptance.]

2. INTRODUCTORY REFLECTIONS TOUCHING THE TWOFOLD FELLOWSHIP OF CHRISTIANS IN SUFFERING AND IN COMFORT.

1: 3-11.

3 Blessed *be* ²the God and Father of our Lord Jesus Christ, the Father of mercies and God of all comfort; 4 who comforteth us in all our affliction, that we may be able to comfort them that are in any affliction, through the

²Or, *God and the Father* See Rom. 15. 6 marg.

3 Blessed be the God and Father of our Lord Jesus Christ, —[The word "blessed" here expresses gratitude and adoration. The phrase is equivalent to praised be God, or is an expression of thanksgiving. It is the usual formula of praise (Eph. 1: 3), and shows entire confidence in God, and joy in him.]

the Father of mercies and God of all comfort;—Paul felt that God was especially full of mercy and comfort to him at this time, in that he had comforted him and them in tribulations and afflictions that they had undergone at Ephesus (Acts 19: 23), and in the troubles at Corinth. They had terminated favorably to him.

4 who comforteth us in all our affliction,—[His affliction was the ground of God's comforting him. He was one of the most afflicted of men. He suffered from hunger, cold, nakedness, stripes, imprisonments; from perils by the sea and land; from robbers, from the Jews and the heathen, so that his life was a continued death or as he expressed it, "I die daily." (1 Cor. 15: 31.) Besides these external afflictions he was overwhelmed with the "anxiety for all the churches." (11: 28.) In the midst of all these, God not only sustained him, but filled him with such a heroic spirit that he actually rejoiced in being thus afflicted. He says: "I take pleasure in weaknesses, in injuries, in necessities, in persecutions, in distresses, for Christ's sake: for when I am weak, then am I strong." This state of mind and heart can be experienced only by those who are filled with the love and devotion to Christ that they rejoice in everything, however painful to themselves, whereby his glory and honor are promoted.]

that we may be able to comfort them that are in any affliction,—God had given Paul comfort so that he would be en-

comfort wherewith we ourselves are comforted of God. 5 For as the sufferings of Christ abound unto us, even so our comfort also aboundeth through
Christ. 6 But whether we are afflicted, it is for your comfort and salvation;
or whether we are comforted, it is for your comfort, which worketh in the

---

abled to comfort others in need of comfort, in the same way
that God had comforted him.

**through the comfort wherewith we ourselves are comforted
of God.**—When this state of mind exists no afflictions can
equal the consolations by which they are attended, and therefore it is added that he was enabled to comfort those who
were in any kind of affliction for the cause of Christ, by the
comfort wherewith he was comforted of God.

5 For as the sufferings of Christ abound unto us,—[Paul
was called to experience the same sufferings which Christ endured (Acts 9: 15, 16); and to suffer in his cause, and in the
promotion of the same object. The sufferings which he endured were in the cause of Christ and his gospel; they were
endured in endeavoring to advance the same object which
Christ sought to promote; and were substantially of the same
nature. They arose from opposition, contempt, persecution,
trial, and want, and were the same as those to which the Lord
Jesus himself was subjected during the whole of his public
life.]

even so our comfort also aboundeth through Christ.—[The
opposition, the persecution, and the cruelties he endured in
the cause of Christ were like those which Christ endured, and
he submitted to them as a servant of Christ, and one who by
faith was identified with Christ. If then, in virtue of this vital
union, he had an abundant share in the sufferings of his Lord,
he was sure that through the same union with Christ he was
receiving an abundant supply of divine comfort.] As we suffer with Christ, suffer as his servants, the consolations that
come from Christ will be bestowed on us as his servants. If
we suffer with him, we shall also reign with him. (2 Tim. 2:
12.)

**6 But whether we are afflicted, it is for your comfort and
salvation;**—The afflictions he had undergone for them would
work out their comfort. [Those who suffer for Christ's sake

patient enduring of the same sufferings which we also suffer: 7 and our hope for you is stedfast; knowing that, as ye are partakers of the sufferings, so also are ye of the comfort. 8 For we would not have you ignorant, brethren, concerning our affliction which befell *us* in Asia, that we were weighed down exceedingly, beyond our power, insomuch that we despaired even of life: 9

---

and with Christ's people, God never fails to comfort, "if so be that we suffer with him, that we may be also glorified with him." (Rom. 8: 17.) It is not of suffering as suffering that Paul here speaks, for there is no tendency in pain to produce holiness. It is only of suffering endured for Christ and in a Christlike manner that it is connected with salvation, or that it tends to work out for those who suffer an eternal weight of glory.]

or whether we are comforted, it is for your comfort,—If he was comforted, it would bring comfort to them, which comfort was wrought out for them through their learning to endure affliction for Christ's sake, by seeing what he endured, and how he was comforted in it.

which worketh in the patient enduring of the same sufferings which we also suffer:—[The sufferings of the Corinthians with those of the apostle, because they sympathized with him in his afflictions, because they in a measure suffered as he did, and because their sufferings were "the sufferings of Christ," in the same sense that his were—they were incurred because those who suffered were Christians.]

7 and our hope for you is stedfast;—He knew if they partook of the afflictions they would share in the consolations.

knowing that, as ye are partakers of the sufferings, so also are ye of the comfort.—[Those who share in our sorrows share in our joys. There are two ideas apparently united here. The one is that the sufferings of the apostle were also the sufferings of the Corinthians because of the union between them. The other is, that his readers were in their measure exposed to the same kind of sufferings. In this two-fold sense they were joint partakers of the same joys and sorrows.]

8 For we would not have you ignorant, brethren, concerning our affliction which befell us in Asia,—Between the writing of the first epistle and this one, Paul had undergone a ter-

³yea, we ourselves have had the ⁴sentence of death within ourselves, that we should not trust in ourselves, but in God who raiseth the dead: 10 who delivered us out of so great a death, and will deliver: on whom we have ⁵set our

³Or, *but we ourselves*
⁴Gr. *answer.*
⁵Some ancient authorities read *set our hope; and still will he deliver us.*

---

rible onslaught made on him at Ephesus by the devotees of the goddess Diana, led by Demetrius, the silversmith. (Acts 19: 23-41.)

[The hostility of Demetrius and his fellow craftsmen, prompted as it was by selfish interests, and the ease with which the mob was collected are enough to account for the deadly peril to which reference is here made. And we can well conceive it prompting some immediate and desperate and well-planned attempt to kill Paul. That Paul felt the danger is proved by his sudden departure (Acts 20: 1) from Ephesus; whereas, a short time earlier, the number of his adversaries had been a reason for his remaining in Ephesus until after Pentecost had prevailed against him (1 Cor. 16: 8, 9).]

that we were weighed down exceedingly, beyond our power, insomuch that we despaired even of life:—He saw no way of escape from death, so in his own mind, he was doomed to death. The danger was so great that he despaired of life.

9 yea, we ourselves have had the sentence of death within ourselves, that we should not trust in ourselves, but in God who raiseth the dead:—His escape was as though delivered from the dead; just as Abraham is said to have acted when "he that had gladly received the promises was offering up his only begotten son; even he to whom it was said, In Isaac shall thy seed be called: accounting that God is able to raise up, even from the dead; from whence he did also in a figure receive him back." (Heb. 11: 17-19.)

10 who delivered us out of so great a death, and will deliver:—Though he had been delivered from instant and a fearful death with which he was threatened, the danger was not over. The plots of his enemies followed him wherever he went, but God's deliverance assured him that he would deliver still.

hope that he will also still deliver us; 11 ye also helping together on our behalf by your supplication; that, for the gift bestowed upon us by means of many, thanks may be given by many persons on our behalf.

---

on whom we have set our hope that he will also still deliver us;—He trusted God still to deliver him from all enemies. [He had been thus far preserved in a most remarkable manner, and his faith led him to the conviction that the Lord would continue to interpose in his behalf until his great purpose concerning him should be fully accomplished.]

11 ye also helping together on our behalf by your supplication;—The Corinthian disciples had prayed for him, and so helped through their prayers, and he trusted that they would still pray for him.

that, for the gift bestowed upon us by means of many,—The deliverance had come through the help of the prayers of many. When one places himself in harmony with the divine law, he puts himself in the place in which he receives all good. He stands where all favoring currents meet; hence Paul says: "We know that to them that love God all things work together for good." (Rom. 8: 28.) It is in securing this harmonious working of the elements of grace and nature for good that prayer comes in to effectually aid and bless the work. For this reason Paul speaks of those who out of ill will toward him preached Christ to add affliction to his bonds. Of their action, he says: "I know that this shall turn out to my salvation, through your supplication and the supply of the Spirit of Jesus Christ." (Phil. 1: 19.) This shows that the prayers of God's children enter into the workings of God's laws and bring good to the person in whose behalf they are offered. God's providences are the results of the working of his laws. The spiritual and natural laws work in harmony for the good of those who love and honor God. To honor God is to obey his laws; to dishonor him is to refuse that obedience. In the spiritual world as in the material, man has it in his power to thwart and hinder the working of his laws, because God has made man with freedom to obey or disobey God. The law of harmony runs through all of God's dealings with man. When Christ said, "According to your faith be it done unto you" (Matt. 9: 29), he recognized this law. Faith, the only faith that God recognizes as anything but mockery, leads to compliance with the law. Hence, if a man's faith is strong he confidently and faithfully complies with the law of God, the blessings will be abundant. If his faith is weak, his compliance will be imperfect and careless and the blessings will be few.

thanks may be given by many persons on our behalf.— Thanks would be given by many for his deliverance, for all who prayed for deliverance would give thanks that deliverance had been effected. [No one ever had more of the spirit of gratitude than Paul. In his epistles he frequently exclaims "thanks be unto God." (Rom. 6: 17; 7: 25; 1 Cor. 15: 57; 2 Cor. 2: 14; 8: 16; 9: 15.) And it seems that to him it was very much desired that a chorus of thanksgivings should be ascending constantly unto God. That which accomplished that end gave him much joy. He counted on the fact that all those who had prayed for his deliverance would render thanks unto God for his deliverance and so another worthy outcome of his troubles would be achieved.]

3. INTEGRITY OF THIS COURSE AND CONSISTENCY OF HIS PURPOSES AND PLANS RESPECTING THE CORINTHIANS.
1: 12-22.

12 For our glorying is this, the testimony of our conscience, that in holi-

12 **For our glorying is this,**—[Paul had been exposed to death. He had been in a situation where he had no hope of life. Then the ground of his glorying and of his confidence was that he had lived a holy life. He had not been actuated by fleshly wisdom, but had been animated and guided by the will of God. His aim had been simple, and his purpose holy. He had the testimony of his conscience that his motives had been right, and he had, therefore, no concern about the result. A holy life through Jesus Christ will enable one always to look calmly into the future.]

the testimony of our conscience,—Though he might be slandered, yet he had the approval of his conscience which had

ness and sincerity of God, not in fleshly wisdom but in the grace of God, we

been enlightened by the word of God, and its decisions were correct. Whatever charges might be brought against him, he knew what had been the aims and purposes of his life; and the consciousness of upright aims, and such a course as the word of God prompted, sustained him. An approving conscience is of inestimable value when we are falsely accused, and when we are in immediate expectation of death.

that in holiness and sincerity of God,—[The holiness and sincerity of which God is the author and gives. Paul uses such expressions as "the peace of God" (Phil. 4: 7; Col. 3: 15), and "joy of the Holy Spirit," meaning the peace or joy of which God or the Holy Spirit is the author, and is bestowed through the provisions made in the gospel. There is a specific difference between spiritual graces and moral virtues, although they are called by the same names. Love, joy, peace, long-suffering, kindness, goodness, faithfulness, meekness, and self-control, when fruits of the Spirit, differ from moral virtues designated by the same terms, as many external things, though similar in appearance, often differ in their inward nature. A devout Christian and a moral man may be very much alike in the eyes of men, though the one is of God and the other of the flesh. Paul here means that the virtues which distinguished his deportment in Corinth were not merely forms of his own excellence, but "the fruit of the Spirit," manifested in a life sincerely devoted to God.]

not in fleshly wisdom—[Not by the principles of cunning and expediency which often characterize men of the world. As used here, the flesh means the perverted human nature, as it is now distinguished from the spiritual. "But ye are not in the flesh but in the Spirit, if so be that the Spirit of God dwelleth in you." (Rom. 8: 9.) As human nature has been corrupted by and perverted by sin, natural and fleshly necessarily involves more or less of the idea of corruption. The natural man, carnal mind, fleshly wisdom, all imply that idea more or less. The fleshly wisdom, therefore, is that kind of wisdom which the man of the world exhibits, wisdom guided by principles of self-interest.]

behaved ourselves in the world, and more abundantly to you-ward. 13 For
we write no other things unto you, than what ye read or even acknowledge,
and I hope ye will acknowledge unto the end: 14 as also ye did acknowledge

but in the grace of God,—This is in contrast with fleshly
wisdom. Paul lived his whole life in the sphere of God's
grace, which led him to straightforwardness and sincere faithfulness to his promises (verses 17-20), even as God is faithful
to his promises.

we behaved ourselves in the world,—Even among the unbelievers, both Jews and Gentiles, he always acted as seeing him
who is invisible.

and more abundantly to you-ward.—[Since his conduct in
his relations to the Corinthians had been of the kind described, he makes a special claim on them for their prayers.
It would have been hyprocrisy to ask their prayers for him
had he been conscious of pursuing a crooked policy. But conscious as he was that he had but one object in view throughout his whole apostolic work, though maligned by self-seeking
enemies, he could freely ask them to unite with him in prayer
for his deliverance from the perils by which he was then surrounded, and the anxieties which were well-nigh weighing
him down.]

13 For we write no other things unto you, than what ye
read or even acknowledge,—The same sincerity and honesty
that characterized his life was characteristic of his letters.
The meaning of his words was always obvious and plain, and
there is no other meaning than that which is on the surface.
They had their own knowledge of him to confirm what he said
of the purity of his life, and they recognized him as a true
apostle of Jesus Christ.

and I hope ye will acknowledge unto the end:—He hoped
they would continue to own him as an apostle, and his teachings to be the truth of God. [Should this bright hope be realized, then in the day of the Lord Jesus it will be the glorying
of the Corinthians that they had the apostle Paul as their spiritual father, and the glorying of Paul that the Corinthians
were his spiritual children.]

us in part, that we are your glorying, even as ye also are ours, in the day of
our Lord Jesus.
15 And in this confidence I was minded to come first unto you, that ye

---

14 as also ye did acknowledge us in part.—A portion of the
church believed him to be sincere and consistent, though there
was a faction that denied it.

that we are your glorying, even as ye also are ours,—They
had acknowledged him when he first went among them to
preach, and then he was honored by them; they gloried in him
as a teacher from God, as he gloried in them as the fruit of his
apostleship.

in the day of our Lord Jesus.—He would glory in them as
the fruits of his labor and the seal of his apostleship. [A similar passage is: "For what is our hope, or joy, or crown of
glorying? Are not even ye, before our Lord Jesus at his coming? For ye are our glory and our joy." (1 Thess. 2: 19, 20.)
In both cases our minds are lifted to that great presence
which Paul constantly anticipated; and as we stand there our
judgments of each other are seen in their true light. No one
will rejoice then that he has made evil out of good, that he has
cunningly perverted the simple actions of others into evil designs, that he has set the saints at variance; the joy will be for
those who have loved and trusted each other, who have borne
each other's infirmities and labored for their healing. The
mutual confidence in all the faithful in Christ will then, after
all its trial, have its exceeding great reward.]

15 And in this confidence—In reliance on the mutual respect and affection which existed between them, he was confident that they would recognize his sincerity, and receive him
with joy, and be benefited by his coming.

I was minded to come first unto you,—[His original intention was to go direct from Ephesus to Corinth before going
into Macedonia; instead of this, he had gone first to Macedonia (1 Cor. 16: 5), and would thus see Corinth only once, on
his way south, whereas had he gone first to Corinth, he would
have paid them a double visit at this time—on his way to as
well as from Macedonia.]

might have a second *benefit; 16 and by you to pass into Macedonia, and again from Macedonia to come unto you, and of you to be set forward on my journey unto Judæa. 17 When I therefore was thus minded, did I show fickleness? or the things that I purpose, do I purpose according to the flesh, that with me there should be the yea yea and the nay nay? 18 But as God is faithful, our word toward you is not yea and nay. 19 For the Son of God,

*Or, *grace* Some ancient authorities read *joy*

---

that ye might have a second benefit;—A second benefit from his teaching and presence. He probably thought of bestowing other and greater gifts on them to further aid them in their Christian life. [The importance of the church of Corinth, its central position, made it very important that he should give them as much as possible of his personal supervision.]

16 **and by you to pass into Macedonia, and again from Macedonia to come unto you, and of you to be set forward on my journey unto Judaea.**—He desired them to set him forward on his way to Judæa. In those days when there were no established modes of traveling, it was customary for the friends of the traveler in one city to send him forward to the next, or at least to escort him on the way. (Acts 15: 3; 20: 38; 21: 5; Rom. 15: 24.) This office of friendship Paul was willing and desirous to receive at the hands of the Corinthians. He was not alienated from them. And his purpose to seek this kindness from them was proof of his confidence in their affection for him.]

17 **When I therefore was thus minded, did I show fickleness? or the things that I purpose, do I purpose according to the flesh,**—Paul had let them know his purpose; had failed to carry it out, and some of them had charged him with fickleness, and some of them claimed that he showed he was afraid to come as he had promised, and this failure to fulfil his promise proved that he was not an apostle.

that with me there should be the yea yea and the nay nay? —Their contention was that he would affirm and deny the same thing; that, like an unprincipled politican, there was no dependence to be placed in his word; that he was so headstrong that when he said he would, he would do it whether best or not, that he was so uncertain that he would break a

Jesus Christ, who was preached among you ¹by us, even ¹by me and Silvanus and Timothy, was not yea and nay, but in him is yea. 20 For how many soever be the promises of God, in him is the yea: wherefore also through him is the Amen, unto the glory of God through us. 21 Now he that estab-

¹Gr. *through.*

promise from a mere whim; that he had no fixed principle; and that he was variable and whimsical.

18 But as God is faithful, our word toward you is not yea and nay.—His word to them did not rest on fleshly whims, but on the will of God. [The connection between this verse and the following shows that reference is made to the word preached concerning Jesus Christ and he argues that as his preaching to them was in all sincerity, so might naturally be regarded all of his expressed purposes concerning them.]

19 For the Son of God, Jesus Christ, who was preached among you by us, even by me and Silvanus and Timothy,— These persons are likely mentioned because Paul refers to his first visit to Corinth when they were his fellow workers. (Acts 18:5.)

was not yea and nay, but in him is yea.—Christ was not yea and nay, variable and changeable. His yea meant yea—was unchangeable. [Those who accepted Christ found him to be "the way, and the truth, and the life." (John 14:6.) He had been made unto them "wisdom from God, and righteousness and sanctification, and redemption." (1 Cor. 1:30.) Christ had not been manifested among them and experienced by them to be uncertain, but he proved himself to be all that was affirmed of him, and continued to be all they had been led to expect.]

20 For how many soever be the promises of God, in him is the yea:—For all the promises of God are "yea," are certain, and will be sure unto the end. [The Judaizers, against whom Paul's reasoning in this epistle is chiefly directed, might see "the yea yea" of the fulfilment of all the promises as "nay" for all the uncircumcised. With Paul the promises of God were all "yea" where Gentiles as well as Jews were embraced. In Christ is full salvation for all who accept him.]

wherefore also through him is the Amen,—Amen here

lisheth us with you ²in Christ, and anointed us, is God; 22 ³who also sealed

²Gr. *into.*
³Or, *seeing that he both sealed us*

means all the promises which are made to men through Jesus Christ the Redeemer shall be certainly fulfilled. They are promises which are confirmed and established, and which by no means fail; but the blessings are assured only to those who give them the "amen" of a practical acknowledgement.

unto the glory of God through us.—[Paul rejoiced that his ministry and that of his fellow laborers contributed to the glory of God, which is identified with the recognition and appropriation by men of his goodness and faithfulness in Jesus Christ.]

21 **Now he that establisheth us with you in Christ,**—[God had established Paul in Christ. Therefore fickleness, duplicity, or deceit was impossible. Observe, too, that he does not assert his truthfulness because of his apostleship, but because of his devotion to Christ, for he associates with himself Sylvanus, Timothy, the Corinthian Christians, and all believers. He does not claim for himself any steadfastness in Christ, or any trustworthiness as dependent upon it, which is not possible to other faithful believers. It is their calling as Christians to be steadfast in Christ. Such steadfastness God is ever seeking to impart through the gospel, and in striving to attain it, every Christian can appeal to him for help. If Christians are letting God have his way with them in this respect, they can be depended upon for conduct in keeping with the goodness and faithfulness of God, into which they have been confirmed by him.]

and anointed us,—Kings, prophets, and priests were anointed when inaugurated in their several offices; to anoint may therefore mean to qualify by divine influence, and thereby to authorize anyone to discharge the duties of any office. In the synagogue at Nazareth the Lord applies to himself the prophecy of Isaiah (61: 1, 2)—"The Spirit of the Lord is upon me, Because he anointed me to preach good tidings to the poor." (Luke 4: 18.) In speaking of Jesus at the house of Cornelius, Peter said: "God anointed him with the Holy

us, and gave *us* the earnest of the Spirit in our hearts.

Spirit and with power." (Acts 10: 38.) Christians are in like manner spoken of as having "an anointing from the Holy One" which abides in them. (1 John 2: 20, 27.) At the conclusion of Peter's sermon on the day of Pentecost, those who heard "were pricked in their heart, and said unto Peter and the rest of the apostles, Brethren, what shall we do? And Peter said unto them, Repent ye, and be baptized every one of you in the name of Jesus Christ unto the remission of your sins; and ye shall receive the gift of the Holy Spirit." (Acts 2: 37, 38.) In the passage before us, when Paul says, "and anointed us," he means that the anointing of the Spirit is common to all Christians.

is God;—God it is who confirms and anoints his people. It is worth noticing that in the New Testament the act of anointing is never ascribed to anyone but God.

22 who also sealed us,—A seal guarantees genuineness, proclaims ownership, is a warrant of safety, and is an impress of likeness. The abiding presence of the Spirit in the heart is a sign that we belong to God. (2 Tim. 2: 19.)

and gave us the earnest of the Spirit in our hearts.—[The earnest is that part which is paid down at the making of the contract, the seal of the bargain, and as a pledge that all that is promised will be paid. This giving of the Spirit in our hearts is, therefore, the seal of God's promise of everlasting life, and the pledge of the fulfillment of that promise. Clearly, then, in addition to all that was extraordinary and miraculous in connection with the outpouring of the Spirit on the day of Pentecost, there was a bestowal of the Spirit of God, as an earnest of the heavenly inheritance to which they were now made heirs; and the fullness of the divine fellowship through the Spirit; such as had not been known before. Thus, the three blessings—the anointing, the sealing, and the pledging of the future—are only different forms or representations of the work of the Spirit.]

4. STATEMENT OF HIS REAL MOTIVES IN CHANGING HIS
PLAN OF VISITATION AND FURTHER INSTRUCTIONS
TOUCHING THE NOW PENITENT OFFENDER
WHOSE CONDUCT MAINLY LED
TO THE CHANGE.
1 : 23 to 2 : 11.

23 But I call God for a witness upon my soul, that to spare you I forbare
to come unto Corinth. 24 Not that we have lordship over your faith, but are
helpers of your joy: for in [4]faith ye stand fast. 1 [5]But I determined this for

[4]Or, *your faith*
[5]Some ancient authorities read *For*.

23 **But I call God for a witness upon my soul, that to spare
you I forbare to come unto Corinth.**—Instead of its being fickleness or fleshly impulse with him, he calls God to witness
that he failed to come directly from Ephesus to Corinth that
he might spare them. He delayed his coming to give them
opportunity to change their course, and that he through his
epistle and the messengers he sent might induce them to
change their course before his arrival.

24 **Not that we have lordship over your faith,**—He did not
claim the right or desire to rule or dictate their faith. [To the
Galatians he said: "But though we, or an angel from heaven,
should preach unto you any gospel other than that which we
preached unto you, let him be anathema." (Gal. 1 : 8.) Faith
comes by hearing the word of God. When we believe that, it
is not man whom we believe. Therefore faith is not subject
to man, but to God alone. The apostles were the instrumen-
talities through whom the Holy Spirit spoke; what they spoke
they could not change or modify in any respect. What they
preached was not under their control. They were as much
subject to that which they preached, and as much bound to
believe and practice it, as were other men.]

but are helpers of your joy:—He wished to help them reach
a condition that his coming would be a source of joy and not
of grief to them.

for in faith ye stand fast.—The only ground of acceptance
was faith in Christ. Nothing stronger can be said of anyone's
faith than that he stands in it; in it he stands justified before
God. "Being therefore justified by faith, we have peace with
God through our Lord Jesus Christ; through whom also we

myself, that I would not come again to you with sorrow. 2 For if I make you sorry, who then is he that maketh me glad but he that is made sorry by me? 3 And I wrote this very thing, lest, when I came, I should have sorrow from them of whom I ought to rejoice; having confidence in you all, that my joy is *the joy* of you all. 4 For out of much affliction and anguish of heart I wrote unto you with many tears; not that ye should be made

---

have had our access by faith into this grace wherein we stand." (Rom. 5: 1, 2.)

2: 1 **But I determined this for myself, that I would not come again to you with sorrow.**—Paul determined not to go to Corinth until he had a good report from them. Until they had improved so that he could come with words of approval rather than of condemnation.

2 **For if I make you sorry, who then is he that maketh me glad but he that is made sorry by me?**—If he blamed them and made them sorry, who would comfort and make him glad, save those he had made sorry? [His first epistle had caused sorrow to himself and to the church. But the sorrow had resulted in repentance, and so, at last, in their joy and Paul's joy. The end had justified the means.]

3 **And I wrote this very thing, lest, when I came, I should have sorrow from them of whom I ought to rejoice;**—In his first epistle he had told them of their wrongs in countenancing the incestuous man, and following false teachers. He most earnestly endeavored to show them their wrongs and bring them to repentance, that he might come to them, not with a rod, but in love and in the spirit of meekness. [He communicated with them by letter, instead of incurring the risk of a painful personal visit, because he was convinced that they would find their own joy in his joy—which, in the present instance, could not but be produced by the doing away of the existing evils according to the instructions contained in his letter.]

having confidence in you all, that my joy is the joy of you all.—[In case they acted according to his instructions their meeting would be one of mutual joy.]

4 **For out of much affliction and anguish of heart I wrote unto you with many tears;**—He had felt deep affliction and anguish of heart to have to write the words of condemnation

sorry, but that ye might know the love which I have more abundantly unto you.
5 But if any hath caused sorrow, he hath caused sorrow, not to me, but in part (that I press not too heavily) to you all. 6 Sufficient to such a one is this punishment which was *inflicted* by ⁶the many; 7 so that contrariwise ye

⁶Gr, *the more.*

---

he had felt compelled to write to them. He wrote them in tears himself, not to grieve them, but out of his deep and abundant love for them.

not that ye should be made sorry,—His love for them led him to seek to deliver them from their errors and sins, lest they should fall under the condemnation of God. [His ultimate and main object was, not that they should be made sorry, but that through sorrow they might be led to repentance, and so to joy.]

but that ye might know the love which I have more abundantly unto you.—True love for any person makes one seek to deliver the loved ones from wrong. Sometimes people uphold their husbands, wives, children, and friends in a wrong course, and say they do it from love. This is not true and helpful love. Love says get them pure and right before God, and insists on the discipline needed to purify them. Not to do this is to encourage them in their own ruin. A selfish determination to uphold one's family or friends in a course of wrong is not love. It is really hatred, in a Bible sense of the word.

5 But if any hath caused sorrow, he hath caused sorrow, not to me, but in part (that I press not too heavily) to you all.— The incestuous person mentioned in the first epistle (5 : 1) is supposed to be here meant. If he had caused sorrow it was not to Paul alone, but they had felt it. The parenthetical clause says it would be too severe condemnation of them to say it had not caused them grief.

6 Sufficient to such a one is this punishment—Paul felt that the guilty person had been sufficiently punished by "the many" putting him away as he had directed.

which was inflicted by the many;—Some expositors thing that "the many" means the majority, and that a vote was taken, and a majority voted to put him away while the minor-

should rather forgive him and comfort him, lest by any means such a one
should be swallowed up with his overmuch sorrow. 8 Wherefore I beseech
you to confirm *your* love toward him. 9 For to this end also did I write,

⁷Some ancient authorities omit *rather.*

ity opposed it. But the record does not show this. He did
not command them to vote on it, but "to deliver such a one
unto Satan." (1 Cor. 5: 5.) It was the question of obeying a
plain command of God given through Paul—God himself decided the case. There is not an intimation that there was a
single objection, or that an objection was called for. They
obeyed; the man was put away. The order of God is that all
Christians shall be of one mind and one voice.

7 **so that contrariwise ye should rather forgive him and
comfort him,**—As he had been sufficiently punished to bring
him to repentance, Paul admonishes them to forgive and encourage him.

**lest by any means such a one should be swallowed up with
his overmuch sorrow.**—Lest he should give up and be lost. It
was a grievous and shameful sin, but not a word is said about
vindicating the honor of the church. The end was to save the
sinner. Indeed, it is possible to vindicate the honor of the
church by giving the children of the church up to ruin.
Sometimes it is necessary for a father and mother to cut off a
hopelessly wayward son from the family, lest he corrupt and
lead the other members of the family into ruin; but it would
be a strange father and mother that would think they had vindicated the honor of the family by giving a child over to hopeless ruin. So a church should feel. The end of discipline,
whether by individuals, or the church as a whole, should be to
save the sinning one by delivering him from his sins.

8 **Wherefore I beseech you to confirm your love toward
him.**—They should show their love by forgiving him, reward-
ing him, cherishing him, and making it evident to him that he
was again recognized as a brother. [The expressions of love to
him ought to be as public and as unmistakable as the expressions of disapproval and condemnation. Confirm here means
public testimony of kind feeling to him by the reversal of his
excommunication.]

that I might know the proof of you, [8]whether ye are obedient in all things. 10 But to whom ye forgive anything, I *forgive* also: for what I also have forgiven, if I have forgiven anything, for your sakes *have I forgiven it* in the [9]presence of Christ; 11 that no advantage may be gained over us by Satan: for we are not ignorant of his devices.

[8]Some ancient authorities read *whereby.*
[9]Or, *person*

9 **For to this end also did I write, that I might know the proof of you,**—One end of his writing of the difficulty instead of coming in person was to test their readiness to obey the will of God in all things, even where their personal friends were involved.

whether ye are obedient in all things.—He found them obedient, and so was filled with joy. This shows that the conclusion under verse 6 is correct.

10 **But to whom ye forgive anything, I forgive also:**—When the church forgave, Paul forgave. That is, he approved what the church did acting under his directions. What he had forgiven he had forgiven for their good.

for what I also have forgiven, if I have forgiven anything, for your sakes have I forgiven it in the presence of Christ;— He did it as a servant of Christ and by his directions. What a church does by the direction of God, God does. When the church puts a man away from among them, in accordance with the law of God, God puts him away. When the church restores following the law of God, God does it. It is a serious matter to a soul to be put away by the church of God.

11 **that no advantage may be gained over us by Satan:**— The advantage that Satan seeks is to get the sinning one entirely under his control. [That Satan is at the bottom of any policy fitted to defeat the work of the church in the struggle against sin is the principle involved in this very definite statement; and the nature of his agency warrants the special attention of all who are laboring for the purity and success of the church. The retention of the openly corrupt in the fellowship of the church, if this can be effected, serves Satan's purpose by contaminating the rest and lowering its standard of purity; but when this fails, through the faithful watchfulness of the guardians of the church (Acts 20: 28-31), the hopelessness of

all restoration to the fellowship even of the manifestly penitent will equally serve his purpose, as it will either harden the
offender of drive him to despair, and thus indirectly weaken
the influence of the church—a lesson to the servants of the
Lord, to beware, both of laxity toward those who walk disor-
derly, and of the relentless severity towards those who, however deep their fall, give good evidence of genuine repentance.]

for we are not ignorant of his devices.—Paul, through the
Spirit was aware of the devices of Satan to lead the discouraged to ruin.

5. HIS FEELINGS TOWARDS THE CORINTHIANS FURTHER ILLUSTRATED BY HIS EXTREME ANXIETY BEFORE MEETING WITH TITUS AND HIS GREAT JOY ON LEARNING THROUGH HIM OF THEIR SPIRITUAL IMPROVEMENT.
2: 12-17.

12 Now when I came to Troas for the [10]gospel of Christ, and when a

[10]Gr. *good tidings*: see marginal note on Mt. 4. 23.

12 **Now when I came to Troas**—[There is here an apparently abrupt transition, but Paul is only resuming the narrative he broke off at verse 4 in order that he might finish the
topic of the painful circumstance under which the first epistle
was written. He now briefly tells the effect that this change
from a personal visit to a letter had upon himself, owing to
the delay which was necessary in hearing from the effect it
had produced. Titus had been sent to Corinth to look after
the collection for the saints of Judea (8: 6). While there he
took an interest in the settlement of the troubles afflicting the
church. Paul depended on him in the matter and expected
him to meet him at Troas and report the condition of the
church, and how they received his letter. Paul, after the up-
roar led by Demetrius, left Ephesus on his intended visit to
Macedonia. He came to Troas, the seaport at which they em-
barked to pass over from Asia to Macedonia.]

for the gospel of Christ,—He did not intend to make a rapid
journey to Corinth, but a regular missionary tour.

door was opened unto me in the Lord, 13 I had no relief for my spirit, because I found not Titus my brother: but taking my leave of them, I went
forth into Macedonia.
14 But thanks be unto God, who always leadeth us in triumph in Christ,

---

and when a door was opened unto me in the Lord,—He
found an opening there for the gospel of Christ, a promise for
good through preaching.

**13 I had no relief for my spirit, because I found not Titus
my brother:**—He was so disappointed in not finding Titus on
his arrival at Troas, and hearing from Corinth, that he could
not tarry there contented. [This seems a singular confession,
but there is no reason to conclude that it was actuated by any
other spirit than the great anxiety he felt for the spiritual welfare of the Corinthian church. The very element in him, in
virtue of which he could act for God at all, was already preoc-
cupied, and though the people were there, ready to receive the
gospel, it was beyond his power to preach it to them. His
spirit was absorbed and possessed by hopes and fears and
prayers for the Corinthians; and as the human spirit is finite,
and only capable of so much and no more, he was obliged to
pass by an opportunity which he would otherwise have gladly
seized. He probably felt that it was more important to secure
the stability and faithfulness of those who were already disciples than make new ones.]

but taking my leave of them, I went forth into Macedonia.
—He hastened on to Macedonia where he met Titus, heard a
good report from Corinth; then sent him with another letter
back to Corinth to complete the raising of the funds for the
poor saints. (8: 6-18.)

**14 But thanks be unto God, who always leadeth us in tri-
umph in Christ,**—He thanked God who always delivered him
from danger and caused him to triumph over his enemies. He
had done this at Corinth, over those denying his claim to be
an apostle, even in his absence. [This sudden outburst of
thanksgiving is very characteristic of Paul. He does not
finish his story, telling where and when he met Titus, but lets
this outburst of feeling imply the meeting and its glad results.
The first characteristic, then, of Paul's ministry is its contin-

and maketh manifest through us the savor of his knowledge in every place.
15 For we are a sweet savor of Christ unto God, in them that [11]are saved,
and in them that [12]perish; 16 to the one a savor from death unto death; to

[11]Or, *are being saved*
[12]Or, *are perishing*

ual triumph; so at least he feels as he rises suddenly out of his
anguish of suspense and learns how fully the Corinthians had
obeyed his instructions and how truly they trust him.]

**and maketh manifest through us the savor of his knowledge
in every place.**—[As in the diffusion of the sweet odor of the
incense; so in the life of Paul, wherever he went there was the
diffusion of the knowledge of Christ. That Christ should be
known was the end of his mission, and was of all things the
most acceptable to God. Wherever he went he presented to
men the knowledge of Christ through his preaching and life.
And this, both when surrounded by those who accepted Christ
and were thus in the way of salvation, and those who rejected
him and were thus perishing (Col. 1: 18). For in each case his
word was acceptable to God, as accomplishing a divine purpose.]

15 For we are a sweet savor of Christ unto God,—[Paul as
a minister and his work of preaching Christ were acceptable to
God whatever might be the result of his labors. God by him
diffused the knowledge of Christ everywhere as a savor, for it
was well-pleasing to God whatever might be the effect it
produced. In the preceding verse the knowledge of Christ is
declared to be a savor as of incense; here Paul is "the sweet
savor of Christ." But it is not Paul as a man, not the purity
or devotion of his life; but as a preacher of the gospel, and
therefore the gospel he preached. In both uses the diffusion
of the knowledge of Christ is said to be well-pleasing to God.
When Paul said he was a sweet odor of Christ, he meant that
wherever he went he was the means of diffusing the knowledge of Christ, and that was acceptable to God.]

in them that are saved, and in them that perish;—Paul was
made a pleasant savor or offering as a servant of Christ unto
God. That savor affected both those who believed and those
who disbelieved. It led one forward to salvation; it confirmed

the other a savor from life unto life. And who is sufficient for these things?

those who believed not to condemnation. This was according to God's will, to save those who believe; to leave those who refuse to believe without excuse in their condemnation.

16 **to the one a savor from death unto death;**—The one class already dead in trespasses and sins, sinking deeper and approaching nearer, by every successive resistance of the truth, to the second death. "Evil men and impostors shall wax worse and worse, deceiving and being deceived." (2 Tim. 3 : 13.)

to the other a savor from life unto life.—These are already alive unto God through Jesus Christ, and through faith in his name, having that life invigorated and developed by every successive welcome given to the word of life, and were thus led from one degree of salvation to another. [In neither case is the final issue as yet seen—the saved are but saved from their past sins and are "guarded through faith unto a salvation ready to be revealed in the last time" (1 Pet. 1 : 5); the lost are neither wholly nor finally lost, but are on the way to it.]

[It is indeed a solemn truth that in the scheme of redemption nothing that God has done or said is indifferent. Everything is a two-edged sword. All Christian privileges, all means of grace, are, according as they are used, either blessings or curses, either an odor of life unto life eternal or of death eternal, to those to whom they come. This double effect of the gospel is set forth in the words of Simeon, when he took the child Jesus in his arms and said: "Behold, this child is set for the falling and the rising of many in Israel" (Luke 2 : 34), and in the words of the Lord himself, "For judgment came I into this world, that they that see not may see; and that they that see may become blind." (John 9 : 39.)]

And who is sufficient for these things?—Who is prepared for such wonderful issues as these? [The question forced itself on Paul's mind as it forces itself on the mind of every true minister of the word of truth. Who can feel qualified for a work which involves such tremendous issues? In himself no

17 For we are not as the many, [18]corrupting the word of God: but as of
[18]Or, *making merchandise of the word of God*   Comp. 2 Pet. 2. 3.

---

one is. But some one must preach the gospel, for the Lord
Jesus, after his resurrection, said: "Go ye into all the world,
and preach the gospel to the whole creation" (Mark 16: 15),
and Paul knew that that responsibility rested upon him, for
the Lord appeared unto him and said: "For to this end have I
appeared unto thee, to appoint thee a minister and a witness
both of the things wherein thou hast seen me, and of the
things wherein I will appear unto thee; delivering thee from
the people, and from the Gentiles, unto whom I send thee."
(Acts 26: 16, 17.) And for this reason Paul accepted the responsibility, and said: "Not that we are sufficient of ourselves,
to account anything as from ourselves; but our sufficiency is
from God; who also made us sufficient as ministers of a new
covenant." (3: 5, 6.) It is obvious that he here assumes his
sufficiency, and proceeds to give the ground of the assumption.]

17 **For we are not as the many,**—"The many" certainly refers to the false teachers who had come among them and
caused much disturbance. [The sense of responsibility as a
preacher of the gospel is not shared by all who claim to be
ministers of the word of truth. To be the bearer and the
representative of a power with issues so tremendous ought
surely to destroy every thought of self; to let personal interest
intrude is to declare oneself faithless and unworthy.]

corrupting the word of God:—[The expressive word rendered here "corrupting" has the idea of self-interest, and especially of petty gain, at its base. The term was originally applied to tavern keeping, and extended to cover all the devices
by which the wine sellers in ancient times deceived their cus-
tomers. Then it was used figuratively as here, and of philoso-
phers of selling the sciences, and in most cases like tavern
keepers, blending, adulterating, and giving short measure. It
is plain that there are two separate ideas here. One is that of
men qualifying the gospel, putting their own meaning into the

sincerity, but as of God, in the sight of God, speak we in Christ.

word of God, temporizing its severity, dealing in compromise. The other is that all such proceedings are faithless and dishonest, because some private interest underlies them. It is as likely to be avarice as anything else. A man corrupts the word of God, makes it the stock in trade of a paltry business of his own, and in many other ways than by subordinating it to the need of a livelihood. When he preaches not that awful message in which life and death are bound up, but himself, his cleverness, his learning, his witticism, his elocution, his fine voice he does so. He makes the word of God minister to him, instead of being a minister of the word; and that is the essence of the sin. It is the same if ambition be his motive, if he preaches to win disciples to himself, to gain ascendency over men, to become the head of a party which will bear the impress of his mind. There was something of this at Corinth; and not only there, but wherever it is found, such a spirit and such interests will change the character of the gospel. It wil not be preserved in that integrity, in that simple, uncompromising, absolute character which it has as revealed in Christ. Have another interest in it than that of God, and that interest will inevitably color it. Thus it will be transformed into that which it was not, and its power is destroyed.]

but as of sincerity,—Paul acted from pure motives and honest feelings, in opposition to corrupting by admixture. He could bear looking at through and through, for he was actuated by unmingled honesty and sincerity of aim.

but as of God,—The source of truth, his authority, and from whom he had received his commission.

in the sight of God,—He was ever conscious of God's presence and that his all-seeing eye was always upon him. [Nothing is better fitted to make a man sincere and honest than this.]

speak we in Christ.—He was one who was united to him, living, moving, and acting as it were in his presence. [What a climax is here presented. All selfishness is excluded.

Molded by God, inspired by his Spirit, in union with and en-
compassed, as it were, with Christ. Such a one speaking
under such conditions was sufficient, for evidently his sufficiency was not in himself, but from God.]

6. CONTRAST BETWEEN THE MINISTRATION OF RIGHTEOUS-
NESS IN THE HANDS OF PAUL AND THE MINISTRA-
TION OF CONDEMNATION ENFORCED BY HIS
JUDAIZING OPPONENTS.
3: 1-11.

1 Are we beginning again to commend ourselves? or need we, as do some,

---

1 **Are we beginning again to commend ourselves?**—[Paul
does not mean by these words to admit that he had been commending himself; but that he had been accused of doing so,
and that there were those at Corinth, who, when they hear
such language as is in this epistle (2: 14-17), will be ready to
repeat the accusation, and obviously his enemies at Corinth
had tried to turn the personal passages in the first epistle
against him by saying: "He is commending himself, and self-
commendation discredits, instead of supporting a cause."
Possibly he had heard of these malicious attacks from Titus,
and in this epistle makes repeated references to them (5: 12;
10: 12, 18; 12: 11; 13: 6). He agreed with his opponents that
self-praise was no honor—"not he that commendeth himself is
approved, but whom the Lord commendeth." (10: 18.) But he
denied that he was commending himself. In distinguishing as
he had done (2: 14-17) between himself who spoke the word
"as of sincerity, but as of God, in the sight of God," and "the
many" who corrupted it, nothing was further from his mind
than to plead his cause with the Corinthians as a suspected
person. Only malignity could suspect any such thing.]

**or need we, as do some, epistles of commendation to you or
from you?**—He possibly refers to the Judaizing teachers (11:
13) who had come to Corinth with letters of commendation
from other churches; and when leaving that city obtained
similar letters from the Corinthians to other churches. The
letter Paul wrote commending Phoebe is a model: "I commend

epistles of commendation to you or from you? 2 Ye are our epistle, written
in our hearts, known and read of all men; 3 being made manifest that ye are

---

unto you Phoebe our sister, who is a servant of the church
that is at Cenchreae: that ye receive her in the Lord, worthily
of the saints, and that ye assist her in whatsoever matter she
may have need of you: for she herself also hath been a helper
of many and of mine own self." (Rom. 16: 1, 2.) Against the
usefulness of such letters in general Paul here says nothing.
Such letters of commendation deserve notice as an important
element in the early church. A Christian traveling with such
a letter from any church was certain to find a hearty welcome
at any other. They guaranteed at once his soundness in the
faith and his personal character, and served to give a reality
of the brotherly love existing between those in Christ. [But
false teachers sometimes used such letters to forward their
unholy purposes, hence John gives the warning: "If any one
cometh unto you, and bringeth not this teaching, receive him
not into your house, and give him no greeting: for he that
giveth him greeting partaketh in his evil works." (2 John 10,
11.) It was absurd to suppose that Paul should ask for a letter of commendation to the church which he had built from its
very foundation, and it was even more so to imagine that he,
their father in the gospel (1 Cor. 3: 10), should need a letter
from them to other churches.]

2 Ye are our epistle,—The church at Corinth, with its spiritual gifts and powers, was his letter of commendation from
God. His work as shown in the life of these brethren commended him instead of letters written on paper.

written in our hearts,—This work was done under great
trial and affliction, so that those who became obedient to the
gospel were very dear unto him and were deeply impressed on
his heart. Reading there he feels that he needs no letter to
them, either from his own or any other pen.

known and read of all men;—Corinth was the center of
Greek civilization, population, and travel. The church there
with its spiritual gifts and powers commended Paul as a
teacher sent from God; was as an epistle from God commend-

an epistle of Christ, ministered by us, written not with ink, but with the Spirit of the living God; not in tables of stone, but in tables *that are* hearts

ing him by the gifts God had bestowed through him, of which Paul says: "I thank my God always concerning you, for the grace of God which was given you in Christ Jesus; that in everything ye were enriched in him, in all utterance and all knowledge; even as the testimony of Christ was confirmed in you: so that ye come behind in no gift." (1 Cor. 1: 4-7.) His ministry among them had not escaped the general observation of the world. Thus he needed no letter of commendation from them, they themselves being the strongest warranty of his genuine apostleship that could be given at large.

3 being made manifest that ye are an epistle of Christ,— This is an elaboration of the preceding verse. [The author of the epistle is Christ; he dictated it.]

ministered by us,—They were openly declared to be an epistle of Christ to the world, ministered or written by the hand of Paul.

written not with ink, but with the Spirit of the living God; —The Spirit made its impress first upon the heart of Paul, then through his preaching what was thus impressed converted them. Christ by the Holy Spirit, and he in his preaching presented it to the Corinthians, and they, like the Thessalonians, received from him the word of the message and accepted it not as the word of men, but, as it is in truth, the word of God, which also worked in them that believed (1 Thess. 2: 13), and as a result became an epistle of Christ to the world that could be read and known that God approved him as his teacher.

not in tables of stone, but in tables that are hearts of flesh. —The Spirit made its impress first upon the heart of Paul, then through his preaching what was thus impressed on his heart to the Corinthians converted them, and they as the result of that teaching became an epistle of Christ to the world that could be read and known of all men. [The material on which this letter was written was not unimpressible stone, as the law of Moses, but the warm susceptible tablets of the heart.

of flesh. 4 And such confidence have we through Christ to God-ward: 5 not that we are sufficient of ourselves, to account anything as from ourselves; but our sufficiency is from God; 6 who also made us sufficient as ministers of a new covenant; not of the letter, but of the spirit: for the letter killeth, but

---

In such an epistle all men could discern that a mighty power had entered into men through the instrumentality of Paul's ministry.]

4 And such confidence have we through Christ to Godward: —What Christ had thus written on his heart by the Spirit caused him to have such trust or confidence in God for them. [Paul had expressed great confidence with respect to what had been accomplished at Corinth through his instrumentality, and he had claimed it as an evidence of his apostolic power. He owed this strong and joyful confidence entirely to Christ; for it was Christ whom he served and under whose influence he accomplished everything he did; and it was therefore through Christ that he had such confidence in what he could do; but this confidence was that God had appointed him, and sent him forth; and confidence that he would still continue to own and bless him.]

5 not that we are sufficient of ourselves, to account anything as from ourselves;—His confidence was not that he was able of himself to think or do anything toward converting men. [He cannot bear the implication that any confidence rests on anything short of the overwhelming sense that he is but an instrument in the hands of God.]

but our sufficiency is from God;—God sent the Spirit who impressed the truth on his heart and led him to preach to them and confirm the teaching "by signs and wonders and mighty works." (12: 12.)

6 who also made us sufficient as ministers of a new covenant;—He had no ability or knowledge save as God bestowed on him the Holy Spirit to guide him into the truth and make him an able minister to set forth the truths of the new covenant. [To appreciate the real force of this passage, we must bear in mind that the ones whom Paul had in view are Judaizers (11: 20-22) who championed the Mosaic covenant. With Jesus, a new covenant came into the world. Paul was fully

the spirit giveth life. 7 But if the ministration of death, ¹written *and* en-
¹Gr. *in letters.*

---

aware of the tremendous difference that Jesus made to history
(1 Cor. 15: 22), and his words cut right into the heart of the
contrast, and lay it bare.]

not of the letter, but of the spirit:—The contrast is between
the epistle written in the heart and that written on stones.
[The letter is the law, which found its most characteristic expression in the commandments engraven upon the tablets of
stone, while the contrast with this is the Spirit, the source of
that new order or constitution of things which was established by Jesus Christ. The contrast is between the law and
the gospel, between Moses and Christ, between laws imposed
from without and from within.]

for the letter killeth,—This evidently refers to the old covenant because it brought the knowledge of sin and death, but
did not give life, because none kept its requirements. [The
law imposed a command to which men were not equal; it virtually condemned them (verse 9)—condemned them to death.
As men could only disobey the law, and life lay alone in obedience, the law could only lead to death. (Rom. 7: 9-11.) In
this sense, therefore, the letter kills.]

but the spirit giveth life.—this was the ministration of life
because it provided for pardon and life in Christ. [The soul
that was slain—shut up to despair and death—by the law is
quickened into life when touched by the Spirit of Jesus. These
words are a vivid summary of Paul's experience under the two
dispensations, both of which he knew so well.] The Spirit is
the author of all true spiritual life. Jesus said: "It is the spirit
that giveth life; the flesh profiteth nothing: the words that I
have spoken unto you are spirit, and are life." (John 6: 63.)
This conveys to us the truth that the word and the Spirit are
closely and essentially associated. He did not say that the
Spirit dwells in the word, but that the words which he spoke
"are spirit, and are life." This expresses a closer relationship
than a mere dwelling in the word; it implies that the Spirit
and the life principle dwell in the word, and, further, that they

graven on stones, came ²with glory, so that the children of Israel could not look stedfastly upon the face of Moses for the glory of his face; which *glory* ³was passing away: 8 how shall not rather the ministration of the spirit be with glory? 9 ⁴For if the ministration of condemnation hath glory, much

²Gr. *in.*
³Or, *was being done away* Comp. 1 Cor. 13. 8, 10. See ver. 7 marg.
⁴Many ancient authorities read *For if the ministration of condemnation is glory.*

are associated and combined as one in work and influence— just as the seed is composed of the material substance and the immaterial life germ that dwells within and is an essential part of the seed.

7 But if the ministration of death, written, and engraven on stones,—The law of Moses written on stones is called the ministration of death, because it could not make the comers thereunto perfect as pertained to the conscience. It condemned all infractions of the law, but gave pardon to none. It, with its sacrifices, pointed forward to Christ as the author of forgiveness; but it could not bring true spiritual life.

came with glory,—[Here begins the comparison of the glory of the ministry of the old covenant with that of the new covenant.]

so that the children of Israel could not look stedfastly upon the face of Moses for the glory of his face;—The outward and visible glory of the appearance of God was such that the countenance of Moses, because he had been face to face with God, shone so that the children of Israel could not bear to look upon his face. (Ex. 34: 29-35.)

which glory was passing away:—All this glory must pass away and have an end.

8 how shall not rather the ministration of the spirit be with glory?—[The ministration of the Spirit is the service performed by the apostles in bringing in the new covenant. The argument is from the less to the greater, from the ministry of death to that of the life-giving Spirit. The glory of the ministration of death was a glory of sight. It was intended to influence the Israelites from without, being addressed to their outward senses, whilst the glory of the ministration of the Spirit is within, from within, unseen for the most part by the

rather doth the ministration of righteousness exceed in glory. 10 For verily that which hath been made glorious hath not been made glorious in this respect, by reason of the glory that surpasseth. 11 For if that which ⁵passeth away *was* ⁶with glory, much more that which remaineth *is* in glory.

⁵Or, *is being done away* See ver. 7 marg.
⁶Gr. *through.*

eye of man, and yet its glory is infinitely greater, for it is the glory of the spirit rather than of the flesh. It is conformity to that which is the highest glory of God, even his loving and righteous character, and as great as the difference between life and death, so great is the difference between the glory of the new covenant and that of the old.]

9 For if the ministration of condemnation hath glory, much rather doth the ministration of righteousness exceed in glory. —For if the ministration which could not bring life, but brought condemnation, inasmuch as it could not free from sin, was glorious, how much rather shall the ministration of the Spirit which brings life be more glorious. The old sought to regulate the life without changing the heart. The lustful impulses dwelling in the flesh hindered this. The new covenant, through Christ, touches the heart with love and so controls the life.

10 For verily that which hath been made glorious hath not been made glorious in this respect, —[Not only does the glory of the dispensation of righteousness exceed that of the ministration of condemnation in that it is moral and spiritual as well as outward and physical, but the glory of the ministration of righteousness far exceeds the glory which preceded it, in this respect that it is permanent.]

by reason of the glory that surpasseth. —The law of Moses, while it was glorious, loses all claims to glory, compared with the greater glory of the ministration of the Spirit that so exceeds it. It is more glorious, as Jesus was more glorious than Moses; as its eternal rewards in heaven are more glorious than the temporal blessings in the land of Canaan.

11 For if that which passeth away was with glory, —[This corroborates the statement just made. The passing of the glory recalls the fading of the glory from the face of Moses, and it is now clear that its vanishing was a symbol of the transitoriness of the Mosaic dispensation, for he applies here the same expression to the ministry which he applied to the glory—"that which passeth away."]

much more that which remaineth is in glory.—[While glory was the accompaniment of the law, it is the permanent element of the gospel. The law was of God; it had a very important function in the economy of God; it was a preparation for the gospel, and shut up men to the acceptance of God's mercy, in Christ as the only hope, and then its work was done. (Gal. 3: 19-25.) In this respect the true greatness of God is revealed, and with it his true glory, once for all. There is nothing beyond the righteousness of God in Christ Jesus for acceptance. That is God's last word to the world—it has absorbed in it even the glory of the law. It is God's chief end to reveal this glory in the gospel, and make men partakers of it. This finality of the new covenant is its crowning glory.]

This is often misunderstood. It does not mean that the moral laws embodied in the law of Moses are not in force now. All the good of the old covenant was brought over into the new covenant, and other truths were added. It is like the adoption of a new constitution by a state. The old constitution has many good wholesome laws, but some have grown ill-adapted to the present condition of the people; a new constitution is adopted. All that was of permanent value in the old is brought over into the new, and when it is adopted, the old is set aside—passes away. The good laws of the old are no longer in force because they were in the old, but because they have been brought over into the new. In like manner the good laws of the Mosaic covenant are no longer in force because they were in it, but because they have been brought over into the new covenant.

7. THE CONTRAST BETWEEN THE COVENANTS CONTINUED, EVINCING THE CLEARNESS AND SUFFICIENCY OF DIVINE KNOWLEDGE THROUGH CHRIST.
3: 12-18.

12 Having therefore such a hope, we use great boldness of speech, 13 and *are* not as Moses, *who* put a veil upon his face, that the children of Israel should not look stedfastly [7]on the end of that which [8]was passing away: 14

[7]Or, *unto*

---

12 Having therefore such a hope,—[This is a comparison and a contrast. His hope is nothing uncertain, but a constant expectation that the splendor of the ministration of the new covenant is an abiding glory.] The law of Moses made nothing perfect, but the bringing of a better hope did. (Heb. 7: 19.) The hope of the freedom from sin in this world, and of an everlasting inheritance in the world to come, was the better hope brought in by Jesus Christ.

we use great boldness of speech,—[This stands opposed to all concealment, whether from timidity or from a desire to deceive; and also to all fear of consequences. It is a frank, open, courageous manner of speech.] In Paul's case it was a firm conviction of his divine mission and of the truth and glory of the gospel which he proclaimed fully, intelligibly, and without regard to consequences, that the people might see the purpose and end of the law.

13 and are not as Moses, who put a veil upon his face, that the children of Israel should not look stedfastly on the end of that which was passing away:—When Moses came down from the mount after his interview with Jehovah, his face shone with such a glory that the people could not look steadfastly upon it, "and when Moses had done speaking with them, he put a veil on his face." (Ex. 34: 33.) This is interpreted to mean that they could not look steadfastly to the end of that dispensation and see Jesus, the end of the law. Their vision was too weak. [The truth concerning man's redemption, Paul says, "in other generations was not made known unto the sons of men, as it hath now been revealed unto his holy apostles and prophets in the Spirit." (Eph. 3: 5.) It was not, therefore, consistent with the ministry of Moses to use the

but their minds were hardened: for until this very day at the reading of the old covenant the same veil remaineth, it not being revealed *to them* that it is done away in Christ. 15 But unto this day, whensoever Moses is read, a veil lieth upon their heart. 16 But whensoever it shall turn to the Lord, the veil

[8]Gr. *thoughts.*   Ch. 4. 4; 11. 3.
[9]Or, *remaineth unlifted; which* veil *is done away*
[10]Or, a man *shall turn*

openness in communicating the doctrines of redemption which is the glory of the ministry of Christ.]

14 but their minds were hardened:—Their minds were blinded or veiled, so that they could not see the full truth concerning the object of the law.

for until this very day at the reading of the old covenant the same veil remaineth,—The same veil that hindered their fathers looking to the end is not taken out of the way.

it not being revealed to them that it is done away in Christ. —The veil is taken away in Christ. He opens up the vision so that they can see the end. As they reject Christ, the veil remains.

15 But unto this day, whensoever Moses is read, a veil lieth upon their heart.—While Jesus has taken away the veil, these Jews in rejecting him retain the veil over their hearts when they read the law of Moses, and so cannot look to the end of the law and see Jesus Christ, the Son of God, and the hope of the world pointed forward to in the law. [They never discovered that the law was given in order that sin might reveal itself under a form in which it could neither be mistaken nor excused. They "had not known sin, except through the law," for "through the law cometh the knowledge of sin," for "through the commandment sin" became "exceeding sinful." (Rom. 7: 7; 3: 20; 7: 13.) This makes it certain that the law was given that they might have a standard, and that under the unmistakable and unyielding demands of the law they might learn their own powerlessness to discharge their obligations to God, and that they might become convinced of their need of a Savior.]

16 But whensoever it shall turn to the Lord, the veil is taken away.—When they shall sleek to know God and his

is taken away. 17 Now the Lord is the Spirit: and where the Spirit of the
Lord is, *there* is liberty. 18 But we all, with unveiled face [11]beholding as in
a mirror the glory of the Lord, are transformed into the same image from
glory to glory, even as from the Lord the Spirit.

[11]Or, *reflecting as a mirror*

---

will, the veil that prevents their seeing that Jesus is the Christ
will be taken away.

**17 Now the Lord is the Spirit: and where the Spirit of the
Lord is, there is liberty.**—[There is here a broad contrast between two covenants, called respectively, "the letter" and "the
Spirit," the one proceeding from the veiled Moses at Mount
Sinai; the other emanting from the unveiled Christ on Mount
Zion. In the expression, "whensoever Moses is read" (verse
15), it is clear that Moses stands for "the letter," or legal covenant which Moses gave, and by force of contrast "the Lord"
stands in the same way for "the Spirit," or gracious covenant
of which he is the author. Fully stated the whole anthithesis
stands thus: Now Moses is "the letter" and where the "letter"
of Moses is there is bondage (Gal. 4: 24, 25); but "the Lord is
the Spirit: and where the Spirit of the Lord is, there is
liberty."]

**18 But we all, with unveiled face beholding as in a mirror
the glory of the Lord,**—With face unveiled beholding as
though looking into a mirror, we are transformed into the
same image of the Lord whom we see. We look unto Jesus
as we look into a mirror; his likeness is reflected back upon
us, and we are transformed into the image which we behold in
him.

are transformed into the same image from glory to glory,—
This image is one of glory. We are raised from one degree of
likeness to another, and it takes place on earth. While it
brings us into a state of glory, it is at best only a partial one,
for we see him imperfectly. The looking into the face of
Jesus as represented in his laws, and seeking to do them,
transforms us by degrees into his likeness. In this world our
vision of Jesus is imperfect, being hindered by the weakness
and infirmities of the flesh; but when these shall all be laid
aside, and in the spirit world, we shall look upon him with

clear, unobscured vision, and see him as he is, in the fullness of his perfections, we shall then be transformed into his perfect likeness, and shall dwell with him forever. "Beloved, now are we children of God, and it is not yet made manifest what we shall be. We know that, if he shall be manifested, we shall be like him; for we shall see him even as he is." (1 John 3: 2.)

even as from the Lord the Spirit.—This is all done for us by the Spirit. The Spirit takes the things of Jesus and declares them unto the world. The New Testament contains the things of Jesus which the Spirit declares. To hear and practice the things taught in the word of God is to be molded by the Spirit into the likeness of Christ. To follow these teachings is to become pure and to begin the transformation on earth that will be perfected into the complete likeness of Christ in the world to come.

8. VINDICATION OF HIS APOSTOLIC MINISTRY IN THE LIGHT OF THE FOREGOING CONTRASTS.
4: 1-6.

1 Therefore seeing we have this ministry, even as we obtained mercy, we

---

1 Therefore seeing we have this ministry,—In this he refers to the ministry of the new covenant (3: 6), which had been committed to him that he might reflect the glory of God upon the Corinthians, that they might be changed into the same image of Christ.

even as we obtained mercy,—It was the mercy of God that so high a trust had been committed to him. He always felt that after his persecuting the church it was a special mercy that God called him and enabled him to preach the gospel. [There was nothing so deep down in his soul, nothing so constantly in his thoughts, as this great experience. No flood of emotion, no pressure of trial, no necessity of conflict, ever drove him from his moorings here. The mercy of God underlay his whole being.]

we faint not:—As God had committed to him so great a trust, he would not be discouraged or disheartened by the great persecution he endured.

faint not: **2** but we have renounced the hidden things of shame, not walking in craftiness, nor handling the word of God deceitfully; but by the manifestation of the truth commending ourselves to every man's conscience in the sight of God. **3** And even if our [12]gospel is veiled, it is veiled in them that

[12]See marginal note on ch. 2. 12.

---

2 but we have renounced the hidden things of shame,— [Those disgraceful and secret arts of carnal wisdom; but his denial by no means implies that he acted in this manner at any time in his life.] The false teachers in their course had committed things so shameful that they sought to hide them from view.

not walking in craftiness,—He did not seek to take advantage of others. [Those who walk in craftiness can do everything, and are willing to do anything, to accomplish their ends. They are shrewd and acute in seeing how things can be done, and unscrupulous as to the character of the means to be employed, which they would be ashamed to avow openly.]

nor handling the word of God deceitfully;—Not perverting and misrepresenting the word of God. This probably refers to the false teachers among them.

but by the manifestation of the truth commending ourselves to every man's conscience—By honest and open declaration of the truth he sought to commend himself to the approval of the consciences of all who were taught by him the word of God. [The truth of God is adapted to man's fallen state, to raise him out of his corruption, and give him power and grace to live as becomes a true child of God. The manifestation of such truth commends itself to the conscience of each man, revealing to him his sin, and showing him at the same time the true remedy.]

in the sight of God.—[This is not an oath, but simply implies that the assertion that he had made respecting his commendation of himself to every man's conscience was entirely pure, inasmuch as he made it under a full sense of God's presence to hear him. He who thus works will work honestly, faithfully, and earnestly. All his work will be profitable to men and acceptable to God.]

¹³perish: 4 in whom the god of this ¹⁴world hath blinded the ⁸minds of the unbelieving, ¹⁵that the ¹⁶light of the ¹²gospel of the glory of Christ, who is the image of God, should not dawn *upon them.* 5 For we preach not our-

¹³Or, *are perishing*
¹⁴Or, *age*
¹⁵Or, *that they should not see the light . . . image of God*
¹⁶Gr. *illumination.*

3 **And even if our gospel is veiled, it is veiled to them that perish:**—This implies that to many the gospel was not perceived. This could not be denied, notwithstanding the plainness and fullness with which its truths were made known; but it was veiled only to those who, by their whole bearing toward the gospel, make it plain that they are not willing to come to Christ that they may be saved.

4 **in whom the god of this world**—The god of this world is Satan. God created the world and all that pertains to it for his own glory and honor. He then created man in his own image as his representative to rule the world, under God's direction, in harmony with God's laws, and for his glory and for the exaltation of his authority. But man betrayed the trust committed to him, and turned from God as his counsellor, guide, and ruler and chose to follow and obey the devil. In doing so, he transferred the allegiance and rule of the world from God to the evil one. Satan, by virtue of this transfer, became "the god of this world." Man chose Satan to be his god and the god of his kingdom instead of the Lord God, the Creator of the heavens and the earth. The devil in his parley with Jesus on the mount of temptation "showed him all the kingdoms of the world," and said unto him: "To thee will I give all this authority, and the glory of them: for it hath been delivered unto me; and to whomsoever I will I give it." (Luke 4: 6.)

hath blinded the minds of the unbelieving,—Satan veils the minds of those under his rule to hinder their seeing the truth of the gospel. [That is, that it might not show its true purport, and its real excellence to them; so that they should neither understand the one, nor appreciate the other. They are blind for lack of faith, and so being unbelieving they are perishing (Eph. 5: 6), seeing that they walk in darkness (John 8:

selves, but Christ Jesus as Lord, and ourselves as your [17]servants [18]for Jesus' sake. 6 Seeing it is God, that said, [19]Light shall shine out of dark-

[17]Gr. *bondservants.*   Comp. 1 Cor. 9. 19.
[18]Some ancient authorities read *through Jesus.*
[19]Gen. 1. 3.

---

12), and in Satan's power (Acts 26: 18). Blindness of heart is both a sin and a punishment of sin.]

that the light of the gospel of the glory of Christ, who is the image of God, should not dawn upon them.—His object in veiling their minds is that the light of the truth of the gospel shall not shine upon their hearts to enlighten and save them. He veils their hearts by filling them with the love of evil things. [So men may have the gospel shining all around them and directed full upon them, and yet be blinded, and blind themselves to it.]

Those who would behold God may see him reflected in the face of his Son, for, as Jesus said to Philip: "He that hath seen me hath seen the Father." (John 14: 9.) [The face of Moses was illumined because he had been in the presence of God, and so Christ reflects perfectly the glory of God, because he is "the effulgence of his glory." (Heb. 1: 3.)]

5 For we preach not ourselves,—He preached not his own thoughts, neither did he preach for his own exaltation, honor, and glory. [By this disclaimer is not meant that he excluded all reference to his own faith, or experience, and maintained an altogether impersonal tone while delivering instruction to the churches. The record of his work indicates the contrary. He freely spoke of his own experience of the mercy of God and sustaining grace of Christ, of his faith, his hope, his sorrows, and joys. He spoke and wrote freely of himself, but did not set himself before his hearers as the leader of the Savior. It was the fault of those factious teachers at Corinth who tried to disparage Paul's work, that they commended themselves, taught their own speculations, and eyed their own advancement, and drew disciples after them. This was what he disclaimed and abhorred, and what all preachers of the gospel must scrupulously and jealously avoid. It is positively fatal to spiritual success to project oneself before the people instead of setting forth the all-sufficiency of Christ Jesus.]

ness, who shined in our hearts, to give the [16]light of the knowledge of the glory of God in the face of Jesus Christ.

---

but Christ Jesus as Lord,—He preached that Christ Jesus is the Ruler and Savior. He must be exalted, honored, and obeyed. [The great end of preaching is to bring men to receive and acknowledge Jesus Christ as the Messiah and Supreme Lord of heaven and earth. It is the only way in which the salvation of men can be attained.]

and ourselves as your servants for Jesus' sake.—Paul presented himself as a servant of the Corinthians for the sake of Jesus, that he might thereby honor and exalt Jesus and save them. He says: "For though I was free from all men, I brought myself under bondage to all, that I might gain the more." (1 Cor. 9: 19.) This was the Spirit of Christ, who made himself to be servant of all that he might save men. He imitated Jesus, and said to them: "Be ye imitators of me, even as I also am of Christ." (1 Cor. 11: 1.)

6 **Seeing it is God, that said, Light shall shine out of darkness, who shined in our hearts,**—He felt the obligation to others on account of what God had done for him. God had given his truth to him that he might teach to others what God had taught him. The truth was revealed through Christ to him, and he made it known to the world.

to give the light of the knowledge of the glory of God in the face of Jesus Christ.—It was presented as light shining from the face of Christ to him, and by him reflected to the world. What the Holy Spirit revealed to him concerning Jesus, he taught the world. [The motive which influenced him to devote himself to the service of the Corinthians was the love of Christ. He always put God before man. A regard for the glory of Christ is a far higher motive than regard for the good of man; and the glory of Christ is the only true source for one's seeking the good of men. All through this verse there is also a clear reminiscence of his own conversion, inasmuch as he had seen the face of Jesus Christ, and the sight of this had changed the darkness of his own life into the light of God through Christ. And, as he walked in that light, conscious of its illumination and obligation, his life became transparent as the day. To such a man artifice, deception, and self-laudation are an impossibility, and he repudiated the charge with earnestness and sorrow.]

9. THE MIGHT OF DIVINE ENERGY COMBINED WITH THE WEAKNESS OF HUMAN INSTRUMENTALITY IN CARRYING FORWARD THIS MINISTRY.
4: 7-18.

7 But we have this treasure in earthen vessels, that the exceeding greatness of the power may be of God, and not from ourselves; 8 *we are* pressed on every side, yet not straitened.; perplexed, yet not unto despair; 9 pursued,

7 **But we have this treasure**—[By treasure is meant his ministry, but it is his ministry as pictured in the preceding paragraph, a ministry of illumination—a turning on the light of the knowledge of the glory of God in the face of Jesus Christ. It was a ministration of life, of power, and glory. It produced the most astonishing effects. It freed men from the condemnation and power of sin, delivered them from the power of the god of this world, and made them heirs of eternal life.]

in earthen vessels,—He possessed this knowledge in an earthen vessel—earthly, perishing body. [Any human body is an unworthy receptacle for so glorious a ministry. And Paul's body, racked and wrecked by all he had suffered (11: 23-27), seemed to him especially unworthy. His outward appearance seems physically not to have been very prepossessing (10: 1, 10), and its many hardships had not made it more so.]

that the exceeding greatness of the power may be of God, and not from ourselves;—All must know that the spiritual light and power he displayed did not pertain to his natural body; that it was given him of God, so that God would receive the honor and glory for all he did. [The frailty of his body made it all the more evident that the source of the power was not in himself, but in God.]

8 **we are pressed on every side, yet not straitened;**—Since the excellency of what he had, the knowledge of what he pos-

yet not [20]forsaken; smitten down, yet not destroyed; 10 always bearing about
in the body the [21]dying of Jesus, that the life also of Jesus may be manifested

[20]Or, *left behind*
[21]Gr. *putting to death.*

sessed, the power over all may be from God while he was
troubled, he did not give way to distress since God was his
shield.

perplexed, yet not unto despair;—He was often perplexed
and troubled; but did not despair, since God rules all things.
[This distinctly suggests inward rather than merely bodily
trials, or at least the inward aspect of these. Constantly at a
loss, he nevertheless always found the solution of his prob-
lems.]

9 **pursued, yet not forsaken;**—He was persecuted of men,
but not forsaken of God. Although God allowed men to per-
secute him, and to seek to destroy his life and usefulness, yet
he never deserted him or gave him up to the power of those
who followed him.

smitten down, yet not destroyed;—Jesus had said to his
apostles: "But when they deliver you up, be not anxious how
or what ye shall speak: for it shall be given you in that hour
what ye shall speak." (Matt. 10: 19.) When men seemed to
have him in their power, God delivered him, and he had confidence in God that he would uphold him in all trials. [This
occurred so often, and in cases so extreme, as to make it manifest that the power of God was exerted on his behalf. No
man left to his own resources could have endured or escaped
so much. This was not an occasional experience, but his life
was like that of Christ, in uninterrupted succession of indigni-
ties and sufferings.]

10 **always bearing about in the body the dying of Jesus,**—
He was always in his body exposed to, and in a manner suffering, the death that Jesus died. [Wherever he went among
Jews or Gentiles, in all his journeyings, he met everywhere
the same kind of treatment which Jesus himself received, and
as his sufferings and deaths were in Jesus' service and for
Jesus' sake, he had no hesitancy in saying that it was the putting to death of Jesus which was the burden his body always

in our body. 11 For we who live are always delivered unto death for Jesus'
sake, that the life also of Jesus may be manifested in our mortal flesh. 12

imposed upon him. He identifies himself with Jesus in his
sufferings and death elsewhere in terms as strong as he uses
here: "I protest by that glorying in you, brethren, which I
have in Christ Jesus our Lord, I die daily" (1 Cor. 15: 31),
"Even as it is written, For thy sake we are killed all the day
long; we were accounted as sheep for the slaughter" (Rom. 8:
36), "That I may know him, and the power of his resurrection, and the fellowship of his sufferings, becoming conformed
unto his death" (Phil. 3: 10), and "Now I rejoice in my sufferings for your sake, and fill up on my part that which is lacking
of the afflictions of Christ in my flesh for his body's sake,
which is the church" (Col. 1: 24). By using another figure he
expresses the same thought: "I bear branded on my body the
marks of Jesus." (Gal. 6: 17.)   The scars which he bore in his
body marked him as a soldier of Jesus Christ, and as belonging to him as his Master, and as suffering in his cause.]

that the life also of Jesus may be manifested in our body.—
That the life that Jesus lived might be reproduced and declared in his body.   [Just as Jesus' sufferings and death had
as their purpose life, so Paul thinks of his own sufferings as
serving the purpose of *manifesting*—making known—the life
which Jesus lives and which he gives.]

11 For we who live are always delivered unto death for
Jesus' sake,—On account of Jesus he constantly encountered
the danger of death.   [The sufferings which came upon him
daily in his work for Jesus were gradually killing him, the
pain and the perils, the spiritual pressure, the excitement of
danger and the excitement of deliverance, were wearing out
his strength, and he soon must die.   In the same way Jesus
had spent his strength and died, and in that life of weakness
and suffering which were always bringing him nearer the
grave, Paul felt himself in intimate sympathetic communion
with his Master.   It was "the dying of Jesus" that he carried
about in his body; but in spite of the dying he was not dead.]

that the life also of Jesus may be manifested in our mortal
flesh.—The mortal body of the believer delivered from death

So then death worketh in us, but life in you. 13 But having the same spirit
of faith, according to that which is written, ²²I believed, and therefore did I
speak; we also believe, and therefore also we speak; 14 knowing that he that

²²Ps. cxvi. 10.

---

represents the resurrection of Jesus from the dead. [The only
variation between this and the corresponding clause in the
preceding verse is that here the phrase "our mortal flesh" is
substituted for "in our body." The word body does not of itself involve the idea of weakness and mortality, but the word
flesh does. Hereafter we are to be clothed with bodies, but
not with flesh and blood. The contrast, therefore, between
the power of the life of Christ, and the feebleness of the organ,
through which that life is revealed, is enhanced by saying it
was manifested in our mortal flesh. In himself Paul was utter
weakness, in Christ he could do and suffer all things.]

12 **So then death worketh in us,**—His labors and teachings
—that they might live spiritually—exposed him to persecution, suffering, and death.

but life in you.—So that death worked in him, but life in
Christ was taught to them. [And as long as spiritual life
was working correspondingly in the Corinthians he was content.]

13 **But having the same spirit of faith, according to that
which is written, I believed, and therefore did I speak;**—Although the afflictions and dangers to which he was exposed
were adapted to discourage and even drive him to despair, he,
however, was not discouraged, but having the same spirit that
faith inspires, appropriated to himself the sentiment of the
psalmist.

we also believe, and therefore also we speak;—[The psalmist was greatly afflicted, the sorrows of death compassed
him, the pain of sheol got hold of him, but he did not despair.
He called on Jehovah and he helped him. He delivered his
soul from death, his eyes from tears, and his feet from falling.
His faith did not fail. He believed, and therefore, in the midst
of his afflictions, he proclaimed his confidence and recounted
the goodness of Jehovah. Paul's experience was the same.

raised up ²³the Lord Jesus shall raise up us also with Jesus, and shall present us with you.   15 For all things *are* for your sakes, that the grace, being multiplied through ¹the many, may cause the thanksgiving to abound unto the glory of God.

²³Some ancient authorities omit *the Lord.*
¹Gr. *the more.*

He also was sorely tried, but retained his confidence in Jehovah.]   Believing the facts of the gospel, Paul could not otherwise than speak them to the world.   The same thought is: "Woe is unto me, if I preach not the gospel." (1 Cor. 9: 16.) His faith constrained him to preach it, although it might bring persecution and even death unto him.

14 knowing that he that raised up the Lord Jesus shall raise up us also with Jesus,—The thing that encouraged him to speak the word of God to them even if it brought death was that he who raised up Christ from the dead would, through Jesus, raise up him and his associates.

and shall present us with you.—They would be the crown of his rejoicing in the day of the Lord.   [He is here exulting in the assurance, however persecuted and downtrodden here, God, who had raised up Jesus, would raise him up and present him with all other believers before the presence of his glory with exceeding joy.   This it was that sustained him, and has sustained so many others of the afflicted of God's people, and given them a peace which passes all understanding.]

15 For all things are for your sakes,—All that God had done for him and all the sufferings and labors he had done for the Corinthians were for their good.

that the grace, being multiplied through the many, may cause the thanksgiving to abound unto the glory of God.— That the abundant mercy and favors shown them might through their much thanksgiving redound to the glory of God. [The more Paul toiled and suffered, the more God's grace was made known and received; and the more it was received the more did it cause thanksgiving to abound to the glory of God. Anything that causes thanksgiving to God is worth all it costs.]

16 Wherefore we faint not; but though our outward man is decaying, yet our inward man is renewed day by day. 17 For our light affliction, which is for the moment, worketh for us more and more exceedingly an eternal weight of glory; 18 while we look not at the things which are seen, but at

16 **Wherefore we faint not;**—Because his sufferings brought glory to God and good to the Corinthians he did not grow discouraged under them.

but though our outward man is decaying, yet our inward man is renewed day by day.—As his fleshly body, day by day, under labors and years, perished, or decayed, the inner spiritual man by these same sufferings and passing years grew stronger and stronger. Paul, never robust, was growing old and feeble in body, but his spiritual man grew stronger day by day.

17 **For our light affliction.**—If we are diligently serving God, the afflictions and troubles of life work out for us greater honors and glories by preparing and qualifying us to enjoy the greater and higher honors God reserves for the faithful in the world to come. As compared with the glory to be gained, the sufferings to be endured are light.

which is for the moment,—As compared with the eternal life which he was to enjoy, the days of his sufferings were but a moment of time.

worketh for us more and more exceedingly an eternal weight of glory;—The sufferings wrought out the glories of Christ. "If we endure, we shall also reign with him: if we shall deny him, he also will deny us" (2 Tim. 2: 12), "but insomuch as ye are partakers of Christ's sufferings, rejoice; that at the revelation of his glory also ye may rejoice with exceeding joy" (1 Pet. 4: 13), "and if children, then heirs; heirs of God, and joint-heirs with Christ; if so be that we suffer with him, that we may be also glorified with him" (Rom. 8: 17). The glory is so great, so past comprehension, he calls it an exceeding and eternal weight of glory, oppressive in its grandeur.

18 **while we look not at the things which are seen,**—The temporal things we see, together with the fleshly body, are temporal—must pass away.

the things which are not seen: for the things which are seen are temporal;
but the things which are not seen are eternal.

**but at the things which are not seen: for the things which
are seen are temporal; but the things which are not seen are
eternal.**—The spiritual things which we see by faith, including
the spiritual body, are eternal. Paul does not look at or prize
the things that are temporal. The bodily sufferings and plea-
sures endure for a time, then cease. He does not let them
weigh upon him or affect his course. The unseen things that
he looks to through faith are eternal. IIe looks to them, lets
them have weight with him, and labors with the view of at-
taining the eternal glories.

All the service God calls on us to perform, every burden he
lays on us to bear, every affliction which we endure are intended for our good, and, if received in the spirit of obedient
and faithful children, will fit us to enjoy the richest blessings
God has in store for them that love him. He calls on us for
no service because he needs it, but because we need it for our
good. The Christian who neglects duties and shirks responsi-
bilities will find himself unqualified for the honors and glories God has in reserve for his faithful servants.

10. MORE SPECIFIC INDICATION OF THE UNSEEN ETERNAL
REALITIES AS STANDING IN CONTRAST WITH THE
PERISHABLE THINGS OF THIS LIFE.
5: 1-10.

1 For we know that if the earthly house of our ²tabernacle be dissolved,

²Or, *bodily frame* Comp. Wisd. 9. 15.

---

1 For we know—This was not the knowledge of experience,
or of human testimony, or of intuition. It was the knowledge
which came to Paul by divine revelation. Only thus could he
know of the resurrection and of the glorified body.

that if the earthly house of our tabernacle—The fleshly
body in which we dwell. The principle of life that pervades
different bodies gives to each the organic form that the life
principle requires. The life principle is the distinguishing and

we have a building from God, a house not made with hands, eternal, in the heavens. 2 For verily in this we groan, longing to be clothed upon with our habitation which is from heaven: 3 if so be that being clothed we shall not

---

controlling factor in the formation and existence of all organic bodies. It distinguishes one body from another. The life principle that gathers and shapes the body must precede the body and must endure when it passes away to give life and form to other like bodies to succeed it. The life principle in man is concentrated in the seed and preserved in the womb until it is brought into favorable conditions for its vivification, and gathers such matter and appropriates to the formation of such a body as the life principle demands.

be dissolved,—This body is perishable, is mortal, will return to the dust. "The body apart from the spirit is dead." (James 2: 26.) When it is dead it ceases to be the abode of the spirit that gave it character, it ceases to be the person. Solomon says: "The dust returneth to the earth as it was, and the spirit returned unto God who gave it." (Eccles. 12: 7.)

we have a building from God, a house not made with hands, eternal, in the heavens.—We have a house or spiritual body from God that endures forever in the heavens. "God giveth it a body even as it pleased him." (1 Cor. 15: 38.) In the eternal world, God will give to each spirit such a body as it is fitted to wear. [Paul entertained no doubt whatever as to the resurrection; "we know" and "we have" is his very positive language, as if it were already an accomplished fact, a present possession. So the prophets and inspired men generally speak of the purposes of God; they seize them by faith as already their own, not as if lying at a distant and uncertain future (cp. Heb. 11: 1). The assurance of apostolic men is remarkable. They never questioned for a moment the majestic revelations of God to them. Real as life, more real than death (for they did not doubt that the Lord Jesus might come again during their lifetime, and they should not die at all) was the certainty of the resurrection and glorification of their bodies.]

2 For verily in this we groan, longing to be clothed upon with our habitation which is from heaven:—In the mortal body we suffer, grow weary. As years and labors press upon

be found naked. 4 For indeed we that are in this ²tabernacle do groan, ³being burdened; not for that we would be unclothed, but that we would be clothed upon, that what is mortal may be swallowed up of life. 5 Now he

³Or, *being burdened, in that we would not be unclothed, but would be clothed upon*

us, we are burdened and sigh for rest. We groan from a sense of weakness, desiring earnestly to be immortalized, or freed from pain and suffering. The Christian through faith in the glory of the future yearns for rest from weariness and sufferings of mortality.

3 **if so be that being clothed we shall not be found naked.**— The earthworm, the larvae, in its chrysalis or cocoon, scarcely shows life or moves. In this state it remains, seems to be burdened by it, but it is protected and shielded by the earthly shell, while its pinions are pluming for a higher life. When this old shell is laid aside and in its new body, it rises and floats upwards toward the skies. The earthly shell has served as a protection, while the more glorious plumage has been growing into fitness for a higher life. While it is necessary to its higher life to lay aside the old shell when the new covering is ready, it would be destruction to it to strip off the old shell before the new body is ready. So as earthworms, we are clothed here for a time with earthly, fleshly bodies, while our spiritual bodies are being made ready for a higher life. When these are ready, and we are ready for them, then the earthly, fleshly bodies are laid aside that in our spiritual bodies we may be borne to the home made ready by the Savior. (John 14: 1-3.) God prepares the immortal covering while we are in the fleshly body serving him, and becoming ready for the spiritual body from heaven. But if we be stripped of the mortal body before the spiritual body is ready, we shall be naked and in a ruined condition.

4 **For indeed we that are in this tabernacle do groan, being burdened;**—In the fleshly mortal tabernacle we suffer and groan.

not for that we would be unclothed, but that we would be clothed upon, that what is mortal may be swallowed up of life. —Not that we would lay aside the outward covering, and be left naked, but that we would be clothed upon with the im-

that wrought us for this very thing is God, who gave unto us the earnest of
the Spirit. 6 Being therefore always of good courage, and knowing that,
whilst we are at home in the body, we are absent from the Lord 7 (for we

mortal in which there will be no more weariness and sorrow.
[Our obedience to the call of the gospel was accompanied by
rejoicing in hope of the glory of God; but this hope was
tested, for it is possible not to hold fast the confidence of the
hope firm unto the end. It is tested or tried by tribulations; if
we receive these tribulations as coming from God and submit
to them, then we have the confidence, the confidence of trial
borne well, and this doubles our hope. We hope not only because of the general promises of the gospel, but because we
are sure of God's having given us such grace to sustain trials
and persecutions that he intends us to partake of the future
glory, according to the words of the apostle: "For if we died
with him, we shall also live with him: if we endure, we shall
also reign with him." (2 Tim. 2: 11, 12.)]

5 **Now he that wrought us for this very thing is God,**—Now
he that prepared and made us ready for this state of immortal-
ity is God. He does this by the training and discipline he
gives those who obey him while here in the flesh.

who gave unto us the earnest of the Spirit.—He sent the
Holy Spirit to train and fit his disciples for the mansions he
prepared for them. An earnest is a pledge or assurance that a
promise will be kept. God has confirmed what he teaches by
"signs and wonders, and by manifold powers, and by gifts of
the Holy Spirit, according to his own will." (Heb. 2: 3, 4.)
Thus God has attested all his promises and all his teaching
concerning all things through the apostles. This assurance or
pledge we now have, filling us with joyous anticipation and
glorious hope of the resurrection and eternal life herein set
forth. "For this we say unto you by the word of the
Lord. . . . . Wherefore comfort one another with these
words." (1 Thess. 4: 15-18.)

6 **Being therefore always of good courage, and knowing
that, whilst we are at home in the body, we are absent from
the Lord**—While Paul had received the Holy Spirit, and this

walk by faith, not by ⁴sight) ; 8 we are of good courage, I say, and are will-
⁴Gr. *appearance.*

help, he was more confident of future blessings, and this made
him feel that while he was on earth in the body he was absent
from the Lord with the eternal glories of the spiritual bodies,
so he desired to be with him.

7 for we walk by faith,—Faith in the promises of God
concerning the future leads man to walk after the things of
God. Faith is seeing by the Spirit. [The condition of our
present state of being is that of believing. We do not know
these things as they appear to the natural eye; it is by faith
that we know them. The faith which "is assurance of things
hoped for" (Heb. 11: 1) is the element in which we live, so
long as we are not present with those things. Being the object of faith, they are of course absent. We are conversant
with the report of the heavenly things, not with the things
themselves. We are absent, not present with the things that
govern our life. Paul says: "That life which I now live in the
flesh I live in faith, the faith which is in the Son of God, who
loved me, and gave himself up for me." (Gal. 2: 20.) By faith
Abraham "looked for the city which hath the foundations,
whose builder and maker is God" (Heb. 11: 10); and by faith
Moses "looked unto the recompense of reward" (Heb. 11: 26).
"These all died in faith, not having received the promises, but
having seen them and greeted them from afar, and having
confessed that they were strangers and pilgrims on the earth."
(Heb. 11: 13.) "Belief cometh of hearing, and hearing by the
word of Christ." (Rom. 10: 17.) Faith is believing fully and
appropriating by obedience whatever God promises or says in
regard to anything. Walking by faith is taking every step we
make according to his directions. We cannot hope for anything which God has not promised, or hope for that which he
has promised without complying with the conditions upon
which his promises are based. We cannot do by faith anything which God has not commanded.]

not by sight) ;—To walk by sight is to walk after the things
of this world. [One walks by sight who makes mammon his
god; lives for getting and hoarding, or else for spending and

ing rather to be absent from the body, and to be at home with the Lord. 9 Wherefore also we ⁵make it our aim, whether at home or absent, to be well-pleasing unto him. 10 For we must all be made manifest before the judgment-seat of Christ; that each one may receive the things *done* ⁶in the body, according to what he hath done, whether *it* be good or bad.

⁵Gr. *are ambitious*. See Rom. 15. 20 marg.
⁶Gr. *through*.

---

squandering; estimates worth by wealth, and will count himself a happy man if he can die rich. A man who walks by sight, who cannot control his appetite or passion, cannot put aside the thing good for food or pleasant to the eyes even for the sake of avoiding tomorrow's sickness, or a life of disgrace, finds himself again and again yielding to a temptation from which he has suffered; weakly lives and miserably dies the slave of that which his better nature condemns and despises, but to which his body of flesh and blood, made a tyrant by long yielding to it, ties and binds him. Again, a man walks by sight who allows himself to live for the admiration of other people. Thus, not only covetousness or self-indulgence in the lowest sense of the word, but vanity and worldliness and vulgar ambition, all have their root in walking by sight.]

8 **we are of good courage, I say, and are willing rather to be absent from the body, and to be at home with the Lord.**—He was willing to leave the fleshly body, or die, and go home to be with the Lord, clothed with the immortal body.

9 **Wherefore also we make it our aim, whether at home or absent, to be well-pleasing unto him.**—Because of his anxiety to be present with the Lord, he labored to live according to God's will so as to be sure of his approval, whether he was absent here in the flesh, or at home with the Lord in heaven.

10 **For we must all be made manifest before the judgment seat of Christ;**—The deeds and courses of all must be laid open to all when we come before the judgment seat of Christ.

that each one may receive the things done in the body,—We shall be judged according to the things done in the body. We cherish secret thoughts and cover up acts of which we are ashamed, but they will be laid open to God, angels, and men. How foolish to conceal things here to have them laid open before the universe.

according to what he hath done, whether it be good or bad.
—Each will be rewarded at that day with good or evil, as the
deeds here have been according to or against the will of God.
[Unto those who through faith in Christ obey him and continue steadfastly in well-doing, seeking for glory and honor
and incorruption, God will give eternal life; "but unto them
that are factious, and obey not the truth, but obey unrigh-
teousness, shall be wrath and indignation, tribulation and anguish, upon every soul of man that worketh evil, of the Jew
first, and also of the Greek; but glory and honor and peace to
every man that worketh good, to the Jew first, and also to the
Greek: for there is no respect of persons with God." (Rom. 2:
8-11.)]

11. FURTHER ACCOUNT OF THE APOSTLE'S MINISTRY SET-
TING FORTH THE PURITY OF HIS MOTIVES AND
BLESSED RESULTS AT WHICH HE AIMED.
5: 11-21.

11 Knowing therefore the fear of the Lord, we persuade men, but we are

11 **Knowing therefore the fear of the Lord,**—[The awe or
reverent fear which the Lord excites or of which he is the object. Hence, it often stands for true devotion to God. "The
fear of Jehovah is the beginning of wisdom." (Prov. 9: 10.)
"So the church . . . walking in the fear of the Lord . . . was
multiplied." (Acts 9: 31.) "Subjecting yourselves one to another in the fear of Christ." (Eph. 5: 21.) Fear in all these
passages means reverence and devotion. Paul's earnest desire to meet with the approval of Christ caused him to always
deport himself in a becoming manner. So it is clear that
Christ was to Paul the object of his devotion; and that he felt
himself responsible to him for his conduct.]

we persuade men,—The awe, the reverent fear which comes
from the thought of the fearful retribution the Lord will inflict on evil caused him to make such diligent efforts to persuade men to turn from their sins so as to escape the wrath.
[His untiring effort was to convince men of the truth.
"He reasoned in the synagogue every sabbath, and persuaded
Jews and Greeks." (Acts 18: 4.) That is, he endeavored to

made manifest unto God; and I hope that we are made manifest also in your consciences. 12 We are not again commending ourselves unto you, but *speak* as giving you occasion of glorying on our behalf, that ye may have wherewith to answer them that glory in appearance, and not in heart. 13 For whether we ⁷are beside ourselves, it is unto God; or whether we are of sober

⁷Or, *were*

---

convince them of the truth concerning Jesus Christ. (Acts 28: 23.)   Hence in the case before us, he means that he was really governed by the fear of the Lord and was sincere and honest, which the false teachers in Corinth had unjustly called in question.]

but we are made manifest unto God;—In doing this for them he commended himself to God as his servant.

and I hope that we are made manifest also in your consciences.—What commended him to God would commend him to the Corinthians, if their consciences were enlightened by the will of God.   [His integrity of purpose and life was made manifest to God, and he desired that it should be also in view of the enlightened consciences of men, and under reverential fear of the Lord in full view of the account to be given before him, he would persuade men of this honesty of heart when, like some of the Corinthians, they were disposed to misjudge him.]

12 We are not again commending ourselves unto you,—He had commended himself as an apostle (3: 1), and now he expresses a wish that his course might commend him to their consciences for good.

but speak as giving you occasion of glorying on our behalf, —He did not commend himself for his own good, but to give them occasion to glory on his account.

that ye may have wherewith to answer them that glory in appearance, and not in heart.—This would enable them to answer his opponents, who gloried in appearance, and were not true in heart.   [These false teachers gloried in the outward appearance of things, such as man's enthusiasms and visions (12: 1, 13), his eloquence (10: 10), his letters of commendation (3: 1), his Jewish birth (11: 22), his personal intimacy in the flesh with the Lord (5: 16).   It was in these things that

mind, it is unto you.   14 For the love of Christ constraineth us; because we thus judge, that one died for all, therefore all died; 15 and he died for all,

---

they placed their confidence, and in them they made their boast.]

13 for whether we are beside ourselves, it is unto God;—It is probable that this is in answer to charges made against him by the false teachers, saying that he was beside himself in his zeal and self-denial.   If he was beside himself it was to promote the honor of God.

or whether we are of sober mind, it is unto you.—If he restrained his zeal, it was to secure their good.   He became all things to all men.   He here looks at the matter as they did, that he might sympathize with them, and help them in their difficulties.

14 **For the love of Christ constraineth us;**—As Christ's servant he partook of the love which Christ has for men.   It constrained him to give up all, that he might persuade some to believe in and obey Christ.   He was willing to be contrasted with those who "gloried in appearance, and not in heart," to be accused by false teachers of being beside himself, because he was constrained by the love of Christ to do so.   [The constraining power of Christian ministration and service is more effective and stable than it would be if it sprang from the fickle and varied affections of men.   Jesus said to his disciples: "Ye did not choose me, but I chose you, and appointed you, that ye should go and bear fruit, and that your fruit should abide: that whatsoever ye shall ask of the Father in my name, he may give it you." (John 15: 16.)]

because we thus judge, that one died for all, therefore all died;—All are dead in trespasses and sins, and need saving, so Christ died for all.   "We behold him who hath been made a little lower than the angels, even Jesus, because of the suffering of death crowned with glory and honor, that by the grace of God he should taste of death for every man. " (Heb. 2: 9.) But not only the fact that Christ died for all, making it possible for God to "be just, and the justifier of him that hath faith

that they that live should no longer live unto themselves, but unto him who
for their sakes died and rose again.   16 Wherefore we henceforth know no
man after the flesh: even though we have known Christ after the flesh, yet
now we know *him* so no more.   17 Wherefore if any man is in Christ, *⁸he is*

⁸Or, there is a *new creation*

---

in Jesus" (Rom. 3 : 26), must be considered, but also the effect
this love should have upon men.

**15 and he died for all, that they that live should no longer
live unto themselves,**—Christ died that he might deliver those
dead in sins from the bondage of sin, and lead them to live for
his honor and glory.   Unless we live such a life as to afford a
steppingstone to a higher life to those who come after us, our
life is a failure.   Jesus gave his life to lift up others and he
expects his disciples to follow his example.   In dying for us,
he has done something for us so immense in love that we
ought to be his forever.   To make us his was the very object
of his death.

but unto him who for their sakes died and rose again.—All
owe their redemption from death to Christ; and whether they
love and obey him or not, they should do so, and should live
no longer unto themselves, but unto him who for their sakes
died and rose again; for none are their own.   "We love, because he first loved us." (1 John 4: 19.)   The goodness of God
leads men to repentance, and every one who does not repent
despises "the riches of his goodness and forbearance and long-
suffering, not knowing that the goodness of God leadeth thee
to repentance." (Rom. 2: 4.)

16 Wherefore we henceforth know no man after the flesh:
—He would follow no man after the flesh or for his family descent.

even though we have known Christ after the flesh,—Some
had been drawn to Christ after the flesh, or because he was
the seed of Abraham.

yet now we know him so no more.—Henceforth we will
know him no more on this ground, but will know him only as
the Son of God, the Redeemer of the world.   [No man became
a Christian, or a child of God, because he was a fleshly descend-

a new creature: the old things are passed away; behold, they are become

---

ant of Abraham, or even of the family of which Christ was born. Even the brothers of Jesus did not at first believe on him and were no better because of kinship to him. But this may mean that "the Word became flesh, and dwelt among us" (John 1: 14); hence, Christ was manifest in the flesh and was known in the flesh; but after he ascended to heaven and is still in heaven in his glorified body, he is not known in the flesh, but is the Savior, Prophet, Priest, and King.]

17 **Wherefore if any man is in Christ, he is a new creature:** —If any man, Jew or Gentile, has died to sin and been raised in Christ, he is a new creature—neither Jew nor Gentile. He has new ends, new purposes; his whole soul, mind, and body are consecrated to the new life in Christ. "We were buried therefore with him through baptism into death: that like as Christ was raised from the dead through the glory of the Father, so we also might walk in newness of life." "Even so reckon ye also yourselves to be dead unto sin, but alive unto God in Christ Jesus." (Rom. 6: 4, 11.) "For as many of you as were baptized into Christ did put on Christ." (Gal. 3: 27.) "If then ye were raised together with Christ, seek the things that are above, where Christ is, seated on the right hand of God." (Col. 3: 1.) Thus before God and man, we take upon ourselves a solemn obligation, to consecrate, devote, and sanctify ourselves to the service of God. The soul, mind, and body with all their faculties and opportunities are buried out of self and raised in Christ Jesus, that we henceforth be his servants to do his will.

the old things are passed away; behold, they are become new.—He has new ends, new aims, new purposes; his whole soul, mind, and body are consecrated to a new life in Christ. [He must abide in Christ, grow in the Christian graces in him. Hence, Paul says: "Put ye on the Lord Jesus Christ, and make not provision for the flesh, to fulfil the lusts thereof." (Rom. 13: 14.) In Christ he finds redemption through his blood, the forgiveness of sins (Col. 1: 14), and all spiritual blessings (Eph. 1: 3).]

new. 18 But all things are of God, who reconciled us to himself through
Christ, and gave unto us the ministry of reconciliation; 19 to wit, that God

---

18 But all things are of God,—All things in the new relation
in Christ are from God. They have come through the love
and grace of God.

who reconciled us to himself through Christ,—In Jesus
Christ God reconciles the world unto himself. God is not
man's enemy. He has no feelings of enmity against him. He
has never harmed or wronged man in any way. "God is
love," and seeks man's greatest good both here and hereafter.
The supreme good of the human race was his consideration in
the creation of all things. When sin and death entered into
the world, through man's transgression, God in grace and love
provided through Christ the way of salvation. Hence, God is
not the one to be reconciled. He is willing and able to save to
the uttermost them that come unto him through Christ. (Heb.
7: 27.) Man must turn from his sins, come to God through
Christ, and in him, by a life of submission to his will, find, and
complete a reconciliation with God.

and gave unto us the ministry of reconciliation;—God committed unto the apostles the ministry of reconciliation. He
gave them the terms on which man could be reconciled to
him, and sent them as ambassadors to make known the terms
of reconciliation to man. The outpouring of the Holy Spirit
on the day of Pentecost and all the miraculous gifts bestowed
on the apostles that enabled them to work miracles were to
confirm them as his apostles, and enable them to show to the
world that they had the right and authority to proclaim the
words of reconciliation. Had Jesus himself ministered the
words of reconciliation after he had commanded the apostles:
"Go ye into all the world, and preach the gospel to the whole
creation" (Mark 16: 15), he would have discredited them and
their mission. God's gifts and calling to a work once bestowed on persons, he does not take them from them (Rom.
11: 29). Once having given the work into the hands of the
apostles to make known the terms of reconciliation, he did not
take it into his own hands, but confirmed them in the work.

was in Christ reconciling the world unto himself, not reckoning unto them

Inasmuch as the Lord desired to make Saul an apostle, to commission him as a coambassador with the other apostles, he must appear unto him for this purpose to enable him to be an apostle. Apostles must have seen the Lord after his resurrection (Acts 1: 22), and be sent by him. He had not delegated that power to others. Paul says: "I thank him that enabled me, even Christ Jesus our Lord, for that he counted me faithful, appointing me to his service." (1 Tim. 1: 12.) "Whereunto I was appointed a preacher and an apostle, . . . a teacher of the Gentiles in faith and truth." (1 Tim. 2: 7.) "And last of all, as to the child untimely born, he appeared to me also. For I am the least of the apostles, that am not meet to be called an apostle, because I persecuted the church of God." (1 Cor. 15: 8, 9.) The appearance to him after death was as to one "untimely born" to be an apostle. Jesus appeared to him to qualify him to be an apostle, but did not take upon himself the work that he had committed to the apostles and prophets. So when Saul had seen Jesus in his glory and learned who he was, Jesus sent him to Damascus to learn from his chosen disciple what he should do to be saved.

19 to wit, that God was in Christ reconciling the world unto himself,—God through Christ has provided the way of salvation, hence he is willing and ready and able to save to the uttermost all who come unto him through Christ. (Heb. 7: 25.) [Sinners are at enmity with God. The friendship with the world is enmity with God. "Whosoever therefore would be a friend of the world maketh himself an enemy of God." (James 4: 4.) The world hates God and Christ and the church. (John 15: 18, 19.) To become reconciled to God is to put away this enmity, to love God, to become obedient to him, to imbibe his spirit, and to live in harmony and unity with him. To influence and induce man to do this, God in his love sent Christ to be the propitiation of our sins.]

not reckoning unto them their trespasses, and having committed unto us the word of reconcilation.—God does not reckon unto men their trespasses, or hold their sins against

their trespasses, and having ⁹committed unto us the word of reconciliation.
20 We are ambassadors therefore on behalf of Christ, as though God
were entreating by us: we beseech *you* on behalf of Christ, be ye reconciled
to God. 21 Him who knew no sin he made *to be* sin on our behalf; that we
might become the righteousness of God in him. 1 And working together

⁹Or, *placed in us*

them, in that he forgives their sins upon their obedience to
Christ. (Heb. 5: 7-9.)

20 We are ambassadors therefore on behalf of Christ,—An
ambassador is ·one entrusted with a message from one sovereign to another. The apostles were ambassadors sent by God
to the world. As ambassadors to men, they, in the state of
Jesus, besought men to accept God's terms of reconciliation.

**as though God were entreating by us: we beseech you on
behalf of Christ, be ye reconciled to God.**—This presents the
picture of God having given his Son to die to redeem man,
still through his chosen ambassadors tenderly beseeching men
to be reconciled to God. This was no selfish good to God, but
knowing the awful doom that awaited the impenitent rebels,
he placed himself in the position of entreating them for their
own good.

21 Him who knew no sin he made to be sin on our behalf;
—God had made Jesus who committed no sin to suffer as
though he had sinned.

that we might become the righteousness of God in him.—
That man who was guilty of many sins might be blessed as
though he had not sinned, and be clothed with the righteousness of God. [Christ was accounted as one sinful and treated
as such in bearing *our* guilt that we might be accounted as
righteous while standing *in him* before God.]

Jesus took our nature and shared our sorrows here on earth,
that we might partake of his nature and share his glories in
heaven. This plea for reconciliation was to the Corinthians
whom he called "saints." This shows that while the reconciliation had begun by their entrance·into Christ, it was not
completed and perfected; and the entreaty was to complete
and perfect the reconciliation. That reconciliation will be
completed and perfected only when man in his heart and life

has been brought into complete harmony with God, "bringing every thought into captivity to the obedience of Christ." (10: 5.)

[Since some preachers speak of themselves as ambassadors of Christ, it is necessary to consider what it takes to constitute an ambassador. An ambassador must be chosen by the head of the government, and be ratified by the chief council of the nation. He must receive a commission and must be sealed with the great seal of the nation or power sending him. Having thus been duly qualified, he receives power at the appointed time to do or transact business in the name and for the government sending him. Not until the appointed time, and at the appointed place, can he act. His power may be either ordinary or extraordinary, according to the terms of the instruction given. Jesus, after he had chosen his apostles, gave them a commission with extraordinary power, saying to them: "Whose soever sins ye forgive, they are forgiven unto them; whose soever sins ye retain, they are retained" (John 20: 23), "What things soever ye shall bind on earth shall be bound in heaven; and what things soever ye shall loose on earth shall be loosed in heaven" (Matt. 18: 18), and to Peter he said: "I will give unto thee the keys of the kingdom of heaven: and whatsoever thou shalt bind on earth shall be bound in heaven; and whatsoever thou shalt loose on earth shall be loosed in heaven" (Matt. 16: 19.) And when he had accomplished his work on earth, just before he ascended to heaven, he appeared to his apostles, and said unto them: "All authority hath been given unto me in heaven and on earth. Go ye, therefore, and make disciples of all the nations" (Matt. 28: 18, 19), and gave them the seal of the court of heaven to their apostleship, saying: "And these signs shall accompany them that believe: in my name shall they cast out demons; they shall speak with new tongues; they shall take up serpents, and if they drink any deadly thing, it shall in no wise hurt them; they shall lay hands on the sick, and they shall recover" (Mark 16: 17, 18).

The record shows how fully and faithfully God bore the apostles witness with signs and wonders and gifts of the Holy

Spirit according to his will, "and, being assembled together with them, he charged them not to depart from Jerusalem, but to wait for the promise of the Father, which, said he, ye heard from me: for John indeed baptized with water; but ye shall be baptized in the Holy Spirit not many days hence" (Acts 1: 4, 5), and when they had received power according to his word, Peter declared that Jesus was sitting at the right hand of God exalted, and having received of the Father the promise of the Holy Spirit, had poured forth that which they saw and heard. Then exclaimed, "Let all the house of Israel therefore know assuredly, that God hath made him both Lord and Christ, this Jesus whom ye crucified. Now when they heard this, they were pricked in their heart, and said unto Peter and the rest of the apostles, Brethren, what shall we do? And Peter said unto them, Repent ye, and be baptized every one of you in the name of Jesus Christ unto the remission of your sins" (Acts 2: 36-38), and no terms of remission of sins were ever proclaimed by any of them except those preached on this occasion. The apostles were and are the ambassadors of Christ. They sustained a relation to the gospel that no other preachers in their day or since sustained or could sustain. They were *the revealers* of the gospel. The rest are simply *proclaimers* of what was *revealed* through the apostles.

No preacher today has any new revelation, nor can he make any valid claim to be a witness of the resurrection. He has no authority to declare the remission of sins, but can only point people to the apostle's declaration on the subject. He may preach the gospel, but he can never reveal it. He has no message that is not already made known. Then he has not the credentials of an ambassador. He cannot work miracles. The apostles were instructed to go into all the world and preach the gospel to the whole creation, to every creature, and it is said: "And they went forth and preached everywhere, the Lord working with them, and confirming the words by the signs that followed." (Mark 16: 20.) Now this gospel that was revealed through Christ's ambassadors is given in trust to the whole church of Christ to proclaim that the whole world may know the manifold wisdom of God. Paul in his instruc-

tion to a preacher of the gospel said, "The things which thou
hast heard from me among many witnesses, the same commit
thou to faithful men, who shall be able to teach others also."
(2 Tim. 2: 2.) We need expect no more gospel ambassadors
until the Lord has a new message for the denizens of earth.
We need expect nor more miraculous performances, because
there is no new divinely appointed message that needs the
credentials of miracles to attest that it is from on high, and
that the men bringing it are ambassadors of God.]

12. PRACTICAL DEMANDS AND SPECIAL CHARACTERISTICS OF HIS MINISTRY AND THE CONTRASTED PHASES OF HIS MINISTERIAL COURSE.
6: 1-10.

with him we entreat also that ye receive not the grace of God in vain 2 (for
.he saith,
　　　　　[10]At an acceptable time I hearken unto thee,
　　　　　And in a day of salvation I succor thee:

[10]Is. xlix. 8.

[In the opening chapters of this epistle, Paul has not an-
swered his enemies directly, as he does in the four closing
chapters. He has rather been supplying his friends, who form
the greater part of the Corinthian church, with grounds on
which they may repel the attacks which his enemies had been
making upon him. This paragraph is inseparable from the
one which precedes it. There he describes his ministry as one
of reconciliation. As an ambassador in behalf of Christ he has
been entreating men to be reconciled to God. Here he shows
that his conduct and experiences as an ambassador of God are
such as to vindicate fully his claims of genuineness, sincerity,
and honesty of purpose.]

1 **And working together with him we entreat also**—Paul
had presented himself as an ambassador sent by God to the
Corinthians entreating them to be reconciled to him. As such
he was a colaborer with God to save them. He entreats them
not to regard the appeal lightly, and pass it heedlessly, but to
hear and respond to it so as to fit themselves to enjoy the glories of the eternal home with God.

behold, now is the acceptable time; behold, now is the day of salvation) : 3
giving no occasion of stumbling in anything, that our ministration be not

---

that ye receive not the grace of God in vain—He fears
lest through the influence of the false teachers among them
their minds should be corrupted from the simplicity and purity that is toward Christ. It would be receiving the grace of
God in vain, if, after having become obedient to the gospel of
Christ which the apostle had taught them, they should turn
unto a different gospel; "which is not another gospel" (Gal. 1:
7)—a perverted gospel—in which these truths had no place.
This is what he dreads and deprecates, both in Corinth and in
Galatia. This is what is meant by receiving "the grace of God
in vain." [This does not, however, preclude from the edifying
application of these words to those who, having received the
truth, do not allow it to inspire and control as Paul shows
himself to have done in the verses that follow. The failure to
do this is too common. But if the mere profession of being a
Christian and an immoral life are the ugliest combination of
which a human being is capable, the force of this appeal ought
to be felt by the weakest and worst.]

2 **(for he saith, At an acceptable time I hearkened unto
thee, and in a day of salvation did I succor thee:**—This is
quoted from Isaiah (49: 8), in which he shows God's willingness to succor and save those who hearken unto his call and
obey him. He does not quote this as a prophecy now fulfilled,
but as the statement of God's willingness at all times to save.

**behold, now is the acceptable time; behold, now is the day
of salvation) :**—God is ever ready and willing to save all who
will submit to him and be saved in God's way. [There is a
"now" running through the ages. For each church and individual, there is a golden present which may never again recur,
and in which lie boundless possibilities for the future.]

3 **giving no occasion of stumbling in anything, that our
ministration be not blamed ;**—Paul endeavored to live in such
a way that nothing in his ministry would prove an obstruction
or a snare in the path of anyone seeking God causing him to

blamed; 4 but in everything commending ourselves, as ministers of God, in much ¹patience, in afflictions, in necessities, in distresses, 5 in stripes, in im-

¹Or, *stedfastness*

---

fall. [This he did not because he feared censure for himself, but "that our ministration be not blamed."]

4 but in everything commending ourselves, as ministers of God,—He showed himself to be a worthy minister of God by teaching the truth under great trials. [Paul's letter of commendation to the Corinthians is his life. This is the letter that should be presented to the people by all ministers of the word of truth. That is the one that will be read in preference to any letter that may be given by men. His life is an open book to the church and to the world. It is vain for him to bid men do as he says, not as he does. What he is thunders so loud in men's ears that they cannot hear what he says. He must meet life as it is, and Paul is not afraid.]

in much patience,—Paul bore patiently all things that came upon him. Jesus forewarned his disciples that they would have much to endure, and had strengthened them by the promise that he that endured to the end would be saved. (Matt. 10: 22.) [Patience, or steadfastness, is among the chief virtues and describes one who has been tested and who cannot be swerved from his course by any opposition or suffering.]

in afflictions,—Pressure from without or within, including everything that presses on the heart or tries the power of endurance or resistance. [This probably includes the griefs endured from the ingratitude of some, and the falling away of others.]

in necessities,—This describes a condition in which one is taxed to the utmost to know what to do or how to bear. A straightened place where one has no room on which to stand or turn, and therefore hope seems hopeless.

in distresses,—This reveals great perplexity as in sickness, loss of friends, and came on him as a servant of God.

5 in stripes,—Paul had already been eight times subjected to ignominy and torture of the lash—five times by the Jews

prisonments, in tumults, in labors, in watchings, in fastings; 6 in pureness, in knowledge, in longsuffering, in kindness, in the Holy Spirit, in love un-

---

and three times by the heathen. (11: 24, 25.) [Stripes were of two kinds—from Jewish whips and Roman rods; but of the five scourgings with Jewish whips not one is mentioned in Acts, and only one of the three scourgings with Roman rods. (Acts 16: 23.)]

in imprisonments,—He was frequently in prison, but Luke only tells us of one of these occasions (Acts 16: 24)—at Philippi; the imprisonment at Cesarea and Rome were subsequent to the time of writing this epistle.

in tumults,—These were normal incidents in Paul's life, both up to this time and for years afterwards. [The word means "tossing to and fro," and refers to his being constantly driven from one place to another, so that he had no quiet abode. (1 Cor. 4: 11.) This occurred at Antioch of Pisidia (Acts 13: 50); at Iconium (Acts 14: 5); at Lystra (14: 19); at Philippi (16: 19); at Thessalonica (17: 5); at Berea (17: 13); at Corinth (18: 12); and at Ephesus (19: 29). Before such manifestation of wrath and power the bravest man often quails. What can one do before an infuriated mob? He was calm and adhered to his purpose.]

in labors,—Working with his own hands, and also in strenuous exertions which he was constantly called upon to make, in traveling and preaching and in caring for all the churches. (11: 28.)

in watchings,—[Probably not vigils, but suggesting, in a large way, all the night toil which was involved in his ministry of the gospel. (Acts 20: 31.) This may also include watchings lest he should fall into some snare of his enemies. (Acts 20: 19.)]

in fastings;—Abstinence from food to which he chose to submit rather than to omit some duty or fail to take advantage of some opportunity of usefulness. The implication is that these hard experiences were not isolated, but frequent and familiar.

6 in pureness,—In this and the following words, he gives

feigned, [7]in the word of truth, in the power of God; [2]by the armor of right-
[2]Gr. *through*.

---

qualities he constantly exercised that no reproach be brought
on his ministry. He does this by following the guidance of
the Holy Spirit, by an earnest and unselfish desire for the
good of all. [By pureness he means not only chastity, which
is certainly included, but also purity of intention and thought,
sincerity and purpose. There is nowhere any trace of an im-
putation against Paul, even from his worst enemies, on the
score of licentiousness.]

in knowledge,—[Knowledge, in this case goes hand in hand
with chastity, and with the requirement of it from all others
as strictly incumbent upon all believers. By mentioning
knowledge he reminds them that he had exhibited no unen-
lightened bigotry in regard to legal cleanness and uncleanness, and so the warning he delivers cannot be attributed to
ignorance or narrow views of moral distinctions.]

in longsuffering,—[He patiently submitted to injustice
and undeserved injuries heaped upon him, and bore long with
the faults and failings of those whom he had converted to the
faith.]

in kindness,—[He endeavored to manifest a kindly spirit to
all, whatever their sin, and whatever might be their treatment
of him. He fully realized that if he would do good he must be
kind and gentle to all.]

in the Holy Spirit,—[By those graces and virtues which it
is the Holy Spirit's office to produce in the heart. Paul here
evidently does not refer to the miraculous agency of the Holy
Spirit, but to such feelings as he produces in the heart of the
children of God. (Gal. 5: 22, 23.)]

in love unfeigned,—[In the preceding clause he refers to the
love manifested to the evil and the good; here it must be that
which is due to those in Christ. "Let love be without
hypocrisy. . . . In love of the brethren be tenderly affec-
tioned one to another; in honor preferring one another."
(Rom. 12: 9, 10.)]

7 in the word of truth,—Paul had kept his private life in fit

eousness on the right hand and on the left, 8 by glory and dishonor, by evil

condition for the ministry, he had likewise demeaned himself publicly as a true apostle. He had kept his heart loyal to the truth, and likewise his tongue faithful to its proclamation,

in the power of God;—[The power of God (4: 7) comprises the whole of his ministerial activity, and the context shows that the power to which reference is made is his disciplinary courage and firmness. It might have seemed ungracious to allude to this here had he not been charged with weakness on one side and severity on the other. He claimed no power of his own, for it was God's, but as he had exercised it decisively in one case (1 Cor. 5: 4), he might use it so again, if his warnings were neglected. At the same time he could not exercise God's power, to wrong, to destroy, or to serve grasping purposes (7: 2), as his adversaries employed their power.]

by the armor of righteousness—[The power of God suggests the weapons by which it is exerted. They are the weapons of righteousness, nor could God's power be put forth by any other. The general idea is best explained in another passage. (10: 3, 4.) In that passage, "mighty before God" corresponds with the "power of God" here, and "we do not war according to the flesh" there is the opposite of "the armor of righteousness" here. This comparison indicates that he means weapons of integrity which smite with perfect impartiality, undirected, and unhindered by fear or favor or any regard for self.]

on the right hand and on the left,—[Paul was no more afraid, as was falsely said, to assail with his right hand pagan corruption than he was to pull down Judaizing strongholds (10: 4, 5), and that he was equally ready to meet with his left hand by all righteous means in his power every blow aimed at him in his office or person.]

8 by glory and dishonor,—He had often been glorifed as god and man. At one time the people were ready to worship him as a god, and immediately afterward they heaped upon him dishonor. (Acts 14: 11-19.) [Notwithstanding this he was always the same—he preached the same things, urged the same

report and good report; as deceivers, and *yet* true; 9 as unknown, and *yet* well known; as dying, and behold, we live; as chastened, and not killed; 10 as sorrowful, yet always rejoicing; as poor, yet making many rich; as hav-

duties, maintained the same principles, whether his preaching was approved or disapproved, whether it secured for him admiration or brought down upon him reproach. He does not mean to say he does not care. He does care very greatly. It stung him to the very depth of his soul. "Being reviled, we bless; being persecuted, we endure; being defamed, we entreat: we are made as the filth of the world, the offscouring of all things, even until now." (1 Cor. 4: 12, 13.) He was not disposed to complain of the conditions of service to Christ. He is the inspiration of all lovers of spiritual truth and freedom in Christ.]

by evil report and good report;—He went through both good and evil report without elation or distress of mind. He was often slandered and calumniated. His motives were called in question and his name aspersed. Others spoke well of him and honored him as a faithful servant of God.

as deceivers, and yet true;—He was often charged with being a deceiver, yet always faithful and true under all trials and temptations.

9 **as unknown, and yet well known;**—He was the same when unknown and well known. [His enemies accused him of being without standing because he had no letters of commendation. To this he replied that he is well known among true believers.]

as dying, and behold we live;—He was stoned and left for dead at Lystra, and often suffered the pangs of death, ye he lived.

as chastened, and not killed;—He was often chastised, beaten, but not killed. (His enemies said his troubles indicated that God was punishing him for his sins. Whether this was true or false, he did not let the opportunity pass to learn what good the chastisement may have for him. God can use these very enemies as a wholesome discipline for him.]

ing nothing, and *yet* possessing all things.

---

10 as sorrowful, yet always rejoicing;—He was sorrowful under his own sufferings and the wickedness of others, but in it all found joy in suffering for Christ and man. Every Christian finds joy and peace in all the sorrows of life endured for Christ. [Sorrow was a real note in Paul's life, but it was interwoven with: "Rejoice in the Lord always: again I will say, Rejoice." (Phil. 4: 4.) To him the sense of the love of God, assurance of his support, confidence in future blessedness, and the persuasion that his present light afflictions would work out for him a far more exceeding and an eternal weight of glory, mingled with his sorrows, gave him a peace which passed all understanding.]

as poor, yet making many rich;—While poor and suffering the want of all things, he brought the riches of life eternal to many. [He worked with his own hands as a tentmaker to support himself and fellow workers so that he could preach the gospel to a world that did not want to hear and that was doing its utmost to defeat him in the effort to do it. But he was of the spirit of the ancient worthies of whom it is said: "They were stoned, they were sawn asunder, they were tempted, they were slain with the sword: they went about in sheepskins, in goatskins; they were destitute, afflicted, illtreated (of whom the world was not worthy), wandering in deserts and mountains and caves, and the holes of the earth." (Heb. 11: 37, 38.) Paul manifested this spirit to make many rich in Christ. Those who accepted the offer of salvation had everything, for they had Christ and God. (1 Cor. 3: 22.) This is the spirit of the faithful preachers of the gospel who have carried the message of love all over the world. Paul did not wait for a place to be made ready for him. He spurned the thought, declaring that he made it his "aim so to preach the gospel, not where Christ was already named, that I might not build upon another man's foundation." (Rom. 15: 20.)]

as having nothing, and yet possessing all things.—While he had nothing of earthly good, the riches of the eternal world were his possession.

**13. MORE EXPLICIT EXPLANATION OF THE PRACTICAL DE-
MANDS OF "THE WORD OF RECONCILIATION."
6: 11 to 7: 1.**

11 Our mouth is open unto you, O Corinthians, our heart is enlarged. 12
Ye are not straitened in us, but ye are straitened in your own affections. 13
Now for a recompense in like kind (I speak as unto *my* children), be ye also
enlarged.

---

11 Our mouth is open unto you, O Corinthians,—Fiiled to
overflowing with the thought of the riches of his possession,
he bursts forth into an expression of love for the Corinthians.
He was ready to teach them; his affections for them grew
mightily.

our heart is enlarged.—His heart was enlarged with love for
them. [Not that he loved them any more dearly than he had
formerly done, but his emotions had broken forth into overflowing expression, and he took the opportunity to assure
them of the great place they had in his heart.]

12 Ye are not straitened in us,—Straitened means com-
pressed in a narrow place. They were not straitened in a narrow place in his affections for them (7: 3; Phil. 1: 7); he assures them that they had ample room there. If there was in
any sense constraint in their relations with him, they could
rest assured that it was altogether on their part, and not at all
on his.

but ye are straitened in your own affections.—They were
straitened by the narrowness of their own love.

**13 Now for a recompense in like kind (I speak as unto my
children), be ye also enlarged.**—Now in turn for his overflowing love for them, he appealed to them to enlarge their affections for him and love him more devotedly as children should
a father—they were his children in the gospel. He asked no
more from them than that candor and love which as his children they should be glad to give. These words show how
deeply pained he was by misunderstanding and reserve on the
part of those whom he loved, and how sorely he hungered for
their affection. He gave them a great place in his own heart,
and he could not bear to have but a little place in theirs.

14 Be not unequally yoked with unbelievers: for what fellowship have

---

14 Be not unequally yoked with unbelievers:—To be unequally yoked would be to be so connected with the unbeliever that the believer would be controlled by the unbeliever. The expression comes from Jehovah's command to the Israelites: "Thou shalt not plow with an ox and an ass together." (Deut. 22: 10.) So persons that do not harmonize in purposes, walk, and life should not be so bound together that the believer would be controlled by the unbeliever. The principle laid down certainly embraces all the relationships in which a Christian will be controlled in his life or business by one not a Christian. While I would not say that this passage is an absolute prohibition of the marriage of a believer to an unbeliever, it certainly discourages it. Paul says: "If any brother hath an unbelieving wife, and she is content to dwell with him, let him not leave her. And the woman that hath an unbelieving husband, and he is content to dwell with her, let her not leave her husband. For the unbelieving husband is sanctified in the wife, and the unbelieving wife is sanctified in the brother: else were your children unclean; but now are they holy." (1 Cor. 7: 12-14.) This is presenting the contingency for a separation where one becomes a believer after marriage in which the believer would be blameless. It seems to me if it had been anticipated that believers would marry unbelievers, such provision would have not have been made for separation when one becomes a believer after marriage.

The whole drift and tenor of the scriptures, both of the Old and the New Testament, is that in the close and intimate relations of life the children of God should seek the companionship of servants of God, that they might help and encourage each other in the service of God. When both are working together, man in his weakness often becomes discouraged; it is greatly worse when the nearest and dearest one pulls from Christ and duty. Then, too, when people marry, they ought to consider the probability of rearing children. It is the duty of Christian parents to rear their children in the nurture and admonition of the Lord. How can one do this when the other

righteousness and iniquity? or what communion hath light with darkness?
15 And what concord hath Christ with *Belial? or what portion hath a be-

*Gr. *Beliar.*

---

sets the example of unbelief and disobedience to God? This passage certainly forbids persons so tying themselves to unbelievers in any business or any relation by which the believer is influenced or controlled by the unbeliever. How can a relationship be found that does this more effectually than the marriage relation?

for what fellowship have righteousness and iniquity?—How can righteousness and iniquity harmonize in the same person and in the same life? Righteousness dwells in the heart and directs the life of the Christian; iniquity in that of the unbeliever. [By righteousness as opposed to iniquity is meant moral excellence in general, conformity to the law of God as opposed to opposition to that law. The opposition intended is that which exists between the righteous and the wicked. People are said to be in fellowship when they are so united that what belongs to the one belongs to the other, or what is true of the other. Incongruous elements cannot be thus united.]

or what communion hath light with darkness?—Since the heart of the believer is filled with light, and that of the unbeliever with darkness, there can be no interest in common between them. [Paul was sent to the Gentiles "to open their eyes, that they may turn from darkness to light and from the power of Satan unto God." (Acts 26: 18.) Of Christians the Holy Spirit said: "Ye are all sons of light, and sons of the day: we are not of the night, nor of darkness." (1 Thess. 5: 5.) The attempt, therefore, of Christians to remain Christians, and retain their inward state as such, and yet to enter voluntarily into intimate fellowship with the world, is as impossible as to combine light and darkness, holiness and sin, happiness and misery.]

15 And what concord hath Christ with Belial?—The believer in heart and life serves Christ. Belial means a worthless fellow; here it is evil personified and means Satan, the

liever with an unbeliever? 16 And what agreement hath a ⁴temple of God
with idols? for we are a ⁴temple of the living God; even as God said, ⁵I will

⁴Or, *sanctuary*
⁵Lev. xxvi. 12; Ex. xxix. 45; Ezek. xxxvii. 27; Jer. xxxi. 1.

---

great antagonist of Christ, and between them there can be no
concord whatever.

or what portion hath a believer with an unbeliever?—The
believer serves God, the unbeliever Satan; hence, with God di-
recting the one and Satan the other, there can be no harmony
or common feeling and interest between them. To the
one Christ is the Son of God, the object of supreme reverence
and love; to the other, he is a mere man. To the one, the
great object is to promote the glory of God and to secure his
favor; to the other, these are objects of indifference.

16 And what agreement hath a temple of God with idols?—
[Were it not for the fact that believers are God's temple, there
would be no propriety in this question. A building consecrated to the service of God is no place for idols. The service
of idols and that of God cannot be combined. Idolatry is such
an insult to God that when an idol comes in God goes out.
We cannot combine the worship of God and the worship of
idols. Idolatry is everywhere in the scriptures represented as
the greatest insult the creature can offer the Creator; and the
grossest form of that insult is to erect idols in God's own temple. Such is the indignity of those, who, while professing to
be Christians, associate themselves with the wicked in their
inward and outward life. It is the introduction of idols into
God's temple. (Col. 3: 5-9.)]

for we are a temple of the living God;—The church is the
temple of God. The temple in Jerusalem, with its corner and
foundation stones, and the comely stones in its walls, was
typical of the temple not made with hands, "built upon the
foundation of the apostles and prophets, Christ Jesus himself
being the chief corner stone; in whom each several building,
fitly framed together, groweth into a holy temple in the Lord;
in whom ye also are builded together for a habitation of God
in the Spirit." (Eph. 2: 20-22.)

even as God said, I will dwell in them, and walk in them;—

dwell in them, and walk in them; and I will be their God, and they shall be my people. 17 Wherefore

---

[God is said to dwell where he specially and permanently manifests his presence. And since he thus manifests his presence in his people collectively and individually, he is said to dwell in all and in each. These words are cited from Leviticus (26: 11, 12), and as they stand here mean something more intimate and profound than they did to Israel. What God speaks, he speaks to his people, and speaks once for all. And if the divine presence in the camp of Israel—a presence represented by the Ark and the Tabernacle—was to consecrate the nation to Jehovah, and inspire them to keep the camp clean, that they might not offend the eyes of his glory, how much more ought those whom God has visited in the person of his Son to cleanse themselves from every defilement and make their hearts a fit place for his habitation. The expression "I will walk in them'" is not simply among them because the presence of God is represented as internal, in the heart: "And if Christ is in you, the body is dead because of sin; but the spirit is life because of righteousness. But if the Spirit of him that raised up Jesus from the dead dwelleth in you, he . . . shall give life also to your mortal bodies through his Spirit that dwelleth in you." (Rom. 8: 10, 11.) And the Lord says the same of every true believer: "If a man love me, he will keep my word: and my Father will love him, and we will come unto him, and make our abode with him." (John 14: 23.) So the human soul is said to be full of God when its inward state, its affection, and its acts are directed and controlled by him so as to be a constant manifestation of his presence.]

and I will be their God, and they shall be my people.—Not only the God whom they worship, but the God who will protect and bless them. This is the great promise of the covenant with Abraham, and with all the true Israel of God. It is for God to be to his people what he designed to be to man when he created him in his own image. The promise contains more than it has ever entered into the heart of man to conceive. The promise that all the nations should be blessed in the seed of Abraham, as unfolded in the mission of Jesus

⁶Come ye out from among them, and be ye separate
saith the Lord,
  And touch no unclean thing;
  And I will receive you,
18 ⁷And will be to you a Father,
  And ye shall be to me sons and daughters, saith the Lord Almighty.

⁶Is. lii. 11.
⁷Hos. i. 10; Isa. xliii. 6.

Christ, comprehends all the blessings in the scheme of redemption.

17 **Wherefore come ye out from among them, and be ye
separate, saith the Lord,**—Since God and Satan cannot walk
together, he tells his children to come out from among them
and be separated and touch no unclean thing.

and touch no unclean thing; and I will receive you,—In the
Mosaic dispensation, the man who touched any unclean thing
could not come into the congregation of Israel until he purified himself. The uncleanness there was of the flesh, now it is
of the spirit. Do not be led into evil associations by the corrupting servants of Satan, for God cannot receive you unless
you be clean from them.

18 **and will be to you a Father,**—God promised that if they
would keep themselves faithful and true to him, he would love
and care for them, with the tender care of a loving Father for
his sons and daughters.

and ye shall be to me sons and daughters,—[The ideal relation of Israel to Jehovah was that of a son to a father; but the
full meaning of such words was reserved for Jesus Christ to
teach who came to reveal the Father (Matt. 11: 27), as their
full blessedness can be realized only by the heirs of the Father's kingdom who overcome at last (Rev. 21: 7).

It is characteristic of Christianity that it was the first system that ever recognized the dignity of women and raised
them generally to the same moral and spiritual level with
men. It was very suitable to notice the unhappy women at
Corinth, where, above all other places in the world, they were
lured to ruin by organized immoralities under the cloak of religion.]

1 Having therefore these promises, beloved, let us cleanse ourselves from all
defilement of flesh and spirit, perfecting holiness in the fear of God.

---

saith the Lord Almighty.—[He has all power, and the term
is applied to God in contrast with the helplessness of idols
that are weak and powerless. The Lord is able to protect his
people, and they who put their trust in him shall never be
confounded.]

7 : 1 Having therefore these promises, beloved,—Having the
promise of God's indwelling, his favors, and that they should
be his sons and daughters, he exhorts them to cleanse themselves from all defilement.

**let us cleanse ourselves from all defilement of flesh and spir-
it,**—Our flesh is defiled when our hands and feet and bodies
do the bidding of sin; our spirits, when we contemplate sin
with pleasure. Paul warns his readers, not only against all
actual contact with sensuality, but also against that consent of
the spirit which often defiles the inner life even where there is
no outward sin. [The work of purification is frequently referred to as the work of God (Acts 15: 9; Eph. 5: 26), but it is
plainly taught that this can be done only as those who are
cleansed cooperate with him in its accomplishment, for the exhortation is: "Work out your own salvation with fear and
trembling; for it is God who worketh in you both to will and
to work, for his good pleasure" (Phil. 2: 12, 13). If God's
love as manifested through Christ does not arouse and direct
us; if it does not create in us the desire for holiness, and the
perseverance to attain it, it is because we refuse to hear and
obey him.]

perfecting holiness—We must go forward in faithful obedience to perfect ourselves in a holy life. [This does not mean
simply to practice, but to complete, to carry to perfection.]

in the fear of God.—To do these things we must look to
God with reverence and fear. [All contact with impurity is in
us a defilement of the temple of God and an insult to the majesty of him who dwells therein. Therefore, fear as well as
hope should prompt us to abstain from all sin.]

14. THE APOSTLE'S JOY OVER THE REFORMATION OF THE CORINTHIANS EFFECTED THROUGH HIS PREVIOUS INSTRUCTIONS AND ADMONITIONS.
7 : 2-16.

2 ⁸Open your hearts to us:⋅we wrong no man, we corrupted no man, we took advantage of no man. 3 I say it not to condemn *you:* for I have said before, that ye are in our hearts to die together and live together. 4 Great is

⁸Gr. *Make room for us.*

2 **Open your hearts to us:**—This refers to the request in 6: 11-13, and he admonishes them to enlarge their hearts with love toward him, and to accept his instructions.

we wronged no man,—He had led no man into sin. [These sudden and unexplained denials must have been prompted by charges against him. Some might have thought that by his strict moral teaching, which required abandonment of idolatry and all unjust gains, he had inflicted loss on his readers. Apparently such an accusation had been laid to his charge.]

we corrupted no man,—The word used here means that he had corrupted no one's morals by his example or arts of seduction; or that he had corrupted no man's faith by false teaching.

we took advantage of no man.—He had taken advantage of no man to make gain or to defraud. He was specially careful to avoid all occasion of all suspicion as to the disposition of the money which he had raised from the churches for the relief of the destitute disciples in Judea (8: 10, 20), and it is quite likely that the false teachers were ready to insinuate that he appropriated the money to his own use (12: 16, 17).

3 **I say it not to condemn you:**—He did not tell them this to reproach or condemn them for having been estranged in their feelings for him, but because he loved them and wished their highest good, and where there is such abundance of affection there is no room for condemnation.

for I have said before, that ye are in our hearts to die together and live together.—He had already told them that his love for them was so earnest and so strong that his heart yearned to live and die with them. So he desired their confi-

my boldness of speech toward you, great is my glorying on your behalf: I am filled with comfort, I overflow with joy in all our affliction.

5 For even when we were come into Macedonia our flesh had no relief, but *we were* afflicted on every side; without *were* fightings, within *were*

---

dence and love. [To have persons so in one's heart that he is ready to die with them, that he has no desire to live without them is one of the strongest tokens of love.]

4 **Great is my boldness of speech toward you, great is my glorying on your behalf:**—Because he loved them he could speak freely to them. He had boasted of them to others. He had great rejoicing over them in view of the course they had pursued and of the report he had now received concerning them.

I am filled with comfort, I overflow with joy in all our affliction.—They had so changed their course that it filled his heart with comfort, and in the deep afflictions that were upon him, gave him joy. Titus, whom he had sent to see how they were, had returned and brought a good report.

5 **For even when we were come into Macedonia our flesh had no relief,**—Here he resumes the narrative which was broken off at 2:13. The sudden thanksgiving there is explained here. Titus, whom he had expected to meet him at Troas, had arrived and brought with him cheering news. He was sadly in need of it. His flesh had no rest until he received the news from Corinth, so that up to that moment the strain had continued. [Flesh as used here is not the seat of sin, but the seat of natural emotions, as dread, anxiety, and fear.]

but we were afflicted on every side;—What the troubles were which surrounded him he does not say, but he implies that they were of two kinds.

without were fightings, within were fears.—The fights without were probably assaults upon himself, or upon the churches, of the nature of persecution; the fears within, his anxieties about how his letter would be received at Corinth. The condition of the church there might well give him dark forebodings.

fears. 6 Nevertheless he that comforteth the lowly, *even* God, comforted us by the ⁹coming of Titus; 7 and not by his ⁹coming only, but also by the comfort wherewith he was comforted in you, while he told us your longing, your mourning, your zeal for me; so that I rejoiced yet more. 8 For though I

⁹Gr. *presence.*   Comp. 2 Thess. 2. 9.

---

6 Nevertheless he that comforteth the lowly, even God, comforted us by the coming of Titus;—While in this harassed state of mind. God, who remembers to comfort the dejected and dispirited, comforted him by the coming of Titus who brought a good report from Corinth.

7 and not by his coming only, but also by the comfort wherewith he was comforted in you,—Titus had apparently gone himself with a sad and apprehensive heart to Corinth; he had been away longer than he had anticipated, and in the interval Paul's anxiety had risen to anguish; but in Corinth his reception had been unexpectedly favorable, and when he returned he was able to cheer Paul with a consolation which had already gladdened his own heart.

while he told us your longing, your mourning, your zeal for me; so that I rejoiced yet more.—Paul was not only comforted, his sorrow had been turned into joy, as he heard Titus tell of the longing of the Corinthians to see him, and their mourning over the pain they had given him by retaining in their fellowship the incestuous man, and of their eagerness to make amends for their conduct, which caused him to rejoice the more. [The word *your* has a certain emphasis which suggests a contrast. Before Titus went to Corinth, it was Paul who had been anxious to see *them,* who had mourned over their moral laxity, who had been passionately interested in cleansing the church he had founded; now it is *they* who are full of longing to see *him,* of grief, and moral earnestness; and it is this which explains his joy. The conflict between the powers of righteousness in one great passionate soul and the powers of evil in a lax and fickle community has ended in favor of the righteous; Paul's vehemence has prevailed against Corinthian indifference, and made it vehement in all good affections, and he rejoices now in the joy of his Lord.]

made you sorry with my epistle, I do not regret it: though I did regret *it* ([10]for I see that that epistle made you sorry, though but for a season), 9 I now rejoice, not that ye were made sorry, but that ye were made sorry unto repentance; for ye were made sorry after a godly sort, that ye might suffer loss by us in nothing. 10 For godly sorrow worketh repentance [11]unto salvation, *a repentance* which bringeth no regret: but the sorrow of the world worketh death.

[10]Some ancient authorities omit *for.*
[11]Or, *unto a salvation which bringeth no regret*

8 **For though I made you sorry with my epistle, I do not regret it: though I did regret it (for I see that that epistle made you sorry, though but for a season),**—This explains why he rejoiced on account of their sorrow. It was not that they sorrowed, but that their sorrow was a godly sort that led them to repentance. The significance of this report from them by Titus was not in the fact of their hurt, but in the fact of their repentance. His epistle in spite of his fears had produced the desired effect.

9 **I now rejoice, not that ye were made sorry, but that ye were made sorry unto repentance; for ye were made sorry after a godly sort,**—[Their repentance was a change of will produced by sorrow for sin which led to a reformation. A change of will produced by other considerations than sorrow for sin, or which fails to produce a change of conduct, is certainly not the repentance of which the apostle spoke.]

that ye might suffer loss by us in nothing.—The infliction of pain is, for the time, a damage or loss, unless it be compensated for by subsequent advantage, but instead of producing any injury, the reproof had resulted in the greatest spiritual good. Note the loving interest in these words concerning the temporary pain as having no right to occasion the least distress unless there was absolute need.

10 **For godly sorrow worketh repentance unto salvation,**—A godly sorrow is produced by faith in God, a sorrow that seeks to please God, to turn from sin to God, so leads to salvation. [God sees sin not only in its consequences, but in itself—a thing infinitely evil, even if the consequences were happiness to the guilty instead of misery. So sorrow for sin is to see sin as God sees it. It is when we let the light of God's truth shine into our hearts and consciences that we may have

11 For behold, this selfsame thing, that ye were made sorry after a godly sort, what earnest care it wrought in you, yea what clearing of yourselves, yea what indignation, yea what fear, yea what longing, yea what zeal, yea

---

wholesome sorrow that worketh repentance and salvation and life.]

a repentance which bringeth no regret:—Such a repentance is not to be regretted as it brings only good.

but the sorrow of the world worketh death.—The sorrow of the world is a sorrow from worldly considerations, fleshly motives. This brings no salvation, but only death. A man steals, he may sorrow for it because he had dishonored God and done wrong to his fellow man. This sorrow would lead to repentance toward God and undo the wrong to man and would save him; but he might sorrow from a worldly motive because it brought on him disgrace, and he might sorrow and cease to steal, and even make restitution in order to gain a good name that he might defraud others. This is worldly sorrow that needs to be turned from because it works death. [Moral and spiritual death, a death which being put in contrast with salvation as the fruit of genuine repentance means eternal death. In the case of many beside Judas, when the sorrow of the world works despair, existence is felt to be intolerable, and self-destruction sends them to their own place. (Acts 1 : 25).]

11 For behold, this selfsame thing, that ye were made sorry after a godly sort,—This is an appeal to their own case to show the happy effects of godly sorrow.

what earnest care it wrought in you,—It led them to an earnest care as to their course, which stands in striking contrast with their former indifference.

yea what clearing of yourselves,—They showed great solicitude to free themselves, as far as could be done from blame, and to remove the evil from among them.

yea what indignation,—Indignation that such a thing should have taken place among themselves, and that they had tolerated it so long.

what avenging! In everything ye approved yourselves to be pure in the matter. 12 So although I wrote unto you, *I wrote* not for his cause that did the wrong, nor for his cause that suffered the wrong, but that your earnest care for us might be made manifest unto you in the sight of God. 13 There-

---

yea what fear,—Fear of what measures Paul might take, if he should come among them "with a rod." (1 Cor. 4: 21.)

yea what longing,—[They dreaded his chastisements, yet longed for his coming, whether to receive the merited correction or a restoration to favor through contrition.]

yea what zeal,—They set about the work in great earnestness to make up for their past indifference.

yea what avenging!—The avenging of those who had led them into wrong.

In everything ye approved yourselves to be pure in the matter.—In everything they had shown that they had repented, and were forgiven in the matter. [Not free from blame, but thoroughly in earnest, straightforward and thoroughgoing in the case. This passage is instructive as presenting a clear exhibition of the intimate nature of the fellowship in Christ. One member committed an offense. The godly sorrow which the apostle describes was the sorrow of the church. The effects which that sorrow wrought was common to the church as such. The believers are one body in Christ Jesus, and "we, who are many, are one body in Christ, and severally members one of another" (Rom. 12: 5), "and whether one member suffereth, all the members suffer with it" (1 Cor. 12: 26), is a matter of common experience.]

12 So although I wrote unto you, I wrote not for his cause that did the wrong, nor for his cause that suffered the wrong, —Among expositors it is a question as to whether the reference is to Paul and his enemy, or to the incestuous man and his father mentioned in 1 Cor. 5: 1. I think it quite likely refers to the incestuous man.

but that your earnest care for us might be made manifest unto you in the sight of God.—He did not write to them out of feeling toward him that did the wrong, nor for him that suffered the wrong; but that his earnest care, that they might

fore we have been comforted: and in our comfort we joyed the more exceedingly for the joy of Titus, because his spirit hath been refreshed by you all. 14 For if in anything I have gloried to him on your behalf, I was not put to shame; but as we spake all things to you in truth, so our glorying also which I made before Titus was found to be truth. 15 And his affection is more abundantly toward you, while he remembereth the obedience of you all, how with fear and trembling ye received him. 16 I rejoice that in every-

---

stand right before God, might be manifest. On their standing before God, their eternal salvation depended. The personal feeling of himself, or others, compared with this was a small matter.

13 **Therefore we have been comforted:**—Inasmuch as they heard him and turned to God and found comfort, he had been comforted in them.

and in our comfort we joyed the more exceedingly for the joy of Titus, because his spirit hath been refreshed by you all. —Paul's joy had been enhanced by the joy of Titus, whose spirit instead of being depressed by his visit to them, as he feared, was refreshed and strengthened by their course. [Evidently Titus had accepted Paul's commission with misgivings. He had spoken encouragingly to Titus of the Corinthians, and he is delighted that their reception of him had shown that his confidence was justified.]

14 **For if in anything I have gloried to him on your behalf, I was not put to shame;**—He had praised them to Titus, and he had not been put to shame by their showing that they were not worthy of the praise he had bestowed upon them. [He cannot refrain from a passing allusion to the charges of prevarication discussed in the first chapter (verses 15-19); he not only tells the truth *about* them as Titus had seen, but he has always told the truth *to* them.]

but as we spake all things to you in truth,—All he had said concerning them had proved to be true.

so our glorying also which I made before Titus was found to be truth.—[Though spoken incidentally, yet the revelation to the Corinthians that Paul had spoken of them in terms of commendation must have convinced them of his love for them. This is one of the objects, as appears from the whole epistle, he had much at heart.]

thing I am of good courage concerning you.

15 And his affection is more abundantly toward you, while he remembereth the obedience of you all, how with fear and trembling ye received him.—And the true spiritual love of Titus for them was increased when he remembered how gladly they received him with fear and trembling lest they had departed from the word of God.

16 I rejoice that in everything I am of good courage concerning you.—His confidence in them as Christians had been completely restored by Titus and that caused him true joy.

SECTION TWO.

CONCERNING A COLLECTION FOR THE POOR SAINTS IN JUDÆA.
8: 1 to 9: 15.

1. ENFORCEMENT OF THE DUTY OF BENEVOLENCE BY THE EXAMPLE OF THE MACEDONIANS AND BY THE ZEAL OF THE CORINTHIANS IN OTHER CHRISTIAN GRACES.
8 1-15.

1 Moreover, brethren, we make known to you the grace of God which hath been given in the churches of Macedonia; 2 how that in much proof of

---

1 **Moreover, brethren,**—This marks the transition to a totally different subject, which Paul introduces with his usual felicity. The term "brethren" is the keynote of this section, as brotherly love is the motive of generosity.

we make known to you the grace of God—The disposition, ability, and opportunity to give was a matter of grace or favor bestowed by God, for which he is to be thanked. Every Christian should regard an opening to do good with his means, his talent, his time an act of kindness. Opportunities to do good are opportunities to make investments that will bear fruit unto eternal life. So every Christian should consider it a favor from God to have an opportunity and ability to give his means to do good as God directs.

which hath been given in the churches of Macedonia;— Contributions were being raised to relieve the suffering saints in Judæa. Directions concerning the raising of this fund were: "Now concerning the collection for the saints, as I gave order to the churches of Galatia, so also do ye. Upon the first day of the week let each one of you lay by him in store, as he may prosper, that no collections be made when I come." (1 Cor. 16: 1, 2.) Contributions under the same directions and for the same purpose were taken up throughout Galatia, Asia, Achaia, and Macedonia. To the Macedonian churches this grace involved more than the opportunity to do good. It was such a matter of grace to them that they were glad to accept the opportunity. They had so progressed in the divine life that they esteemed it a privilege to be permitted to give.

affliction the abundance of their joy and their deep poverty abounded unto the riches of their [1]liberality. 3 For according to their power, I bear wit-

[1]Gr. *singleness.* See Rom. 12. 8.

They had learned that "it is more blessed to give than to receive." (Acts 20: 35.) The churches of Macedonia founded by Paul were those of Philippi, Thessalonica, and Berea.

2 how that in much proof of affliction—In great afflictions which were a severe test of their sincerity and devotion. These afflictions arose from persecutions. Of them it is said: "And ye became imitators of us, and of the Lord, having received the word in much affliction, with joy of the Holy Spirit" (1 Thess. 1: 6), and "ye, brethren, became imitators of the churches of God which are in Judæa in Christ Jesus: for ye also suffered the same things of your own countrymen, as they did of the Jews" (2: 14).

the abundance of their joy—The joys arising from the pardon of their sins and the grace of God which arose above their sorrows.

and their deep poverty—Joy and poverty together poured out a rich stream of liberality. Strange as it may seem, it is not to those to whom the gospel comes easily, and on whom it imposes little, who are most generous in its cause. On the contrary, it is those who have suffered for it, those who have lost by it, who are, as a rule, the most liberal.

abounded unto the riches of their liberality.—Their poverty abounded unto their liberality, because it was seen to be great in relation to it—their liberality made their poverty, by contrast, appear even greater. The poor thoroughly in earnest can do much; the rich, lukewarm, do but little. [The marginal reading *singleness* is not to be preferred to *liberality*, but it throws light on the real significance of the word. The same word is rendered *liberality* (9: 11, 13; Rom. 12: 8), *singleness* (Eph. 6: 5; Col. 3: 22), *simplicity* (11: 3), and these are its only occurrences in the New Testament. In the Sermon on the Mount Jesus uses the adjective *single,* "If therefore thine eye be single" (Matt. 6: 22), where the meaning is that the eyes of the heart (Eph. 1: 18), like the eyes in the

ness, yea and beyond their power, *they gave* of their own accord, 4 beseeching us with much entreaty in regard of this grace and the fellowship in the
ministering to the saints: 5 and *this,* not as we had hoped, but first they gave
their own selves to the Lord, and to us through the will of God. 6 Insomuch

head, must focus and see like a single eye, if the vision is to be
perfect. The eye must not attempt to look in two directions
at the same time. So *singleness* is the faculty of undivided attention; it is the faculty of seeing straight. As applied to giving, *singleness* is that liberality which gives without grudging
(9: 7) and gives disinterestedly. It does not look in two directions at the same time.]

3 **For according to their power, I bear witness, yea and beyond their power, they gave of their own accord,**—To the full
extent of their ability and beyond what Paul expected or what
would be required of them, they had given freely. They were
moved in this not by persuasion and entreaty of others, but
were willing of themselves to do so.

4 **beseeching us with much entreaty in regard of this grace
and the fellowship in the ministering to the saints:**—They not
only moved in it without persuasion from Paul, but they did it
of their own will, then besought Paul to take their bounty to
Jerusalem and see that it was distributed to the saints that
needed it.

5 **and this, not as we had hoped,**—He does not mean to say
he had not hoped that they would give, but that they had
gone beyond what he had hoped. He knew their poverty and
needs, and he had only hoped that they would give a small
amount.

**but first they gave their own selves to the Lord, and to us
through the will of God.**—To give themselves to God was to
consecrate all they had to his service, and this was according
to his will. When we do this, he bestows the fullness of his
blessings upon us. [Thus we see that in every relative estimate bearing the stamp of inspiration even the richest gifts of
money are always subordinate to the vastly superior value of
the soul of the giver. In fact, there is only one thing which
man can give that reaches to the point of highest value, and
that is that he gives himself.]

that we exhorted Titus, that as he had made a beginning before, so he would
also complete in you this grace also. 7 But as ye abound in everything, *in*

---

6 **Insomuch that we exhorted Titus, that as he had made a
beginning before, so he would also complete in you this grace
also.**—This example of the Macedonian churches was used by
Paul to urge the Corinthians to greater zeal, so he exhorted
Titus, who, when among them, had begun the work with so
much zeal, to complete it. We are often surprised how slow
Christians are to do work without a living voice to encourage
them, but it seems to have been the same in Paul's day. He
could not trust his letters to stir them up to activity. [Paul
made a wise use of the example of the Macedonians. He did
not appeal to pride, vanity, or any such selfish feeling, but
simply presented this remarkable case of Christian liberality.
Had he said: "Be not beaten by those Macedonians"; had he
called natural prejudices into play—a Corinthian to yield to a
Macedonian!—then all the evil passions of their nature would
have been stimulated. Emulation is a true principle if properly used. The danger lies not in the thing itself, but in its
abuses, and particularly in the encouragement in which it may
afford to false rivalry and jealousy. In a large measure, the
spirit and conduct of others make the social atmosphere we
breathe, nor can we live in the world without contact with it.
Excellence assumes its most attractive forms in noble examples, and, except for these, our ideals, if they existed at all,
would be very imperfect. Consistently, then, with his purpose of stimulating a higher degree of Christian excellence, he
sets before them in most vivid colors the liberality of the
Macedonian churches.]

7 **But as ye abound in everything,**—On the Corinthians had
been bestowed many spiritual gifts, and notwithstanding the
evils that prevailed in the church, the Christian graces or virtues practiced, which are also placed among the gifts of God,
were cultivated among them. Many were faithful and true,
and cultivated the sturdy Christian virtues. Paul had remained
with them a year and six months, had fully taught them, and
bestowed on them all needed spiritual gifts (1 Cor. 1: 5; 12:
13, 14).

faith, and utterance, and knowledge, and *in* all earnestness, and *in* [2]your love to us, *see* that ye abound in this grace also. 8 I speak not by way of commandment, but as proving through the earnestness of others the sincerity also of your love. 9 For ye know the grace of our Lord Jesus Christ, that,

[2]Some ancient authorities read *our love to you.*

---

in faith,—A faithful adherence to the truth. Their abounding in this was their animation, assurance, and activity in faith.

and utterance,—The ability to speak the gospel in different tongues.

and knowledge,—The spiritual gift that brought to their mind all the knowledge needful to salvation, that Paul taught them, and the power of imparting it to others by the gift of tongues had been freely bestowed on the memebers of the church at Corinth.

and in all earnestness,—The energy or vigor of their spiritual life, of which their love was one manifestation.

and in your love to us,—The love which flowed from them to Paul, and which he felt in himself toward them.

see that ye abound in this grace also.—Inasmuch as they possessed all other graces, he urges them to abound in the grace of liberality also.

8 I speak not by way of commandments,—He did not give this as a commandment, for God loves freewill offerings and cheerful givers. As God left it to their free will, Paul would not give a specific command.

but as proving through the earnestness of others the sincerity also of your love.—He uses the forwardness of the brethren in Macedonia to arouse them, and to revive the purpose or will in them to freely give to relieve the suffering brethren in Judea. The sacrifices they made would be a proof of their sincerity as followers of Christ. Jesus shows this clearly in his speech to the disciples on the Mount of Olives: "Then shall the ·King say unto them on his right hand, Come, ye blessed of my Father, inherit the kingdom prepared for you from the foundation of the world: for I was hungry, and ye gave me to eat; I was thirsty, and ye gave me drink; . . . And the King shall answer and say unto them, Verily I say unto

though, he was rich, yet for your sakes he became poor, that ye through his
poverty might become rich.   10 And herein I give *my* judgment: for this is

---

you, Inasmuch as ye did it unto one of these my brethren,
even these least, ye did it unto me." (Matt. 25: 34-40.)
And John says: "But whoso hath the world's goods, and beholdeth
his brother in need, and shutteth up his compassion from him,
how doth the love of God abide in him?" (1 John 3: 17.)

9 For ye know the grace of our Lord—The unmerited and
spontaneous love of the supreme and absolute Lord, whom
they acknowledged to be their rightful sovereign and posses-
sor, who was theirs, belonged to them, in so far as the care,
protection, and support of his almighty power was by his love
pledged to them.

Jesus Christ,—He who was theirs was their Lord and Savior, and the Christ, God's anointed, and invested by him with
supreme dominion and heir of all things. (Heb. 1: 2.)

that, though he was rich,—In possession of the glory which
he had with the Father before the world was. (John 17: 5.)

yet for your sakes he became poor,—This does not refer to
what he did while on earth, but to what he did when he came
into the world.   As he said to the Philippians: "Have this
mind in you, which was also in Christ Jesus: who, existing in
the form of God, counted not the being on an equality with
God a thing to be grasped, but emptied himself, taking the
form of a servant, being made in the likeness of men; and
being found in fashion as a man, he humbled himself, becoming obedient even unto death, yea, the death of the cross."
(Phil. 2: 5-8.)   That is, he so far laid aside the glory of his
divine majesty that he was to all appearance a man, even a
servant, so that men refused to recognize him as divine, but
despised, persecuted, and at last crucified him, as a man. He
who was rich in the plentitude of all divine attributes and prerogatives thus became poor and despised.

that ye through his poverty might become rich.—Believers
are made rich in the possession of that glory which Christ laid
aside. Had he not submitted to all humiliation while in the
flesh, we should forever have remained poor and destitute of
all holiness, happiness, and glory.   No one can enter into the

expedient for you, who were the first to make a beginning a year ago, not only to do, but also to will. 11 But now complete the doing also; that as *there was* the readiness to will, so *there may be* the completion also out of your ability. 12 For if the readiness is there, *it is* acceptable according as *a man* hath, not according as *he* hath not. 13 For I *say* not *this* that others

---

meaning of this verse or feel its power, without being thereby made willing to sacrifice himself for the good of others. It is vain for any person to imagine that he loves Christ, if he does not love the brethren and is not liberal in relieving their needs.

10 **And herein I give my judgment: for this is expedient for you,**—While Paul as an apostle would not give command as to what they should give, he did give his advice as to what was best for them—what they ought to do.

who were the first to make a beginning a year ago, not only to do, but also to will.—When Paul wrote his first epistle, they had not only begun, but were forward themselves to engage in the work. Now he advises (he does not command, wants it to be a freewill offering on their part) to complete the work which they began, not only to do, but to show a zeal.

11 **But now complete the doing also;**—As there was a readiness to will—as they were forward to begin—let there be a continuance in the work until it is completed.

that as there was the readiness to will, so there may be the completion also out of your ability.—This is an admonition that the completion should correspond to the promise. It often occurs that when an earnest advocate of a cause goes before the people, lays the needs before them, stirs their feelings, they promise great things; but when the excitement subsides, they grow cold and indifferent and fail to fulfil their promise.

12 **For if the readiness is there**—What is given must be given of a willing mind; it must be an offering of consecration. This is fundamental. It is clearly a self-deception for an individual to think he pleases God under the perfect dispensation of Christ while doing less than the Israelites did under the typical dispensation. "And Jehovah spake unto Moses, saying, Speak unto the children of Israel, that they

may be eased *and* ye distressed; 14 but by equality: your abundance *being a supply* at this present time for their want, that their abundance also may become *a supply* for your want; that there may be equality: 15 as it is written. [8]He that *gathered* much had nothing over; and he that *gathered* little had no lack.

[8]Ex. xvi. 18.

take for me an offering: of every man whose heart maketh him willing ye shall take my offering." (Ex. 25: 1, 2.) What the child of God gives is the response of gratitude to our gracious Redeemer, and if it does not have this character he does not want it. If there is a willing mind the rest is easy; if not, there is no need to go on—it is not accepted.

it is acceptable according as a man hath,—Readiness is the acceptable thing. If we cannot give much, then a ready mind with even a little is acceptable. Only let us remember that readiness always gives all that is in its power. The readiness of the poor widow in the temple could only give two mites, but the mites were all her living (Mark 12: 41-44); the readiness of the Macedonians was in the depth of poverty, but they gave themselves to the Lord. The widow's mites are an illustrious example of sacrifice; yet it has been profaned many times to a cloak of the meanest selfishness.

not according as he hath not.—The poorest as well as the richest are included. None were exempted because they were poor. If one is able to give one dime or one cent and fails to give it he is just as culpable before God as is the man who is able to give a thousand dollars and fails to give it to the Lord. God values, blesses, and rewards gifts according to the sacrifices made, not according to the amount given.

13, 14 For I say not this that others may be eased and ye distressed; but by equality: your abundance being a supply at this present time for their want, that their abundance also may become a supply for your want; that there may be equality:—He does not mean that the brethren in Judea may be relieved and the Corinthians burdened: but that now while they have an abundance, they should help those in Judea who are in need, that sometime when the Corinthians needed others may help them, so that there will be equality.

15 **as it is written, He that gathered much had nothing over; and he that gathered little had no lack.**—When God gave the manna in the wilderness, no matter how much they gathered, there was nothing left, and no lack. (Ex. 16: 18.) The lesson taught is, if each will give freely to help others, none will want. Give what we have over to supply the lack of others.

2. COMMENDATION OF THOSE WHO WERE ENGAGED IN SU-
PERINTENDING THE COLLECTION.
8: 16-24.

16 But thanks be to God, who putteth the same earnest care for you into the heart of Titus. 17 For he accepted indeed our exhortation; but being himself very earnest, he went forth unto you of his own accord. 18 And we have sent together with him the brother whose praise in the ⁴gospel *is spread*

⁴See marginal note on ch. 2. 12.

16 **But thanks be to God, who putteth the same earnest care for you into the heart of Titus.**—Titus had undertaken this business from being exhorted to it by Paul. He had gone to Corinth and had become acquainted with their spiritual condition and their great need. While the collection was for the poor saints in Judea, their taking part in it was a great benefit to them. [From this it appears that God controls the feelings and acts of faithful men without interfering with their liberty or responsibility. The zeal of Titus in this matter was the spontaneous outburst of his own heart and was an element of his own character. Yet God put that zeal into his heart.]

17 **For he accepted indeed our exhortation; but being himself very earnest, he went forth unto you of his own accord.**—Titus had already such an earnest care that they should possess this grace, that while he accepted the exhortation of Paul to go, he had of his own accord before made ready to go to Corinth. His own desire led to the ready acceptance of the exhortation.

18 **And we have sent together with him the brother whose praise in the gospel is spread through all the churches;**—He sent with Titus one whom he does not name, but describes him as one whose praise in the service of the gospel was spread abroad throughout all the churches. Some think this

through all the churches; 19 and not only so, but who was also appointed by
the churches to travel with us in *the matter of* this grace, which is ministered by us to the glory of the Lord, and *to show* our readiness: 20 avoiding
this, that any man should blame us in *the matter of* this bounty which is

---

was Luke, and the gospel was his written gospel, then distributed throughout all the Gentile churches; that Luke wrote for
the Gentiles under the preaching of Paul. This epistle was
written from some point in Macedonia, when Luke was not
with him. Luke had gone with him and Silas over this country on his first visit to Macedonia. In his account of the journey, as given in Acts, in referring to the company he uses
"we" until they reach Philippi. (16: 12.) Then he changes to
"they," showing that he remained in Philippi. When Paul and
his fellow messengers, six years later, came to Philippi on the
way to Jerusalem with the alms, Luke joined them, and the
"they" is changed to "we." (Acts 20: 6.) During this time it
is thought that the gospel was written by Luke and largely
distributed through these Gentile churches, and so his praise
in the gospel was spread abroad. But this is conjecture without much ground on which to base it. But the next verse
says that this brother was appointed to travel with Paul to
distribute this grace, and Luke in company with others did
travel with him.

19 and not only so, but who was also appointed by the
churches to travel with us in the matter of this grace,—This
brother was entitled to confidence, and might safely be received, not only on the ground of general reputation, but also
because he had been appointed by the churches for the purpose of assisting Paul in the collection and delivery of the
bounty which Paul and his companions carried and delivered.

which is ministered by us to the glory of the Lord,—The
design was to promote the glory of the Lord by the manifestation of the power of the gospel in their lives.

and to show our readiness:—It afforded the opportunity of
evincing his readiness to do good to others and to promote
their welfare.

20 avoiding this, that any man should blame us in the matter of this bounty which is ministered by us:—Paul was care-

ministered by us: 21 for we take thought for things honorable, not only in the sight of the Lord, but also in the sight of men. 22 And we have sent with them our brother, whom we have many times proved earnest in many things, but now much more earnest, by reason of the great confidence which *he hath* in you. 23 Whether *any inquire* about Titus, *he is* my partner and *my* fellow-worker to you-ward; or our brethren, *they are* the [1]messengers of the churches, *they are* the glory of Christ. 24 [2]Show ye therefore unto them

[1]Gr. *apostles.*
[2]Or, *Show ye therefore in the face . . . on your behalf unto them.*

---

ful that others should accompany him in the gathering and the delivering of these gifts that no man should blame him in the handling of the bounties.

21 for we take thought for things honorable, not only in the sight of the Lord, but also in the sight of men.—He set an example in this by which every Christian ought to profit. He was not willing to handle means, save under safeguards that he should not be charged with malfeasance in the handling of it. This he desired to do not only in the sight of the Lord, but also in the sight of men. [In handling money it is always best to keep on the safe side. If most men are too readily suspected by others, it only answers to the fact that most men are too ready to trust themselves. We have an infinite confidence in our own honesty; and when auditors are appointed to examine their books, the inexperienced are apt to think it needless, and even impertinent. If they were wise, they would welcome it as a protection against suspicion and even against themselves.]

22 And we have sent with them our brother, whom we have many times proved earnest in many things, but now much more earnest, by reason of the great confidence which he hath in you.—In addition to the brother already mentioned as going with Titus, he sent with them another brother. He had proved him often, in many things, and found him uniformly earnest and faithful, and now much more so since he had heard the good report of Titus, his confidence in the Corinthians made him more earnest than ever.

23 Whether any inquire about Titus, he is my partner and my fellow-worker to you-ward;—Titus had been with Paul much at Corinth, and he so testifies to them. They knew him personally, but he gave his relation to him and his fellows.

in the face of the churches the proof of your love, and of our glorying on
your behalf.

---

or our brethren, they are the messengers of the churches,—
These messengers of the churches were sent by the churches,
and sustained the same relation to the churches sending them
as the apostles sent by Christ sustained to him. The apostles
of Christ were sent by him to deliver a message. They had
no authority except to deliver the message and perform the
work Christ sent them to do. They had no authority as delegates. They had no right to confer one with another to determine how the Lord should act. They had no right to change
or modify any decision, sit in judgment upon the will or work
or order of God. They had no right to legislate for God. The
messengers of the churches had no more right to assemble,
confer, determine what was best for the churches than the
apostles had the right to legislate for or determine how or
what Christ and God should do. The messengers of the
churches were sent to carry the message and do the specific
work the church sent them to do, without direction or power
to change or otherwise direct the work of the churches.
Messengers have no right to meet other messengers and orga-
nize a body, nor to consider or determine what is best, nor to
form a new organization, nor to legislate. Scriptural messengers carried a message or gift, went to do a work and return.
Their power was limited to this. Churches sent messengers
to deliver their messages and receive others and to bear their
gifts. Messengers were sent to the churches in Judea to bear
the gifts of those sending. They were sent with gifts to Paul,
were sent by him to the churches to urge them to make gifts,
to tell how it was with him, and to learn how the churches
did, or receive gifts and return. Paul and Barnabas were sent
as messengers to the apostles at Jerusalem to report the troubles and facts about the circumcision question to them, to receive their response and report it to the church.

they are the glory of Christ.—They by their work promoted
the glory of Christ. [Their character was so well known and
established for piety and devotion to the cause of Christ that
they led men to see the excellence of Christ, whose image

they bore. Nothing more genuinely complimentary was ever by way of introduction said of anyone.]

24 **Show ye therefore unto them in the face of the churches the proof of your love,**—This is an exhortation to so receive these messengers as to give proof of their love in a liberal contribution, and thus justify Paul's glorying in their behalf. [These were the messengers of the churches, and what the Corinthians showed to them, therefore, they showed before the churches. The love meant is the love for their brethren.]

and of our glorying on your behalf.—He urges them to prove by actual demonstration that their love for Paul was genuine, and that all glorying regarding them to the messengers was warranted.

3. ADDITIONAL INDUCEMENTS PRESENTED TO THE CORIN-
THIANS TO RENEW THEIR READINESS IN THIS BENEF-
ICENCE BY A PROMPT RESPONSE TO TITUS
AND HIS COMPANIONS.
9: 1-15.

1 For as touching the ministering to the saints, it is superfluous for me to write to you; 2 for I know your readiness, of which I glory on your behalf to them of Macedonia, that Achaia hath been prepared for a year past; and

1 **For as touching the ministering to the saints, it is super-fluous for me to write to you:**—[While saying this, he does write further on this very subject, not because they were igno-rant, but because the subject is of such importance that it will bear repetition. He was so full of the importance of the sub-ject, and with a single aim of doing good, that it caused him to make this repetition.]

2 **for I know your readiness, of which I glory on your behalf to them of Macedonia, that Achaia hath been prepared for a year past;**—[Having urged the example of the generosity of the Macedonians (8: 1-5), he now very tactfully states that he has been using the readiness of Achaia to stimulate the Mace-donians, glorying that Achaia had been in readiness to take part in the work for the past year.]

and your zeal hath stirred up very many of them.—[He now tells them that the zeal of Achaia, as he had presented it,

³your zeal hath stirred up ⁴very many of them. 3 But I have sent the brethren, that our glorying on your behalf may not be made void in this respect;
that, even as I said, ye may be prepared: 4 lest by any means, if there come
with me any of Macedonia and find you unprepared, we (that we say not,
ye) should be put to shame in this confidence. 5 I thought it necessary
therefore to entreat the brethren, that they would go before unto you, and
make up beforehand your aforepromised ⁵bounty, that the same might be

³Gr. *emulation of you*
⁴Gr. *the more part.*
⁵Gr. *blessing.*

had been largely instrumental in stimulating the Macedonians
to their splendid liberality.]

3 **But I have sent the brethren, that our glorying on your
behalf may not be made void in this respect;**—He sent Titus
and his two companions lest they should fail to complete the
work of which he had gloried, and his glorying would seem to
be without ground.

that, even as I said, ye may be prepared:—So these brethren were sent to them to urge them that they might be ready.
[It is plain that he could not have told the Macedonians that
the collection at Corinth had already been made, because he
not only knew that such was not the fact, but in this very passage refers to the work as yet to be accomplished. The fact is
that he had said the Corinthians were ready to do their part in
the business, now he urges them to complete it.]

4 **lest by any means, if there come with me any of Macedonia and find you unprepared, we (that we say not, ye)
should be put to shame in this confidence.**—Lest any of those
from Macedonia who had heard Paul glorying of the churches
of Achaia, especially of the Corinthians, come and find that
they had done but little, he would, to say nothing of them, be
put to shame for having gloried in their readiness.

5 **I thought it necessary therefore to entreat the brethren,
that they would go before unto you, and make up beforehand
your aforepromised bounty,**—He wished them to do it deliber-
ately and willingly, so he sent beforehand these brethren to
teach and encourage them that their hearts might be willing
and so have it all ready as a cheerful gift. In this way it
would bring a blessing to them, as well be one to the needy.

ready as a matter of bounty, and not of ⁶extortion.
6 But this I *say,* He that soweth sparingly shall reap also sparingly; and
he that soweth ⁷bountifully shall reap also ⁷bountifully. 7 *Let* each man *do*

⁶Or, *covetousness*
⁷Gr. *with blessings.* Comp. ver. 5.

that the same might be ready as a matter of bounty, and not
of extortion.—If Paul and his company reached there on the
way to Judea with the gifts, and did not find them ready, and
it was raised under pressure, it would seem to be extorted
from unwilling hearts. [Here *bounty* stands in opposition to
extortion, the former meaning that which is given generously
and the latter that which is extorted or wrested from one unwilling to give. So far as the Christians are concerned, no
amount of money obtained from them as a mere extortion
would have done any good. The element of cheerfulness and
generosity must be in the gift before the giver himself can be
blessed. At another time he said: "Not that I seek for the
gift; but I seek for the fruit that increaseth to your account."
(Phil. 4: 17.) Here, as elsewhere, the value and usefulness of
money are freely admitted, but the matter of still higher value
and more serious consequence, "the fruit that increaseth to
your account," is brought prominently to the front and sol-
emnly emphasized.]

6 But this I say, He that soweth sparingly shall reap also
sparingly;—He lays down the principle of God's dealings,
both in nature and grace. He that sows a scanty measure of
seed in his soil will reap a scanty harvest. The giving to the
Lord is one way of sowing spiritual seed; and he that sows
with a penurious hand will reap blessings sparingly.

and he that soweth bountifully shall reap also bountifully.
—He who gives to the Lord liberally will reap a bountiful
harvest of blessings from God. This principle applies only to
those in Christ, who, in his name, give help to those in need.
When we give to be seen of men to gain honor, or from any
selfish motive, we receive our reward in the praise of men.
What constitutes bountiful giving in the Lord's esteem? We
cannot determine for ourselves what is liberal. At least we
cannot expect God to adopt each man's standard. God is to be
the judge. There is but one way, and that is to go to the Old

according as he hath purposed in his heart: not [8]grudgingly, or of necessity: for God loveth a cheerful giver. 8 And God is able to make all grace

[8]Gr. *of sorrow.*

Testament and see what he expected of the Jews, who were less blessed than we are. He cannot require of us less than he did of them. Indeed the scriptures abound with clear intimations that he expects much more than he did of them. He demands of us our all, if his honor and the good of man require it.

7 Let each man do according as he hath purposed in his heart:—Every man is required to give, no one is exempt; but what is given must be the purpose of the heart, not having it forced from him so as to cause him pain to think of the sacrifice made.

not grudgingly,—It is not to proceed out of a reluctant state of mind, grieving after what is given as so much lost. God will not accept a gift grudgingly and unwillingly made.

or of necessity:—Not constrained by circumstances to give, when one prefers not to do it. Oftentimes the giving is done sorrowfully, when the giver is induced to give by regard to public opinion, or the stress of circumstances.

for God loveth a cheerful giver.—A cheerful giver is one to whom giving is a delight, who does it with joy. The messengers, then, were to convince them that it was right to make a sacrifice so that their hearts would be willing to give. This is the work that ought to be done. This is the work that should be done in every congregation. They should not be begged to give against their will; but their hearts should be made willing by teaching the will of the Lord on the subject.

All gifts to be acceptable to God must be freewill, voluntary gifts. The giver must be pleased with the opportunity and ability to give. It must be the purpose of the heart. Certainly, with these admonitions, it will appear to every thoughtful child of God, that it is as necessary that offerings should be freely given in order to be acceptable to the Lord as that baptism should be freely entered into to be acceptable to him. A forced baptism, one submitted to unwillingly—one in

abound unto you; that ye, having always all sufficiency in everything, may abound unto every good work: 9 as it is written,

---

which the subject is entrapped—would be just as acceptable to God as offerings made unwillingly or extracted from men by worldly and fleshly appeals, or secured by indirect means. They all defile and corrupt the spiritual temple of God and make it an unfit "habitation of God in the Spirit." (Eph. 2: 22.)

8 And God is able to make all grace abound unto you;— This was a promise to them if they would faithfully do as God directed in relieving the poor and carrying forward his work, he would make all favors and blessings abound unto them.

that ye, having always all sufficiency in everything, may abound unto every good work:—This as clearly teaches as any passage in the Old Testament that God bestows temporal blessings under the new dispensation as well as spiritual, and that he does it in response to a free and hearty consecration to the Lord on our part. All grace here is favor in temporal good, that the Christian having all sufficiency may abound unto every good work. To the Philippians, Paul says: "I have all things, and abound: I am filled, having received from Epaphroditus the things that came from you, an odor of a sweet smell, a sacrifice acceptable, well-pleasing to God. And my God shall supply every need of yours according to his riches in glory in Christ Jesus." (Phil. 4: 18, 19.)

In these things it may be asked: "Does God violate his laws to bless his children?" Nay, I do not believe God violates his laws to do anything. But his laws are multiform and far-reaching. One law acting alone might produce one result, another law working in harmony with it would greatly modify that result. A law working without prayer or a life of consecration on our part might produce one result, acting in harmony with the influence growing out of prayer and self-sacrifice to God and that result is greatly modified. The prayer and consecration so harmonize with all the laws of God that the working of every law bears blessings to him who prays and consecrates himself to God.

⁹He hath scattered abroad, he hath given to the poor ;
His righteousness abideth for ever.   .
10 And he that supplieth seed to the sower and bread for food shall supply
and multiply your seed for sowing, and increase the fruits of your righteousness : 11 ye being enriched in everything unto all ¹⁰liberality, which worketh
through us thanksgiving to God. 12 For the ministration of this service not

⁹Ps. cxii. 9.
¹⁰Gr. *singleness.* Comp. ch. 8. 2.

---

9 **as it is written, He hath scattered abroad, he hath given to
the poor ;**—This teaches as clearly as any passage in the Old
Testament that God bestows temporal blessings as well as
spiritual, and that he bestows them in response to a free and
hearty consecration to the Lord.

His righteousness abideth for ever.—[Righteousness here
means general excellence or virtue, as manifested in beneficence. When it is said that his beneficence shall abide forever,
the meaning is that he can go on giving from a constantly re-
plenished store.]

10 **And he that supplieth seed to the sower and bread for
food, shall supply and multiply your seed for sowing,**—Whatever is done through the working of God's laws, God does.
Through the laws of God, seed is given to him that sows.
[When a man sows seed in his field, God provides him with the
means of sowing again. He not only gives him a harvest, but
blesses him also in giving him the ability to sow again.]

and increase the fruits of your righteousness :—God gives
freely to him who gives freely to others. So God multiplies
what is given and increases the means of doing good.

11 **ye being enriched in everything unto all liberality,**—Con-
necting back with verse 8, he means that the blessings of God
will be enriched so that the giver may be enabled to abound in
liberality.

which worketh through us thanksgiving to God.—Liberality being administered through the Corinthians to the needy
will cause them to render much thanksgiving to God. [So the
good effects of the liberality of Christians is not limited to the
relief of the temporal necessities of their brethren; it had the
higher effect of promoting gratitude and praise to God.]

only filleth up the measure of the wants of the saints, but aboundeth also through many thanksgivings unto God; 13 seeing that through the proving *of you* by this ministration they glorify God for the obedience of your confession unto the [11]gospel of Christ, and for the [10]liberality of *your* contribution unto them and unto all; 14 while they themselves also, with supplication on your behalf, long after you by reason of the exceeding grace of God in you.

[11]Gr. *good tidings.* See marginal note on ch. 2. 12.

---

12 **For the ministration of this service not only filleth up the measure of the wants of the saints,**—The distribution of this service not only supplied the wants of the needy, but caused the thanksgivings of many to abound to God. [These results were evident, for by thus showing their liberality to the Jewish Christians they proved to them that they were indeed true and obedient believers in Christ.]

but aboundeth also through many thanksgivings unto God; —It carried the thought that the gifts ascended to God through the thanksgiving of those helped. [Unfeigned generosity is in its very nature a sacrifice of praise to God—the answer of our love to his; and it has its best effects when it evokes the thanksgivings to God of those who are the recipients of it. Wherever love is, he must be first and last.]

13 **seeing that through the proving of you by this ministration they glorify God for the obedience of your confession unto the gospel of Christ, and for the liberality of your contribution unto them and unto all;**—Seeing their obedience and fidelity to the gospel of Christ, and their liberality to the poor saints in Jerusalem in the offerings they made, prompted them to glorify God for their professed subjection to the gospel of Christ, and their beneficence to all men, for their liberality showed that they excluded no Christian from their fellowship.

14 **while they themselves also, with supplication on your behalf, long after you by reason of the exceeding grace of God in you.**—[Since such a time had passed (8: 6; 9: 2) since the collection was first mooted, it is most likely that the news of it had reached the saints in Judea, and was already working this thanksgiving and affection. They made the contribution the object of their earnest prayer, with a genuine affection and longing for them which added effectiveness to their petitions.

15 Thanks be to God for his unspeakable gift.

This was one of the blessings accruing to the liberal givers.]

15 **Thanks be to God for his unspeakable gift.**—The unspeakable gift of God is Jesus Christ, which inspires love for man in those that believe in Jesus. Jesus is the manifestation of God's love to man, and his love for man inspires those who trust him to love and serve others. [The wisdom and love of God as displayed in man's redemption are unspeakable, and unsearchable, passing knowledge. It is to this Paul's mind goes back instinctively, as he contemplates what has flowed from it in the particular case before him; but it is the great divine gift, and not its fruits in the lives of men, however rich and various, that passes the power of words to characterize.]

SECTION THREE.

RENEWAL OF PAUL'S DEFENSE OF HIS AUTHORITY AND EFFICIENCY WITH A VIEW TO AN UNSPARING EXPOSURE OF HIS IRRECONCILABLE TRADUCERS.
10: 1 to 13: 14.

[In this section Paul defends his apostolic authority against his detractors and slanderers who sought by all means, whether fair or foul, to undermine his authority and destroy his influence, and thus the more certainly capture the churches he had been instrumental in founding, and impose upon them the Judaistic and legal principles and practices they advocated. There was a small minority in the churches under their influence; some were living, apparently, in gross sin. (12: 20, 21.) The one resource with which he had to encounter the situation—his own standing ground alike against the church and those corrupting it—was his apostolic authority; and to the vindication of this he first addresses himself.]

1. HIS MEANS OF ACHIEVING A CONQUEST OVER ALL ADVERSARIES OF THE GOSPEL.
10: 1-6.

1 Now I Paul myself entreat you by the meekness and gentleness of

---

1 **Now I Paul myself**—Up to this point in this epistle, Paul has used the plural *we,* now he not only uses the singular, but *I Paul myself,* and in these concluding chapters there is a severity, which is in striking contrast with the gentleness manifested in the preceding chapters, in which he was addressing the church which had cleared itself of guilt; but there was a faction who joined with the Judaizers, who denied his being an apostle. He now deals with them. This explains his change in tone. His authority and apostleship have been challenged; and with boldness he puts his personality into the forefront of the discussion.

entreat you by the meekness and gentleness of Christ,— This is one of the few references in Paul's epistles to the earthly life and character of Jesus. There can be no doubt

Christ, I who in your presence am lowly among you, but being absent am of good courage toward you: 2 yea, I beseech you, that I may not when present show courage with the confidence wherewith I count to be bold against some, who count of us as if we walked according to the flesh. 3 For though we

---

that it is to the life of Jesus he refers. Jesus was at times most stern and outspoken in his demonstrations. The language which follows is very strong, but he reminds them that the motive which inspires it is the highest; he speaks in the name and spirit of Christ who claimed to be meek and lowly. (Matt. 11: 29, 30.)

I who in your presence am lowly among you, but being absent am of good courage toward you:—His enemies charged that he was a coward in close quarters, a brave man at a distance; he was one who could write bold letters, but lacked authority and courage when he came in person—such was their description of Paul. We have already seen that he was accused of fickleness and indecision (1: 17); his conduct was easily misrepresented by those who had no love for him, and did not understand his inspiring motives. His caution and tenderness were mistaken for cowardice. Courage was the motto of his life (4: 16; 5: 6, 7), and his courageous life is the best answer to this charge of cowardice (Acts 19: 30; 21: 13; 24: 24, 25).

2 yea, I beseech you, that I may not when present show courage with the confidence wherewith I count to be bold against some,—He beseeches them that he may not be compelled by their course to show courage and boldness toward some who charged him with walking after fleshly desires and purposes. He expected to be severe toward the leaders in evil; but he besought the members not to force him to be severe toward them. [He had determined in his own mind that if persuasion failed to bring his opponents to a right state of mind, he would resort to that power with which God had armed him to put down all opposition. These "some" are the cause of the whole trouble.]

who count of us as if we walked according to the flesh.—It seems that they charged that he had an undue regard for the opinion of others and acted with inconsistency in his efforts to

walk in the flesh, we do not war according to the flesh 4 (for the weapons
of our warfare are not of the flesh, but mighty before God to the casting
down of strongholds) ; 5 casting down [12]imaginations, and every high thing

[12]Or, *reasonings* Rom. 2. 15.

please them. A man of whom all this could truthfully be said
would be without spiritual authority, and it was to discredit
him in the church that the vague and damaging charge was
made. He certainly showed no want of courage in meeting it.
That he walked in the flesh, he could not deny. He was a
human being, wearing the weak nature, and all its maladies
were incident to him. He spent his life in this nature, with all
its capacity for unworthy conduct, but in his Christian warfare he was not ruled by it—he had conquered it and it had no
power over him. [He said to them: "I was with you in weakness, and in fear, and in much trembling. And my speech and
my preaching were not in persuasive words of wisdom, but in
demonstration of the Spirit and of power." (1 Cor. 2: 3, 4.)]

3 **For though we walk in the flesh, we do not war according
to the flesh**—Though he lived and walked in the flesh, he was
not led by the fleshly feelings and lusts. He was not under
human leadership; it was no human war in which he was engaged.

4 **(for the weapons of our warfare are not of the flesh,**—This
shows that he was not actuated by fleshly motives, nor seeking fleshly good, nor did he use weapons of carnal strife.

but mighty before God to the casting down of strongholds) ;
—Many think the miraculous powers by which he was enabled to cast out demons, and demonstrate superiority to the
wicked one, are meant; others think it means the sound scriptural reasoning, teaching, and motives used in turning men
from Satan to God. It probably means both. The spiritual
weapons are the only ones the child of God can use, and they,
through the power of God that goes with and is in them, are
mighty to the overturning of the strongholds of sin. The
Christian can lawfully use no other. And God's power to
overturn the strongholds of sin cannot go with one using
fleshly or carnal weapons. For a Christian to use these is to
drive God out of the battle he wages. These things are true if

that is exalted against the knowledge of God, and bringing every thought
into captivity to the obedience of Christ; 6 and being in readiness to avenge

there is truth in the Bible. We weaken our strength in ap-
pealing to the civil power. There is not one word in the New
Testament giving man direction as ruler or participator in the
management of human government. That means he has no
place in this work.

5 casting down imaginations,—This brings out the truth
that the lifework of the Christian is to cast down all the imaginations and everything that exalteth itself against the knowledge of Christ and casting these out of his heart; bring every
thought of his heart to the obedience of Christ. No heart is
actually clean in the sight of God until the very thoughts and
feelings and impulses of the heart are brought into subjection
to the will of Christ. It takes a lifework to accomplish this,
but too often the Christian life is so neglected that the heart
never becomes purified for a habitation of God through the
Spirit.

and every high thing that is exalted against the knowledge
of God,—The teaching of the word of God is to bring to
nought the mere reasonings of the mind, and everything that
sets itself up against the revelation of God. [In reference to
this Paul had already triumphantly asked: "Where is the
wise? where is the scribe? where is the disputer of this
world?" (1 Cor. 1: 20.) But what was seen then is often repeated today. The vain reasonings of the modernists, puffed
up with the conceit of their own wisdom, are exalted against
the infallible teaching of the Son of God and his inspired
apostles. And Paul's admonition is no less appropriate now
than when it first came with burning energy from his earnest
soul. "Let no man deceive himself. If any man thinketh that
he is wise among you in this world, let him become a fool,
that he may become wise." (1 Cor. 3: 18).]

and bringing every thought into captivity to the obedience
of Christ;—The end sought is to bring every thought of the
heart and mind into obedience to Christ, which is a difficult
thing to do. Evil thoughts will arise in our minds, excited
by fleshly lusts, yet by constant prayer, watchfulness, and per-

all disobedience, when your obedience shall be made full. 7 [18]Ye look at the things that are before your face. If any man trusteth in himself that he is

[18]Or, *Do ye look . . . face?*

severing effort the very thoughts that spring from the heart can be brought into subjection to the will of Christ. The heart can be so trained that the thoughts that arise in it will be of God, of our duties and obligations to him, and of the high and exalted privileges and blessings that are bestowed on us as his children.

6 and being in readiness to avenge all disobedience,—When he speaks of his "readiness to avenge all disobedience," he certainly did not have in mind those to whom he writes, and whose repentance and obedience filled him with so much joy (7: 6-13); but only to the rebellious remnant who had persisted in their disobedience.

when your obedience shall be made full.—He would wait till all who were willing had repented and were willing to obey. He does not indicate what form of vengeance he would administer, but possibly such severe discipline as that indicated by delivering to Satan (1 Cor. 5: 5; 1 Tim. 5: 20, with a view, if it were possible, to their ultimate restoration (13: 3-10).

2. THE CONTRAST BETWEEN HIS OWN COURSE AND THAT OF HIS OPPONENTS.
10: 7-18.

7 Ye look at the things that are before your face.—I think the marginal reading—"Do ye look at the things that are before your face?"—more fully brings out the thought. It certainly was addressed to the members of the church, and with reference to the claims which had been set up by the false teachers, warning them not to be carried away with appearances. Looking at the work of the false teachers it was strictly manifest that Paul had showed more of the signs of an apostle in the miracles of power and the good he had accomplished than any of them.

Christ, let him consider this again with himself, that, even as he is Christ's, so also are we. 8 For though I should glory somewhat abundantly concerning our authority (which the Lord gave for building you up, and not for casting you down), I shall not be put to shame: 9 that I may not seem as if I would terrify you by my letters. 10 For, His letters, they say, are

---

If any man trusteth in himself that he is Christ's, let him consider this again with himself, that, even as he is Christ's, so also are we.—[At this point Paul only claims bare equality; as the argument advances, he advances his claims as in 1 Cor. 9: 1-27, by pointing to his success at Corinth, or to his vision of the risen Christ, as in 1 Cor. 15: 9; the proof, which he adduces later (11: 21-30), lies in what he had suffered for the gospel's sake.]

8 **For though I should glory somewhat abundantly concerning our authority (which the Lord gave for building you up, and not for casting you down),**—The authority Paul had was given him to build them up, not to cast them down. In this he intimates that he would be sorry to so use it as to punish them.

I shall not be put to shame:—Were he to glory somewhat abundantly concerning this power, he would not be put to shame thereby. The power he had would bear out the glorying. [He was quite sure, without any shadow of misgiving, that if he should be forced to proceed to the extreme step of delivering his detractors to Satan, the result which he contemplated would follow.]

9 **that I may not seem as if I would terrify you by my letters.**—That he might not seem to make a boast in his letters to terrify them when he had no power to carry out the boast when present. [There is evident allusion to the representations made by the false teachers, that Paul wrote in the authoritative tone which he assumed merely to frighten his readers, having neither power nor the purpose to carry his threats into execution.]

10 **For, His letters, they say, are weighty and strong;**—[Allusive references to what had been said of Paul at Corinth by the false teachers have already appeared in this epistle (1: 17; 3: 1; 5: 12, 13.) Here for the first time the very words are

[1]weighty and strong; but his bodily presence is weak, and his speech of no account. 11 Let such a one reckon this, that, what we are in word by letters when we are absent, such *are we* also in deed when we are present. 12 For we are not bold [1]to number or compare ourselves with certain of them that commend themselves: but they themselves, measuring themselves by them-

[1]Gr. *to judge ourselves among, or to judge ourselves with.*

quoted. The scorn conveyed in them had deeply wounded him; and we have here the nearest approach which the New Testament presents of the passionate complaints poured forth by David. (Psalm 69: 1-21; 109: 1-5.) We note the common element of a burning indignation under the sense of wrong; but also the absence from his feelings of the maledictory element which is so prominent in David. The meekness and gentleness of Christ had not been without their effect in tempering even the most vehement emotions.]

but his bodily presence is weak, and his speech of no account.—His enemies said that his letters were brave and strong, but when present in body he was cowardly and subservient. [These words give remarkable significance to a passage in an epistle written shortly after this, which says: "Ye know that because of an infirmity of the flesh I preached the gospel unto you the first time: and that which was a temptation to you in my flesh ye despised not, nor rejected; but ye received me as an angel of God, even as Christ Jesus." (Gal. 4: 13, 14.) There is manifestly a contrast present to his thoughts between the mean insults of his opposers at Corinth and the affection which the Galatians had once manifested, and which made their subsequent alienation all the more painful to him.]

11 Let such a one reckon this, that, what we are in word by letters when we are absent, such are we also in deed when we are present.—He warned those who so charged that, as he wrote, he would when present act with vigor and promptness.

12 For we are not bold to number or compare ourselves with certain of them that commend themselves:—This charge of self-commendation Paul's opponents had leveled at him (3: 1; 5: 12), whereas it was they themselves who were guilty of

selves, and comparing themselves with themselves, are without understanding. 13 But we will not glory beyond *our* measure, but according to the
measure of the ²province which God appointed to us as a measure, to reach

²Or, *limit* Gr. *measuring-rod.*

the practice. He boldly asserts that he has not the courage to
range himself among such boasters.

**but they themselves, measuring themselves by themselves,
and comparing themselves with themselves,**—Men who commend themselves, having nothing but themselves with which
to measure themselves, can only end by boasting immeasura-
bly; and Paul frankly confesses, that he has not the courage
to join such a company.

are without understanding—They who so measure themselves are foolish. Wisdom tests all things by the will of
God. The only wise way is to lose confidence in self, and earnestly seek the standard God has given. The heart that loses
sight of its own ways, and comes to trust to divine guidance
and light is wise. The great trouble with most religious people is that they desire to honor God, but desire to do it in
their own way. They have confidence in their own ability to
invent ways that will please God. They please themselves,
satisfy their own conscience, and take this as satisfactory evidence that they please God. This is a fatal mistake. Christ,
to correct this error, said: "He that rejecteth me, and receiveth
not my sayings, hath one that judgeth him: the word that I
spake, the same shall judge him in the last day." (John 12:
48.) We are not to be judged in the last day by our conscience, by our standards of right, by what we have been
taught, nor by the agreement of public sentiment, but by the
word spoken by the Lord to guide man. The great difficulty
with man is to bring himself to the point that he sincerely desires to do the will of God.

**13 But we will not glory beyond our measure, but according
to the measure of the province which God apportioned to us
as a measure,**—God gave Paul a rule by which he walked, and
worked, and by that rule he measured himself, and he did not
boast of anything without this measure. [In opposition to the
false teachers, who not only boasted of gifts which they did

even unto you.   14 For we stretch not ourselves overmuch, as though we reached not unto you: for we ³came even as far as unto you in the ⁴gospel of Christ: 15 not glorying beyond *our* measure, *that is,* in other men's labors;

³Or, *were the first to come*
⁴Gr. *good tidings.* See marginal note on ch. 2. 12.

not possess, but appropriated to themselves the fruits of other men's labors by intruding into churches which they had not founded, Paul says he did neither the one nor the other. His glorying was neither immoderate, nor was it founded on what others had done. He invaded no man's sphere of labor. It was his settled purpose to preach the gospel where Christ had not been named, and not to build on another man's foundation. (Rom. 15: 20.)]

to reach even unto you.—[Acting on this principle he had the right to regard Corinth as legitimately within his field. His assigned limit of labor reached at least that far. He founded the church at Corinth; others built thereon. (1 Cor. 3: 10.) The church was his work in the Lord.]

14 For we stretch not ourselves overmuch, as though we reached not unto you:—He did not go beyond his measure when he came to them. The work he performed by the measure God gave him brought him unto them.

for we came even as far as unto you in the gospel of Christ: —Walking by the rule God gave him he came unto them in preaching the gospel of Christ. [The idea involved in over-extension is as in verse 12 of a commensurateness between the person and the place which he holds, such as exists between a man and a fitting garment. If anyone wishing to be great undertakes a province which he cannot fill, he overmeasures himself. This was not the case with Paul, for God gave him his province, and he filled the Corinthian district of it, having taken possession before anyone else had set foot on it.]

15 not glorying beyond our measure, that is, in other men's labors;—He did not boast of things not accomplished by himself working by this rule, or accomplished by other men.

but having hope that, as your faith groweth, we shall be magnified in you according to our province unto further abun-

but having hope that, as your faith groweth, we shall be magnified in you according to our ²province unto *further* abundance, 16 so as to ⁵preach the gospel even unto the parts beyond you, *and* not to glory in another's ²province in regard of things ready to our hand. 17 ⁶But he that glorieth, let him glory in the Lord. 18 For not he that commendeth himself is approved, but whom the Lord commendeth.

⁵Gr. *bring good tidings.* Comp. Mt. 11. 5.
⁶Jer. ix. 24.

dance,—After he had trained them and gone to other points of labor, he would receive help from them, as he had from the Philippians, who sent to him once and again (Phil. 4: 14-17.)

16 **so as to preach the gospel even unto the parts beyond you,**—He hoped that when their faith was strengthened they would enable him in accordance with this rule to preach the gospel in regions beyond them. That is, that they would assist him while he was preaching in the regions beyond them.

and not to glory in another's province in regard of things ready to our hand.—Paul did not like to build upon another man's foundation. It was his ambition to preach where the gospel was not known. So he did not boast of work done by others as these false apostles had done, taking his work, perverting it, and boasting of it as though done by themselves. Paul could not do this. When he said God had given him this rule, he did not mean that God required him to work without being chargeable to those to whom he preached, but that he had enabled him to work by it successfully.

17 **But he that glorieth, let him glory in the Lord.**—Paul would not glory in what others had done. He would only glory in what the Lord had enabled him to do. What he did under the direction of the Lord, the Lord did through him— he enabled him to do it. (Jer. 9: 24.) Paul reproved in this those who came, entered into his work, decried him, boasted in, and perverted what he had done.

18 **For not he that commendeth himself is approved, but whom the Lord commendeth.**—The Lord commends those through whom he works. He commended the apostles by his presence and power in spiritual gifts bestowed. [Paul did not commend himself; his claims were not founded on the suggestions of self-conceit; neither did he rely on the commendation

of others, his eyes were fixed on God. If he could secure his favor, it was to him a small matter to be judged by man's judgment (1 Cor. 4: 3).]

3. IRONICAL GLORYING OF THE APOSTLE IN HIS MINISTE-RIAL WORK IN OPPOSITION TO THE EMPTY BOASTING OF THE JUDAIZERS.
11: 1-15.

1 Would that ye could bear with me in a little foolishness: [7]but indeed ye do bear with me. 2 For I am jealous over you with [8]a godly jealousy: for I espoused you to one husband, that I might present you *as* a pure vir-

---

[7]Or, *nay indeed bear with me*
[8]Gr. *a jealousy of God.*

---

1 **Would that ye could bear with me in a little foolishness:** —[Paul has been forced by the challenge of the Judaizers into an argument which to him was very distasteful. In this case it was indeed necessary; but he describes it as foolishness, and he asks the Corinthians to bear with him a little longer, as the matter which has extorted his self-vindication from him is one of the greatest importance.]

but indeed ye do bear with me.—He turns from a request to an assurance that, on account of their love for him, they bear with him while he asserts his apostolic mission and authority.

2 **For I am jealous over you with a godly jealously:**—A godly jealousy is a pious zeal of which God is both the author and the object, and is such a zeal as he has. The feeling which Paul had for the church was no selfish or mercenary interest, but such as arose from his desire that the church should be faithful to Christ, and not turn aside to another.

for I espoused you to one husband, that I might present you as a pure virgin to Christ.—In this the church is represented as a virgin espoused to Christ, arranged by Paul who promoted the espousal, desiring that she should be a chaste virgin who had not lavished her affections on others when Jesus shall come to take her to himself and abide with her. If the espoused cannot comply with the terms and conditions imposed, she cannot stand the test he has made, and is rejected as a spurious and unreal love.

gin to Christ. 3 But I fear, lest by any means, as the serpent beguiled Eve
in his craftiness, your ⁹minds should be corrupted from the simplicity and the
purity that is toward Christ. 4 For if he that cometh preacheth another
Jesus, whom we did not preach, or *if ye* receive a different spirit, which ye

⁹Gr. *thoughts.* See ch. 3. 14.

**3 But I fear, lest by any means, as the serpent beguiled Eve
in his craftiness,**—The false teachers who came into their
midst and turned the disciples away from their true love to
God and an unshaken fidelity to his word, to things Paul had
not taught, is compared to the evil one entering Eden and
turning Eve from her loyalty to God. [The New Testament
writers sanction and confirm the historical verity of the Old
Testament record. The account of the temptation as recorded
in Genesis is regarded by the inspired writers of the New Testament not as a myth, or an allegory, or fiction, but a true
story.]

**your minds should be corrupted from the simplicity and the
purity that is toward Christ.**—Satan operates through his
word, institutions, and appointments to accomplish his work.
Every rebel against God is a minister of Satan; every word of
opprobrium, reproach, or disparagement of the church of
Christ, every discouraging word spoken, or influence exerted
against faithful obedience to the gospel in its spirit and pre-
cepts, is the devil working and speaking through his ministers. The kingdoms of earthly mould, the institutions of man's
framing, the fashions, the public sentiment of the world, are
all institutions of Satan to divert men's heart from God.
Every institution and appointment that is not God's planting
is a means through which Satan exerts his influence to wean
man from God. Whoever comes into the church of God, and
with fair promises leads men away from a strict loyalty to
God and his word to things not taught, is used by the evil one
to corrupt their minds from the simplicity of the truth revealed in Christ.

**4 For if he that cometh preached another Jesus, whom we
did not preach, or if ye receive a different spirit, which ye did
not receive, or different gospel, which ye did not accept, ye
do well to bear with him.**—Exactly what the false teachers

did not receive, or a different [10]gospel, which ye did not accept, ye do well to bear with *him*. 5 For I reckon that I am not a whit behind [11]the very chief-

[10]Gr. *good tidings.* Comp. ch. 2. 12.
[11]Or, *those preëminent apostles*

---

taught is not clear. They denied that Paul was an apostle and sought to supersede his influence and authority among them, and probably sought to reinstate the law of Moses, yet this is not clear. This shows that men may acknowledge many of the leading truths of the Christian religion, yet so pervert the teachings as to make it another gospel. If he who comes should preach another Jesus, or if they received a different spirit bestowing miraculous powers, or a different gospel plan of salvation from that they received from Paul, then they might bear with him. But these teachers came with nothing different, acknowledging the Jesus that Paul preached, the same spirit, the same plan of salvation, yet denied that Paul, working miracles by the Spirit, was a teacher from God, and so perverted the teachings of the Spirit. Paul seems to think there was more inconsistency in acknowledging Jesus and the Holy Spirit, and then changing their teachings, than in denying outright that Jesus is the Christ, or that the Spirit was sent from God. Many now do as these false teachers did—acknowledge Jesus and the Spirit, and the gospel from God, yet change and pervert the teaching. They are placed by Paul as he did these early teachers, in company with the serpent in Eden deceiving Eve.

[The import of this verse is not quite clear, and commentators differ in their interpretation. But it is clear enough that the reference is to the Judaizing teachers who threatened to carry away the Galatian Christians. (Gal. 1: 6-9.) In this case the import is that Paul might well be jealous over them, for they seemed ready to drink in the teaching of these men. In the interpretation of the passage it is necessary to bear in mind that Paul begins this paragraph with the wish that the Corinthians would "bear with me" in the constrained "foolishness" of boasting, to which he adds, "but indeed ye do bear with me." He gives us a reason for this earnestness, his "godly jealousy," which fills him with great anxiety as to

est apostles. 6 But though *I be* rude in speech, yet *am I* not in knowledge;

their spiritual welfare. He then adverts (verses 3, 4) to the source of his fear of their estrangement from Christ through the perverse teaching of those who were preaching "another Jesus" than the crucified and risen Christ whom he himself had preached to them, and were consequently inculcating "a different gospel" from that which they had received from him. What now could be more appropriate and more closely connected with this than to end with the enforcement of the earnest entreaty which begins this train of thought by saying, "ye do well to bear with me" in his anxious effort to expose every such adversary of the truth and to hold them in steadfast loyalty to the redeeming Christ of the gospel which he preached. He had said in full form of expression, "but indeed ye do bear with me," and after presenting his argument in justification of this entreaty repeats it in elliptical form, and according to usage the word to be supplied is the one that is found in the complete form of expression already employed. To suppose that Paul, after speaking of the false teachers who would preach "a different gospel" for his, *ironically* says, "ye do well to bear with *him*," is absurd; for this would require emphasis upon the pronoun and hence demand its actual appearance in the sentence. The simple construction is that Paul, after entreating them to bear with him in his efforts to detach them from false teachers, shows from the character of their teaching that the Corinthians would do well to bear with *him* in his effort and accordingly urges them to do so.]

5 **For I reckon that I am not a whit behind the very chiefest apostles.**—He had shown all the powers that the very chiefest of the apostles, Peter, James, and John, possessed. God had given his testimony to Paul as an apostle as fully as he had to them. He was behind them in no qualification, and greatly surpassed them in the extent of his labors and sufferings for the cause of Christ.

6 **But though I be rude in speech, yet am I not in knowledge;**—Paul was a scholar, learned and wise in the use of

¹²nay, in every way have we made *this* manifest unto you in all things. 7 Or did I commit a sin in abasing myself that ye might be exalted, because I ¹³preached to you the gospel of God for nought? 8 I robbed other churches, taking wages *of them* that I might minister unto you; 9 and when I was

¹²Or, *nay, in everything we have made it manifest among all men to you-ward*
¹³Gr. *brought good tidings.* See ch. 10. 16.

knowledge. He was plain and direct in speech and fearlessly denounced wrongs and perverters of the word of God. [They charged him with being rude and rough, and not following the rhetorical style of reasoning. He accepted this as true, but said he was not deficient in knowledge and the truths he preached, having received them by direct revelation from heaven. (Gal. 1: 12; Eph. 3: 4, 5.)]

nay, in every way have we made this manifest unto you in all things.—In everything he had made himself plain, intelligible, and had given ample proof of his knowledge of the gospel to all men while in their midst.

7 Or did I commit a sin in abasing myself that ye might be exalted, because I preached to you the gospel of God for nought?—The only thing Paul had done that the other apostles did not was that he had not been chargeable to any of them while preaching to them. He worked with his own hands to supply his wants. He calls this abasing himself that they might be free from charge and that he might save the more. [In suggesting that it was perhaps a sin to preach the gospel of God for nought, Paul is using the language of bitter irony, compare 12: 13, where the allusion is the same—"forgive me this wrong." He was deeply hurt by the ungenerous construction of his generosity. The grace of God is more eloquently proclaimed by the preacher who illustrates it in his own conduct.]

8 I robbed other churches, taking wages of them that I might minister unto you;—He accepted assistance from other churches while preaching to the Corinthians, but he does not mean that what he received was against the will of those helping him; but he deprived others of their goods by receiving help from them while preaching to the Corinthians. [There is a pointed contrast between *others* and *you;* and the language

present with you and was in want, I was not a burden on any man; for the
brethren, when they came from Macedonia, supplied the measure of my
want; and in everything I kept myself from being burdensome unto you, and
so will I keep *myself*. 10 As the truth of Christ is in me, no man shall stop
me of this glorying in the regions of Achaia. 11 Wherefore? because I love

is very vigorous; the contribution from other churches he
characterizes as *robbery*—the motive of which was service to
you—though from another point of view it is simply wages. (1
Cor. 9: 7.) In Corinth, as the sequel shows, the most scrupu-
lous care must be taken to give no offense, and Paul would be
less exposed to reproach, if he accepted nothing from the Corinthians for his services.]

9 and when I was present with you and was in want, I was
not a burden on any man;—When he needed, and what his own
labor did not furnish, the churches supplied. [This recalls
with almost tragic force his laboring among the Corinthians,
how earnestly and successfully they knew well, and yet in
want.]

for the brethren, when they came from Macedonia, supplied
the measure of my want;—He instances the brethren coming
from Macedonia and supplying his wants when he began to be
in need. [The Philippians had sent supplies to him while he
was in Thessalonica "once and again" (Phil. 4: 15, 16), and it
was a natural sequence that they should send to him also at
Corinth.]

and in everything I kept myself from being burdensome
unto you, and so will I keep myself.—He had not been chargeable to any of them, nor did he intend to be. [He accepted
with gratitude free gifts from a distance. For these he felt to
be a meet expression of spiritual life.]

10 As the truth of Christ is in me, no man shall stop me of
this glorying in the regions of Achaia.—This is a solemn form
of earnestly saying he will not be stopped from this privilege
of boasting that he preached the gospel without charge. (1
Cor. 9: 18.) That is, in the regions of Achaia he did not intend to take help that would prevent his boasting. He desig-
nates this region because there his course had been attacked.

you not? God knoweth. 12 But what I do, that I will do, that I may cut
off ¹⁴occasion from them that desire an occasion; that wherein they glory,
they may be found even as we. 13 For such men are false apostles, deceitful
workers, fashioning themselves into apostles of Christ. 14 And no marvel;

¹⁴Gr. *the occasion of them.*

---

11 Wherefore? because I love you not? God knoweth—
He appeals to God as to how strong his love was for them.

**12 But what I do, that I will do, that I may cut off occasion
from them that desire an occasion;—**He did not refuse their
help because he did not love them, but because he had determined to cut off all occasion for his enemies to charge that he
was seeking gain of them.

that wherein they glory, they may be found even as we.—
[Paul's enemies desired that they should be on an equality
with him. But they accepted support while Paul did not;
though it pleased them to construe this as an admission that
he was not a true apostle, the obvious unselfishness of Paul's
policy was, to candid men, a sufficient refutation of this argument. Paul therefore in this respect had a distinct advantage
over them, and he was determined to retain it. The apostolic
equality with him to which they aspired he rendered impossible by adopting an unselfish policy which their avarice would
not let them imitate.]

13 For such men are false apostles,—False apostles were
those who claimed to be apostles. They claimed to be what
they were not, and usurped an authority which did not belong
to them.

deceitful workers,—They were workers in so far as they
were preachers or teachers; but they were not honest; they
availed themselves of every means to deceive and pervert the
people. They were workers; but with hidden, selfish, and
wicked motives.

fashioning themselves into apostles of Christ.—[Though
their real object was not to advance the kingdom and glory of
Christ, and although they were never commissioned for that
work, they gave themselves out as Christ's messengers and
servants, and even claimed to have more intimate relation

for even Satan fashioneth himself into an angel of light. 15 It is no great
thing therefore if his ministers also fashion themselves as ministers of righteousness; whose end shall be according to their works.

---

with him, and to be more devoted to his service than Paul
himself.]

**14 And no marvel; for even Satan fashioneth himself into
an angel of light.**—Satan pretends to be an angel of light to
men, seeking their good. So he appeared to Eve and deceived
her. He generally comes in the garb of righteousness pre-
tending to seek the good of those he would ruin.

**15 It is no great thing therefore if his ministers also fashion
themselves as ministers of righteousness;**—Since this is true
of Satan, it is not a strange thing that his servants should follow his example and claim to be ministers of light. These impostors claiming to be apostles were an example of this.
They yet do it. Every one who seeks to turn the children of
God from his appointed ways is a minister of Satan, even
though he thinks he is serving God. [This fearful description
implies that Paul's opponents, though church members and
professed followers of Jesus Christ, were bad men, deliber-
ately deceiving the Corinthian Christians. Therefore since
Satan even assumes the garb of righteousness in order to en-
snare men, it is no wonder that these men assumed a garb
which was not their own.]

whose end shall be according to their works.—The end of
all such shall correspond to their works; evil works bring an
evil end. [They are guilty of the deepest sort of lie, and their
punishment will be as terrible as their sin.]

4. CONTINUANCE OF IRONICAL GLORYING IN A MORE EX-
TENDED COMPARISON WITH THE JUDAIZERS.
11: 16-33.

16 I say again, Let no man think me foolish; but if ye do, yet as foolish

---

16 I say again,—[Paul had made three attempts to begin his
glorying. First (10: 7), he stops to give attention to the
empty glorying of his opponents; second (11: 1), he pauses to
express his anxiety for the Corinthian Christians under the in-

receive me, that I also may glory a little. 17 That which I speak, I speak
not after the Lord, but as in foolishness, in this confidence of glorying. 18
Seeing that many glory after the flesh, I will glory also. 19 For ye bear
with the foolish gladly, being wise *yourselves*. 20 For ye bear with a man, if

---

fluence of false teachers; and third (11: 6), he stops again to
answer the charge of not accepting support. Now he returns
to the point and expresses himself fully as far as 12: 13.]

**Let no man think me foolish; but if ye do, yet as foolish re-
ceive me, that I also may glory a little.**—While averring that
his course was not that of a foolish, self-boaster, he tells them
that if they think he is, receive him as such, as bear with him
to see if he has not as much of which to boast as those whom
they had received in their boasting.

17 **That which I speak, I speak not after the Lord, but as in
foolishness, in this confidence of glorying.**—[The words rendered "after the Lord" possibly mean according to the spirit
of the Lord, "who never boasted in this manner." Self-praise,
in itself considered, is not the spirit of the Christian; it is not
a work to which the Spirit of Christ impels the believer. But,
when it is necessary to the vindication of the truth or the
honor of Christ, it becomes a duty.] What Paul now says, he
does after the manner of the boasters, to show that he has
much stronger claims than they do to be received, even on
their own grounds.

18 **Seeing that many glory after the flesh, I will glory also.**
—As the false apostles gloried in their fleshly relation to
Abraham, he meets them on this ground. [Here for the first
time, he tells just what course his glorying is to take. It is to
his claim to honor as a man. It includes his ancestry, his endurance of physical hardships in his ministry, and the special
visions and revelations which had been granted to him. His
opponents so magnified themselves and their services, and so
depreciated him and his labors, that he was forced, in order to
maintain his influence as the advocate of the pure gospel, to
set forth his claims to the confidence of the people.]

19 **For ye bear with the foolish gladly, being wise yourselves.**—Before presenting his claims as a child of Abraham,

he bringeth you into bondage, if he devoureth you, if he taketh you *captive,* if he exalteth himself, if he smiteth you on the face. 21 I speak by way of disparagement, as though we had been weak. Yet whereinsoever any is bold (I speak in foolishness), I am bold also. 22 Are they Hebrews? so am I.

---

he tells them that they are wise (in their own conceits), that they can afford to bear with him while he meets the foolish on their own ground to show that he has greater claims than they.

20 **For ye bear with a man, if he bringeth you into bondage, if he devoureth you, if he taketh you captive, if he exalteth himself,**—This is given as a reason why they should bear with him in his boasting. A reason personal to them. The false apostles had brought them into bondage; they had become lords over God's heritage; they had devoured their substance; they had taken them captive by bringing them around to serve their ends. They had borne all these things from the false apostles. They certainly could bear a little boasting from him.

if he smiteth you on the face.—[To smite on the face was the highest indignity; as such it was offered to our Lord (Luke 22: 64), and to Paul (Acts 23: 2). Such was the treatment to which the Corinthians submitted from the hands of false teachers. They really took away their freedom is Christ as much as if they had been abject slaves. It is only the pure and undefiled of our Lord Jesus Christ that gives perfect freedom. All heathens are slaves to their priests; all those who embrace error are slaves to those who are their guides.]

21 **I speak by way of disparagement, as though we had been weak.**—In this boasting he ironically brings reproach upon himself, or disparges himself as though he were weak, but he was not weak

Yet whereinsoever any is bold (I speak in foolishness), I am bold also.—In this he refers to the reproach cast upon him, as a weak preacher, because he showed none of that proud and insolent bearing which the false teachers did. But he could be as bold as they, and with much better reason too. [Now follows that incomparable burst of indignant eloquence, embodying particulars of history, or rather bare allusions to facts in

Are they Israelites? so am I.   Are they the seed of Abraham? so am I.   23

his apostolic history—extending over about fourteen years, without any of those details which we should be so glad to have.]

22 Are they Hebrews?—This then was their boasts. [They were Jews of Palestine, speaking Aramaic, reading the law and the prophets in the original.]

so am I.—His answer is that he too was a Hebrew [or as he puts it, "a Hebrew of Hebrews." (Phil. 3: 5.) What he means is obviously that his parents were Jews of Palestine and that the accident of his birth had not annulled his claim to that nationality. As a matter of fact, it made him able to unite things that were commonly looked upon as incompatible, and to be both a Hebrew and a Hellenist.]

Are they Israelites?—They claimed to be members of the nation which traced its origin to Jacob (Gen. 32: 28), and which had, through all its history, been a nation whose God was Jehovah.

so am I.—His response to this was that he too was an Israelite of the purest blood and the accident of his having been born in Tarsus did not annul his claim to that nationality, neither did it prevent his being brought up in Jerusalem at the feet of Gamaliel their great teacher. (Acts 22: 3.)

Are they the seed of Abraham?—They boasted that they were the descendants of Abraham. This will all the Jews was regarded as a distinguished honor (Matt. 3: 9; John 8: 39), and no doubt the false apostles gloried in it as eminently qualifying them to engage in the work of the ministry.

so am I.—The mention of the "seed of Abraham" to Paul was an equivalent to "heirs according to the promise" (Gen. 12: 1-3; 22: 17; Gal. 3: 8, 29); it describes the Jewish people as directly and immediately interested in "this salvation of God" (Luke 2: 30; Acts 28: 28). [No one can read Romans 9: 4, 5 without feeling that pride of race as pride in his people —and in their special relation to God and their special place in the history of redemption—was among the strongest passions in his heart; and we can understand the indignation with

Are they ministers of Christ? (I speak as one beside himself) I more; in
labors more abundantly, in prisons more abundantly, in stripes above mea-

---

which he regarded men who trailed him over Asia and Europe,
assailed his authority, and sought to undermine his work, on
the ground that he was faithless to the lawful prerogatives of
Israel. There was not a son of Abraham in the world prouder
of his birth, with a more magnificent sense of his people's glories than the apostle to the Gentiles. And it provoked him beyond endurance to see the things in which he gloried debased,
as they were debased, by his enemies—made the symbol of
paltry vanity which he despised, made barriers to the universal love of God by which all the families of the earth were to
be blessed. Driven to extremity, he could only outlaw such opponents from the Christian community, and say to the Gentile
Christians: "We are the circumcision, who worship by the
Spirit of God, and glory in Christ Jesus, and have no confidence in the flesh." (Phil. 3: 3.)]

23 **Are they ministers of Christ?**—They called themselves
apostles and ministers; but Paul called them false apostles
and ministers of Satan. [This defines fairly accurately who
they were. They claimed to be more genuinely ministers of
Christ than Paul. That is, they were Judaizers seeking to
ground all Christian faith, first of all in Jewish form and ceremony.]

(I speak as one beside himself)—[This is a strong expression, and is said out of the consciousness of ill desert and
utter insufficiency. Feeling himself to be in himself both im-
potent and unworthy, this self-laudation, though having reference only to his infirmities and to what God had done in him
and by him, was in the highest degree painful and humiliating
to him.]

I more;—He claimed to be something beyond the ordinary
servant of Christ. [This is the frantic boast which he proceeds to justify in a fragment of biography which must ever
be accounted as the most remarkable and unique in the
world's history.]

in labors more abundantly,—More abundant in labors necessary to propagate the gospel and more indefatigable in it.

sure, in deaths oft.   24 Of the Jews five times received I forty *stripes* save

[The comparison between himself and them were reference to
these conclusively shows how far they were from being ministers of Christ. They did not labor, but claimed the fruits of
his labor. (10: 15, 16.) But comparison, in fact, was out of the
question—the sufferings of Paul in laboring for the advancement of the cause of Christ were unparalleled and alone. The
few lines he devotes to them are the most vivid light on the
apostolic age and the apostolic career.]

in prisons more abundantly,—[Luke mentions only one imprisonment of Paul before this time. That was at Philippi.
(Acts 16: 23-39.) But we must remember that many things
which actually occurred were omitted by Luke. He does not
profess to give an account of all that happened to Paul.]

in stripes above measure,—[This probably refers to scourgings inflicted by the heathen, which were not limited to forty
stripes save one to which the Jews were restricted.]

in deaths oft.—He suffered as though he died, "for we who
live are always delivered unto death for Jesus' sake, that the
life also of Jesus may be manifested in our mortal flesh" (4:
11). No one familiar with his life can doubt that he was often
in danger of death.

24 Of the Jews five times received I forty stripes save one.
—[None of these occasions are mentioned in Acts but he may
have been whipped at Damascus on his conversion, and then
at Jerusalem, and again at Antioch. The chiefs of the synagogue had the power to inflict stripes on their own people,
and would often exercise the jurisdiction against Paul, who
was in the habit of preaching in the synagogue what was regarded as heresy. The number of stripes was not to exceed
forty (Deut. 25: 3); whence the Jews took care not to exceed
thirty-nine (Josephus, Ant. iv. 8, sec. 21). The convict was
stripped to the waist and tied in a bent position to a low pillar, and the stripes with a whip of three thongs were inflicted
on the back between the shoulders. (Acts 22: 25.) A single
stripe in excess subjected the executioner to punishment.
The fortieth was omitted that they might not by mistake ex-

one. **25** Thrice was I beaten with rods, once was I stoned, thrice I suffered
shipwreck, a night and a day have I been in the deep; **26** *in* journeyings
often, *in* perils of rivers, *in* perils of robbers, *in* perils from *my* ¹countrymen, *in* perils from the Gentiles, *in* perils in the city, *in* perils in the

¹Gr. *race.*   Comp. Acts 7. 19.

ceed the number allowed. The infliction was severe and frequently resulted in death.]

25 Thrice was I beaten with rods,—This was the Roman
mode of scourging, and this also sometimes resulted in death.
Only one of these three cases is recorded in Acts. (16: 22-24.)
In Paul's case it was an illegal act, and inflicted barbarously
and with cruel aggravation, the bleeding backs of him and his
companion being left to smart on the floor of a dark dungeon,
while their feet were fast in stocks.

once was I stoned,—This was the usual mode of punishment among the Jews for blasphemy. The instance referred
to here occurred at Lystra. After stoning him, they "dragged
him out of the city, supposing that he was dead." (Acts 14: 19.)

thrice I suffered shipwreck,—[None of these are recorded,
but Paul was frequently on the seas in the course of his labors, and from defective navigation and unskilled shipbuilding, and from want of the mariner's compass, wrecks were frequent.]

a night and a day have I been in the deep;—It is probable
that in this Paul refers to some time, when having been shipwrecked, he was saved by supporting himself on a plank or
fragment of the vessel until he obtained relief. Such a situation is one of great peril, and he mentions it, therefore, among
the trials which he had endured.

26 in journeyings often,—[Traveling in those days was both
arduous and dangerous. Journeyings seem to introduce the
various forms of peril, just as labors introduced the experiences with magistrates and mobs.]

in perils of rivers,—[In all countries which, like parts of
Syria, Asia Minor, and Greece, abound in unbridged mountain
torrents, journeys are constantly accompanied by deaths from
drowning in the sudden rush of swollen streams.]

wilderness, *in* perils in the sea, *in* perils among false brethren; 27 *in* labor and travail, in watchings often, in hunger and thirst, in fastings often, in cold

in perils of robbers,—Some of the mountain regions through which he passed are known to have been infested by robbers, and it is probable that he was often attacked and his life was endangered.

in perils from my countrymen,—The Jews in most cases were the first to stir up opposition and to excite the mob against him. This was the case at Damascus (Acts 9: 23), at Jerusalem (9: 29), at Antioch in Pisidia (13: 50), at Iconium (14: 5), at Lystra (14: 19), at Thessalonica (17: 5), at Berea (17: 13), and at Corinth (18: 12). They had deep enmity against him as an apostle, and he was in constant danger of being put to death by them.

in perils from the Gentiles,—The Gentiles were generally stirred up against him by the Jews, but sometimes by interested idolaters, as at Iconium (Acts 14: 5), at Philippi (16: 19-24), at Ephesus (19: 23-31).

in perils in the city,—Damascus (Acts 9: 23), Jerusalem (9: 29), Antioch in Pisidia (13: 50), Iconium (14: 5), Lystra (14: 19), Philippi (16: 19), Thessalonica (17: 5), Berea (17: 13), Corinth (18: 13), and Ephesus (19: 23).

in perils in the wilderness,—[In traveling through the wild waste tracts of land between Perga and Antioch in Pisidia, or thence to Lystra and Derbe; or over the mountain of Taurus into the cities of Galatia where he would be exposed to the attacks of wild beasts, or to hunger and want.] He met with constant danger wherever he was, whether in the busy haunts of men or in the solitude and loneliness of the desert.

in perils in the sea,—He had encountered many storms, shipwrecks, and had most likely been beset by pirates.

in perils among false brethren;—It is probable that this refers to the treachery of those who professed to be his brethren in Christ, and yet endeavored to deliver him into the power of his enemies. [This was the crowning danger and trial to Paul, as it is to all others. A man can better bear danger by land and sea, among robbers and in deserts, than he can bear

and nakedness. 28 ²Besides those things that are without, there is that which

²Or, *Besides the things which I omit* Or, *Besides the things that come out of course*

---

to have his confidence abused, and to be subjected to the actions and the arts of spies upon his conduct.]

27 in labor and travail,—Wearisome toil and consequent exhaustion and suffering resulting from the hard work wherever he preached.

in watchings often,—He pursued the labor and travail by night as well as by day and so incurred the want of sleep. He also sacrificed sleep for teaching and preaching (Acts 20: 31), as well as for prayer and meditation (1 Thess. 3: 10).

in hunger and thirst,—The hunger and thirst endured was through lack of necessary food.

in fastings often,—The fastings were abstinence practiced when he preferred the service of Christ and labor for the salvation of men to the satisfaction of physical want. (6: 5.)

in cold and nakedness.—All these hardships were the necessary accompaniments of a life spent in traversing half-civilized countries, such as Syria, Asia Minor, and Greece. [He was insufficiently clad. In his labors his clothing became old and badly worn, and he had no friends to replace them, neither had he money with which to buy new ones.]

[In all this we cannot resist the impression of triumph with which Paul records the "perils" he had faced; so many they were, so various and so terrible, yet in the Lord's service he had come safely through them all. It is a commentary from his own hand on his own words—"As dying, and behold, we live." (6: 9.) In the retrospect all these perils show not only that he was a true servant of Christ, entering into fellowship with his Master's sufferings to bring blessings to men, but that he was owned by Christ as such. The Lord had delivered him from deaths so great; yes, and he would deliver him; and his hope was set on him for every deliverance he might need. (1: 10.) In all their kinds and degrees—violence, privation, exposure, fear—they are a historical testimony to the devotion with which Paul had served Christ. He bore in his body the marks which they had left, and to him they were

presseth upon me daily, anxiety for all the churches. 29 Who is weak, and I am not weak? who is caused to stumble, and I burn not? 3 If I must needs glory, I will glory of the things that concern my weakness. 31 ³The God

³Or, *God and the Father* See Rom. 15. 6.

"the marks of Jesus" (Gal. 6: 17) ; they identified him as Jesus Christ's bond servant.]

28 **Besides those things that are without, there is that which presseth upon me daily, anxiety for all the churches.**—In addition to all these bodily afflictions, one harder to be borne was that he, as the apostle to the Gentiles, felt the care of all the churches resting upon him. The anxiety which he had for them was more real and intense than that which the ordinary man has about food and raiment. This came as a daily and a constant burden—to see that they were properly taught and trained in the way of the Lord. Each epistle which he wrote manifested different causes of anxieties, and different admonitions, and different thanksgivings, so that he must have kept himself perfectly alive to the spiritual necessities of each.

29 **Who is weak, and I am not weak?**—Paul, in sympathy with all men, felt their weaknesses and infirmities. He became all things to all men. He felt and bore the weaknesses of the body with them.

who is caused to stumble, and I burn not?—Who was led into sin that he did not feel the shame and sorrow with him? Paul, like Jesus, bore the sins and weaknesses of the children of God with them. Yet despite all these sufferings in spirit and body, sorrows and burdens, Paul rejoiced as few men have rejoiced. Jesus was "a man of sorrows, and acquainted with grief," on whom the stripes of all were laid, suffered as never man suffered, yet beyond all doubt was the happiest being who ever trod this earth. Happiest because he did and suffered most to make others happy. After Jesus, Paul was the happiest man on earth because he suffered more to make others happy. This is a new way of happiness opened by Jesus to man that we learn so slowly. Yet the truest happiness of earth comes from denying self to help others. This is akin to the happiness of heaven.

30 **If I must needs glory, I will glory of the things that con-**

and Father of the Lord Jesus, he who is blessed [4]for evermore knoweth that I lie not. 32 In Damascus the [5]governor under Aretas the king guarded the city of the Damascenes in order to take me: 33 and through a window was I let down in a basket by the wall, and escaped his hands.

[4]Gr. *unto the ages.*
[5]Gr. *ethnarch.*

cern my weakness,—As Paul was forced to glory, he gloried in what he had suffered for God and man. This was a new theme for glorying, it was a new way to prove his apostleship and power from God. How strange, how unanswerable, how crushing to his enemies. It was like the Master. He proved his love for men by what he suffered for them.

31 **The God and Father of the Lord Jesus, he who is blessed for evermore knoweth that I lie not.**—[Paul's glorying was so different from the common glorying among men that he felt that some would not appreciate his deep feelings, and would listen to his words with astonishment and doubt; but this solemn affirmation is in keeping with the fervid character of the whole passage. It is thrown in somewhat independently, having reference to what precedes and what follows.]

32 **In Damascus the governor under Aretas the king guarded the city of the Damascenes in order to take me:**— From the mass of his past endurances for Christ, he selects as a specimen and proof of all the rest this great fact, occurring at the beginning of his Christian career—a fair note to the whole—to show his sufferings and deliverances as an apostle. [Paul saw enacted in Damascus a scene like some in which he had played a part in Jerusalem, but with his own part reversed. He experienced some of the ill-treatment which he had heaped upon others. From the account given by Luke (Acts 9: 23-25), we learn that when he heard of their plot to kill him he hid himself; but his enemies, thinking that he would try to escape through one of the gates of the city, and that they would be sure of finding him, kept constant watch for him. This watching also became known to his friends, which shows that they too were on the watch, and they provided for him another mode of escape.]

33 **and through a window was I let down in a basket by the wall, and escaped his hands.**—[Along the wall of Damascus

some of the houses were built against the wall, with upper stories of wood resting on the top of the wall. Out of a window in one of these he was let down by the side of the wall in a basket. This attempt to kill him was the effect of his preaching on unbelieving Jews. The effect was seen "when many days were fulfilled" (Acts 9: 23), an indefinite expression which might mean a few weeks, a few months, or a few years. But we learn from Paul's own statement (Gal. 1: 17, 18) that his escape occurred three years after his conversion and within this period he had made a sojourn into Arabia. How far he had gone into Arabia, or how long he had remained there, he does not say; but he does say that after the excursion he returned to Damascus, and it is easy to see that the attempt to kill him occurred after his return. He also says that "the governor under Aretas the king guarded the city of the Damascenes" in order to take him, which shows that Damascus was then under the dominion of Aretas, who was king of Arabia, and that the Jews had his cooperation in the attempt to arrest Paul in the gates. Furthermore, as Damascus was at that time under the king of Arabia, the country of and adjacent to it must have been overrun by his forces, and for the time in which he held it it would be styled a part of Arabia. Saul's sojourn there, then may have been into this region for the purpose of preaching in its cities and villages; and it may have been his activity in this work which aroused the Jewish opposition to its highest pitch, and at the same time enabled them to enlist the Arabian government in their plot. For many reasons unknown to us the danger in Damascus, and the escape from it, had a peculiar interest for Paul. He gloried in what he had endured there in imminent peril and in the undignified escape alike—as in things belonging to his weakness. Another might choose to hide such things, but they are precisely what he tells. In Christ's service scorn is glory, ignominy is honor; and it is the mark of loyalty when men rejoice that they are counted worthy to suffer shame for his name.]

5. REFERENCE TO HIS VISIONS AND REVELATIONS AS IN-
VOLVING EXTRAORDINARY FAVOR, BUT OF WHICH
HE WILL GLORY ONLY AS THEY STAND RELATED
TO HIS AFFLICTIONS AND WEAKNESS.
12: 1-13.

1 [6]I must needs glory, though it is not expedient; but I will come to visions and revelations of the Lord. 2 I know a man in Christ, fourteen years
ago (whether in the body I know not; or whether out of the body, I know
not; God knoweth), such a one caught up even to the third heaven. 3 And I

[6]Some ancient authorities read *Now to glory is not expedient, but I will come &c.*

---

1 **I must needs glory, though it is not expedient;**—While it
was not commendable for him to boast, it was necessary that
he should do so. That is, while boasting or glorying was not
ordinarily becoming, the false teachers had forced him to do it
to vindicate his apostleship and superiority to them. He had
already told them of his Hebrew blood, the Spirit with which
he was endowed; and the toils, imprisonments, sufferings, and
burdens he had borne.

but I will come to visions—Visions were appearances presented to a person in a supernatural manner, whether awake
or asleep.

and revelations of the Lord.—Revelations were a disclosure
of truth, instruction, concerning things before unknown—
especially those relating to salvation—given by God himself,
or by the risen and glorified Christ, and so to be distinguished
from other methods of instruction. These were marks of his
apostleship.

2 **I know a man in Christ, fourteen years ago**—According to
the received chronology, this epistle was written near the
close of the year 57, and "fourteen years ago" would place this
vision about the time he and Barnabas were sent forth from
Antioch on the first tour among the Gentiles. (Acts 13: 1-3.)
Verses 6 and 7 show that Paul himself was the subject of the
vision.

**(whether in the body, I know not; or whether out of the
body, I know not; God knoweth),**—In this vision Paul could
not tell whether he was carried bodily or was transported in
the spirit.

know such a man (whether in the body, or apart from the body, I know not; God knoweth), 4 how that he was caught up into Paradise, and heard unspeakable words, which it is not lawful to a matter to utter. 5 On behalf of

such a one caught up even to the third heaven.—The Jews held the idea of three heavens: (1) The air or atmosphere where clouds gather (Gen. 2: 1, 19); (2) the firmament in which sun, moon, and stars are fixed (Deut. 18: 3; Matt. 24; 29); and (3) God's dwelling place (Matt. 5: 12, 16, 45, 48). Paul was caught up to the throne of God.

3 **And I know such a man (whether in the body, or apart from the body, I know not; God knoweth),**—This seems to be a repetition to give emphasis to the statement.

4 **how that he was caught up into Paradise,**—The meaning of the word Paradise has been a question of doubt. It is probably a term for "the third heaven." It is not a common word in the New Testament, found only here and in Luke 23: 43, and Rev. 2: 7. It originally meant a park, then a pleasure park. It was used in Genesis 3: 1, 8, 23, 24, for the Garden of Eden, and came in later to be applied to the abode of the righteous after death. Here it is usually regarded as the same as the "third heaven."

and heard unspeakable words, which is not lawful for a man to utter.—While there he heard words unspeakable. Not that it was impossible to utter them, but not lawful to speak them. [The veil which conceals the mysteries and glories of heaven God has not permitted to be raised. It is enough that we know that in that world the saints shall be made perfectly happy and perfectly blessed in the full enjoyment of God forever.]

I cannot tell with any degree of certainty what was the object of granting this wonderful vision to Paul. He himself could not tell exactly the condition or circumstances of the vision. He was transported to the third heaven, and saw wonders, "and heard unspeakable words, which it is not lawful for a man to utter." While he could not reveal the secrets of that state of bliss, yet the knowledge might be of great service to him in giving zeal, earnestness, and devotion in the work, knowing the glories that were in store for him in that blessed

such a one will I glory: but on mine own behalf I will not glory, save in *my*
weaknesses. 6 For if I should desire to glory, I shall not be foolish; for I
shall speak the truth: but I forbear, lest any man should account of me
above that which he seeth me *to be*, or heareth from me. 7 And by reason
of the exceeding greatness of the [7]revelations, that I should not be exalted
overmuch, there was given to me a [8]thorn in the flesh, a messenger of Satan

[7]Some ancient authorities read *revelations—wherefore, that &c.*
[8]Or, *stake*

state. The fact that we do not know the object for which God
does a thing is no evidence that he did not have a wise purpose in doing it. It may be that he at this time received an
increased measure of the Spirit, saw Jesus, and became more
completely qualified and fully endowed for the apostolic work.
[It certainly braced him for the whole heroic career of unparalleled success which lay before him as a herald of the cross.]

5 **On behalf of such a one will I glory:**—It was not glorying
on his own behalf to glory in a man in Christ, who had been
so honored as to be carried up to the throne of God and shown
the unspeakable glories of heaven.

**but on mine own behalf I will not glory, save in my weak-
nesses.**—Yet as to his personal fleshly self, he only gloried in
his weaknesses. He always recognized himself as nothing.
He was what he was by the grace of God.

6 **For if I should desire to glory, I shall not be foolish; for I
shall speak the truth:**—Boasting was foolish only when it was
a boast in self. Yet on account of the revelations God had
given him and the blessings he had bestowed, it would not be
foolish for him to boast in these things that God had done for
him.

**but I forbear, lest any man should account of me above that
which he seeth me to be, or heareth from me.**—But he fore-
bore these boastings that were lawful lest some·should think
concerning him more than they could find in him.

7 **And by reason of the exceeding greatness of the revelations, that I should not be exalted overmuch,**—Paul recognized in his fleshly weakness that he might be exalted above
measure, uplifted with pride himself. The same feeling is expressed in the following: "I buffet my body, and bring it into
bondage; lest by any means, after that I have preached to oth-

to buffet me, that I should not be exalted overmuch. 8 Concerning this

---

ers, I myself should be rejected." (1 Cor. 9: 27.) He felt that the very greatness of the blessings and the honors entrusted to him might excite a pride that would be his ruin.

there was given to me a thorn in the flesh,—God provided against the danger by permitting Satan to give him a thorn in the flesh to keep him humble. [That the affliction was bodily seems evident from the words "in the flesh"—an expression that does not indicate the principle of evil still in him, as some think, nor yet his mind or spirit, as others, but his physical being alone. It was something personal, affecting him individually, and not as an apostle; causing him acute pain and shame. That the affliction was humiliating and loathsome is evident from the following reference to it: "Ye know that because of an infirmity of the flesh I preached the gospel unto you the first time: and that which was a temptation to you in my flesh ye despised not, nor rejected; but ye received me as an angel of God, even as Christ Jesus." (Gal. 4: 13, 14.) The term for rejected is very strong, literally "spat out," as the marginal reading. Its effect was to excite the scorn and aversion of the beholder, so that it supplied a severe test of the candor and generosity of the Galatians who had witnessed Paul's abject condition under its infliction. The precise nature of the malady has been concealed perhaps that all afflicted ones may be encouraged and helped by Paul's unnamed, yet painful, experience.]

a messenger of Satan—In God's government of his people and of the world, Satan is sometimes permitted to afflict bodily suffering upon men. (Job 2: 7; Luke 13: 16.)

to buffet me,—[Buffet seems to carry the idea that the affliction was outward, visible, and such as would have a tendency to prejudice his hearers against him, and so against his ministry. This removes the affliction, whatever it was, from the sphere of the mind, where some expositors would place it, and locates it in the body.]

that I should not be exalted overmuch.—This indicates that bodily suffering is sometimes allowed to keep the fleshly im-

thing I besought the Lord thrice, that it might depart from me. 9 And he
hath said unto me, My grace is sufficient for thee: for *my* power is made
perfect in weakness. Most gladly therefore will I rather glory in my weak-

---

pulses down to promote the spiritual well-being of the individual.

**8 Concerning this thing I besought the Lord thrice, that it
might depart from me.**—God heard this thrice repeated prayer
as he heard that of Jesus, but he did not grant the petition of
either as asked. He heard both petitions; and while not removing the evil, he strengthened each to bear what he was
called upon to suffer. God, no doubt, answers many of our
prayers in the way that he sees will bless us and carry out his
will and his purposes. It is not good that we formulate methods and ways in which we desire God to grant our petitions;
but we should make our wants and supplications known to
God, and leave him to answer as he will. In our blindness
and lack of faith, we often think God has not heard us, when
he has blessed us above that we asked.

9 And he hath said unto me, My grace is sufficient for thee:
—The Lord did not grant his request, but told him that his
grace would be sufficient to enable him to bear the temptation,
and still labor and enjoy his service. [This is Christ's contin-
ous, as well as final, answer to Paul's prayer. He has been
made to understand that the "thorn" must remain in his flesh,
but along with this he has received the assurance of an abiding love and help from the Lord. He can no more ask for the
removal of the thorn—it was the Lord's will that he should
submit to it for high spiritual ends. But it is no longer an
unrelieved pain and humiliation; he is supported under it by
the grace of Christ which finds in the need and abjectness of
men the opportunity of showing in all perfection its own con-
descending strength.]

for my power is made perfect in weakness.—The Lord's
power to help is called out by the weakness of man   [With
many professed Christians the word "grace" has no particular
meaning, but in the promise of the Lord, it is his strength bestowed on men for timely succor; it finds its opportunity in

nesses, that the power of Christ may ⁹rest upon me.   10 Wherefore I take
pleasure in weaknesses, in injuries, in necessities, in persecutions, in distresses, for Christ's sake: for whem I am weak, then am I strong.

11 I am become foolish: ye compelled me; for I ought to have been commended of you: for in nothing was I behind ¹the very chiefest apostles,

⁹Or, *cover me*   Gr. *spread a tabernacle over me.*   See Rev. 7. 15.
¹Or, *those preëminent apostles*

---

our extremity; when our weakness makes us incapable of
doing anything it gets full scope to work.]

**Most gladly therefore will I rather glory in my weaknesses,
that the power of Christ may rest upon me.**—Paul gladly endured the fleshly weakness that called out the strength of the
Lord on him to strengthen him.   When he was weak within
himself, the Lord's strength became his strength.

**10 Wherefore I take pleasure in weaknesses, in injuries, in
necessities, in persecutions, in distresses, for Christ's sake:**—
Because his weakness and helplessness secured to him the
strength of Christ, he rejoiced in his weaknesses, injuries, and
sufferings for Christ's sake.   [His thoughts go back to the sufferings of which he had spoken fully. (11: 16-33.)   One new
word is added, *injuries,* which elsewhere in the New Testament meets us only in Acts (27: 10, 21), in the sense of material damage inflicted by the violence of the storm.   Here the
reference is to the wrong springing from violence, injury, af-
front, and insult, to which there are frequent allusions in this
epistle. (1: 17, 3: 1; 7: 8; 10: 10; 11: 6, 8, 16.)   He was able to
bear even these with satisfaction when he was bearing them
for the glory of Christ.]

for when I am weak, then am I strong.—When he was
weak for Christ, Christ's strength was on him.   [He had
learned to add another paradox to those of 6: 10, and to feel
that the greatest weakness was not only compatible with the
highest strength, but might be the very condition of its energy.]

11 I am become foolish:—He had said that glorying was
foolishness, and painful to his feelings; but he was forced to
do it.

**ye compelled me; for I ought to have been commended of
you: for in nothing was I behind the very chiefest apostles,**—

though I am nothing. 12 Truly the signs of an apostle were wrought among
you in all ²patience, by signs and wonders and ³mighty works. 13 For what

²Or, *stedfastness*
³Gr. *powers.*

All the fault of this foolish boasting was theirs. They knew
him intimately. They had derived great benefit from his ministry, and they were bound in gratitude, and from a regard to
right and truth to vindicate him. But they had not done so;
and hence through their fault, he had been compelled to go
into this unpleasant vindication of his own character.

though I am nothing.—[He felt that what was the effect of
grace, or free gift of God, was no ground of self-exultation. (1
Cor. 4: 7; 15: 8-10.) There was therefore united in himself a
deep sense of his own unworthiness and impotence, with the
conviction and consciousness of being full of knowledge,
grace, and power, by the indwelling of the Holy Spirit.]

**12 Truly the signs of an apostle were wrought among you
in all patience,**—Especially they should have recognized him
as an apostle because in their midst all the signs of an apostle
were wrought by him, in patient suffering of the persecution
brought upon him.

by signs and wonders and mighty works.—The signs of
God's presence with him as an apostle were signs and wonders and mighty works of the Spirit of God which was in him.
[By the three terms, Paul does not mean three classes of action, but he uses them to describe the same phenomena. He
means the miracles he wrought, which were signs because
they signified God's approval of what he taught; they were
called wonders, because they excited wonder in those who
witnessed them; and they were called mighty works, because
wrought by the immediate power of God. These three terms
occur three times in connection with one another (Acts 2: 22;
2 Cor. 12: 12; 2 Thess. 2: 9), although on each occasion in a
different order. They are all descriptive of different aspects
of the same works rather than themselves different classes of
works. An example of one of the miracles of Jesus will illustrate this. The healing of the paralytic (Mark 2: 1-12) was a
wonder, for they who beheld it were all *amazed";* it was a

is there wherein ye were made inferior to the rest of the churches, except *it be* that I myself was not a burden to you? forgive me this wrong.

power, for the man at Christ's command "arose, and straight-way took up the bed, and went forth before them all"; it was a *sign,* for it proclaimed that one greater than men deemed was present before them; it stood in connection with a higher power of which it was a seal and sign, being wrought that they might "know that the Son of man hath authority on earth to forgive sins."]

13 **For what is there wherein ye were made inferior to the rest of the churches,**—If they had all the teaching and re-ceived all the gifts bestowed by the apostles on the churches, why should they think him inferior to other apostles?

except it be that I myself was not a burden to you?—He in-timates that it would have been best for the church at Corinth had he required them to help him from the beginning, but bet-ter for him and the truth that he refrained from burdening them with the support of him and his companions in labor. He sent Titus and others to Corinth, but none of them bur-dened the church with their support.

forgive me this wrong.—If he meant it was an injury, he considered that other good was accomplished which more than compensated for the injury done them.

6. AN EARNEST AND AFFECTIONATE EFFORT TO RECLAIM THOSE WHO WERE DISAFFECTED BY THE JUDAIZERS. 12 : 14-21.

14 Behold, this is the third time I am ready to come to you; and I will

14 **Behold, this is the third time I am ready to come to you;** —This epistle was written to prepare them for this visit, so that he would find them ready to receive him with gladness and affection.

and I will not be a burden to you:—He felt for them such affection that he was again refusing to accept any support at their hands.

not be a burden to you: for I seek not yours, but you: for the children ought
not to lay up for the parents, but the parents for the children. 15 I will

---

for I seek not yours, but you:—He was ready to give his
very life for them, but was not willing to accept gifts from
them. [In view of the fact that on this very occasion when he
used this language, he was soliciting a contribution of money
to help the poor saints in Judea, and in this he positively tells
them that he seeks not *theirs,* but *them.* In the face of such
facts, it is proper to ask the question, if he sought not theirs,
but them, how, while asking for their money, could he consistently say he sought not theirs? In the light of the context,
and all the word of God elsewhere on the subject, there can be
but one proper explanation, and it is found in the fact that he
was expressing the truth only as to the comparative importance or value of a Christian man, on the one hand, and a
Christian man's earthly possessions, on the other hand. In
such a comparison, the mere possessions of a Christian are as
nothing. In this relative estimate of the two things, he could
very properly say that, in point of real and permanent value,
their possessions were as nothing, and that the real object of
his seeking was the Christian man himself, and not his possessions. He was seeking that which was permanent and enduring, and not a mere material consideration, which, ever so important as a means to an end, is nothing in comparison with a
human being. Hence, while it was true that their gift of
money could be used for good in helping the poor, it was also
true that the desired help for the poor could be obtained from
other sources; but it was not true that the essential good at
this point for the Christians themselves could be secured
without they would give of their means to help in the cause of
the Lord; and hence, after all, the real object for which Paul
sought in this case was the Corinthian Christians themselves.]
**for the children ought not to lay up for the parents, but the
parents for the children.**—He stood to them in the relation of
a parent, in the course of nature, it was the parents' office to
provide for the children, and not the children for the parent.
He sought that they would allow him the parent's privilege.
[Thus gracefully and tenderly does the apostle reconcile a

most gladly spend and be ⁴spent for your souls. If I love you more abundantly, am I loved the less? 16 But be it so, I did not myself burden you; but, being crafty, I caught you with guile. 17 Did I take advantage of you by any one of them whom I have sent unto you? 18 I exhorted Titus, and I sent the brother with him. Did Titus take any advantage of you? walked we not ⁵in the same spirit? *walked we* not in the same steps?

⁴Gr. *spent out.*
⁵Or, *by the same Spirit*

seemingly ungracious act with the kind feelings which he cherished in himself and desired to excite in others.]

15 **And I will most gladly spend and be spent for your souls.**—As their father in the gospel (1 Cor. 4: 14-16) he would most gladly spend and be spent for his children, if he could save their souls. Because of his great love for them, he admonished and reproved them.

If I love you more abundantly, am I loved the less?—Thus he concludes his long boast of love by words of love, the greatest we can conceive, a love not destroyed; but moved by greater sacrifice by the unloving spirit of those loved. Such is the love revealed in God's gift of his Son for rebellious man.

16 **But be it so, I did not myself burden you:**—If his greater love for them caused them to love the less, he was willing; but he would love them anyhow.

but, being crafty, I caught you with guile.—It seems that his enemies insinuated that even though he did not receive any financial support from them, he shrewdly managed to obtain it through craft and guile.

17 **Did I take advantage of you by any one of them whom I have sent unto you?**—It appears by this statement that his contemptible enemies endeavored to undermine the confidence of the Corinthian Christians in him, not only by stating that he did not dare to accept a support, but even by the mean insinuation that there was something very suspicious about the collection which he was making, and that there was much probability that in this reputed offering he had a secret personal interest.

18 **I exhorted Titus, and I sent the brother with him. Did Titus take any advantage of you? walked we not in the same spirit? walked we not in the same steps?**—By this series of

19 *Ye think all this time that we are excusing ourselves unto you. In the sight of God speak we in Christ. But all things, beloved, *are* for your

*Or, *Think ye . . . you?*

---

questions he reminds his readers of the course of unselfish service which he and his messengers had followed. From first to last, his dealings with the Corinthians had shown only devotion and self-forgetfulness and love.

[That Paul should think it necessary to guard against insinuations so ungenerous and so unfounded is proof of his wisdom in refusing to give such antagonists the least occasion to question the purity of his motives, and at the same time exposed their selfish ends in the course they pursued.]

19 **Ye think all this time that we are excusing ourselves unto you.**—They thought it was to them that he was making his defense; but he repudiated the idea that he had any wish to enter into such a vindication. He had explained his conduct (1: 15-24; 8: 20-24; 11: 7-12), but he did not acknowledge that he stood before their judgment seat. [It would have been impossible, under any circumstances, for an apostle to place himself before a human tribunal for judgment (1 Cor. 2: 15; 4: 4), but it was strikingly necessary to repudiate the jurisdiction of that section of his readers which he was then addressing, because they had shown a bias in favor of his accusers.]

In the sight of God speak we in Christ.—The motive which really prompted him to speak as he had spoken was not the wish to clear himself from aspersion, but before God in Christ —under a profound sense that God was his judge, and that Christ is, as it were, the sphere in which his thoughts revolve.

But all things, beloved, are for your edifying.—[All he had done was for their welfare. The vindication of his character, and his effort to free their minds from prejudices, had been that they might have unwavering confidence in the gospel, and be built up in their faith in Christ.]

20 **For I fear, lest by any means, when I come, I should find you not such as I would,**—It was his fear that the disorders would not be removed, and that they would not have cor-

edifying. 20 For I fear, lest by any means, when I come, I should find you
not such as I would, and should myself be found of you such as ye would
not; lest by any means *there should be* strife, jealousy, wraths, factions,
backbitings, whisperings, swellings, ⁷tumults; 21 lest again when I come my

⁷Or, *disorders*

rected the errors which prevailed, and for which he had rebuked them.

and should myself be found of you such as ye would not;—
That is, that he should be compelled to administer discipline,
and that his visit would not be as pleasant as they would desire.

lest by any means there should be—Something of the old
anxiety which had led him to postpone his visit (1 Cor. 4: 21)
comes back upon his spirit.

strife,—Contention, altercation connected with anger and
heated zeal, even to bloodshed.

jealousy,—This word denotes, properly, any fervor of mind,
and may be applied to any exacting and agitating passion.
The jealousy here referred to was that which arose from the
superior advantages and endowments which some claimed to
possess over others. Jealousy everywhere is a fruitful cause
of strife. Most contentions in the church are somehow usually connected with jealousy.

wraths,—Anger or animosity between contending factions,
the usual effect of forming parties.

factions,—Split into parties, embittered with mutual recrim-
inations and reproaches.

backbitings,—Calumniating, slandering, or speaking evil of
those who are absent.

whisperings,—Whisperers declare secretly, and with great
reserve, the supposed faults of others. Backbiters proclaim
them publicly and avowedly.

swellings,—Undue elation; being puffed up; disposed to
look upon others with contempt; and to seek to depress and
humble them.

tumults;—Disorders and confusion arising from the existence of parties. Paul, deeply sensible of the evils of all this,

God should humble me before you, and I should mourn for many of them that have sinned heretofore, and repented not of the uncleanness and fornication and lasciviousness which they committed.

---

endeavored in this epistle to suppress it, that all things might be peaceful and harmonious in the Lord's work.

21 lest again when I come my God should humble me before you, and I should mourn for many of them that have sinned heretofore,—Lest by these evils among them, God should humiliate him, and he be forced to mourn for many who had sinned and refused to repent of the evils enumerated.

and repented not of the uncleanness and fornication and lasciviousness which they committed.—[Repentance results from sorrow for sin, and leads to reformation of life; there is no difficulty in ascertaining what it is; for the only result of sorrow for sin which leads to reformation is a change of the will in reference to sin. The primary meaning of the Greek word is a change of the mind; and in this sense it is used when it is said that Esau "found no place for a change of mind in his father, though he sought it diligently with tears." (Heb. 12: 17.) What he sought was a change in his father's mind with reference to the blessing already bestowed on Jacob; consequently the word in this instance is translated "change of mind." If the change of will designated by the word is not a result of sorrow for sin, but of some considerations of mere expediency, it is not the repentance required; and if it stops short of reformation of life on the part of the penitent, it falls short of the blessings of forgiveness. Repentance, then, fully defined, is a change of will produced by sorrow for sin, leading to a reformation of life, and this is the thing for which Paul was earnestly pleading.]

7. WARNING OF THE SEVERITY TO WHICH HE MAY BE DRIVEN THROUGH THEIR IMPENITENCE COMBINED WITH FURTHER EXHORTATION TO SPARE HIM THIS NECESSITY.
13: 1-10.

1 This is the third time I am coming to you. At the mouth of two witnesses or three shall every word be established. 2 I have said [8]beforehand, and I do say [8]beforehand, [9]as when I was present the second time, so now, being absent, to them that have sinned heretofore, and to all the rest, that, if I come again, I will not spare; 3 seeing that ye seek a proof of Christ that speaketh in me; who to you-ward is not weak, but is powerful in you: 4 for

[8]Or, *plainly* Comp. 1 Thess. 3. 4.
[9]Or, *as if I were present the second time, even though I am now absent*

---

1 **This is the third time I am coming to you.**—We have no record of but one visit to Corinth. (Acts 18: 1-18.) But this, with 12: 14, makes it clear that he made a visit of which we have no record.

At the mouth of two witnesses or three shall every word be established.—Moses gave the law that no man should be put to death or punished except on the testimony of two or three witnesses. (Num. 35: 30; Deut. 17: 6; 19: 15.) This law received a fresh prominence from our Lord's reproduction of it in giving directions for the discipline of his disciples (Matt. 18: 16), and what was more natural than that Paul should conform to this law? The things to be established were the sins of which they had been guilty in opposing him, perverting the gospel, and corrupting the church.

2 **I have said beforehand, and I do say beforehand, as when I was present the second time, so now, being absent, to them that have sinned heretofore, and to all the rest, that, if I come again, I will not spare;**—When he was with them the second time, he dealt gently with them, but then warned them, if they persisted in their course, when he returned again, he would deal severely with them. He now repeats that he will not spare them if he still finds them obdurate in their sins. [The repeated warning includes those to whom it was first and who since then had similarly sinned.]

3 **seeing that ye seek a proof of Christ that speaketh in me;** —They had lightly spoken of his humble manner, and lack of apostolic power and authority, and challenged him to show

he was crucified through weakness, yet he liveth through the power of God. For we also are weak [10]in him, but we shall live with him through the power of God toward you. 5 Try your own selves, whether ye are in the faith;

[10]Many ancient authorities read *with*.

his power by miraculous gifts, the presence of Christ in him by exhibition of power.

who to you-ward is not weak, but is powerful in you:—The powers had been manifested with might toward them. Paul had both worked miracles before them, and had bestowed gifts upon them. [There had been evidences enough, even in the church at Corinth, that God's power was unmistakably in Christ. These evidences wre chiefly those of Christian character, developed by the power of the gospel.]

4 for he was crucified through weakness,—The crucifixion of Christ was the result of human weakness. He meekly submitted to wrong, patiently bore suffering unto death. And the dread reality of these words must not be set aside lightly. The weakness of Christ here is the same that Paul has attributed to himself—the weakness of passive endurance, and humble service; the weakness of human condition, subjected to the power of his enemies. [We must conceive therefore the Word taking on himself and dwelling among men (John 1: 14) in a mode inconceivable to us, but divine, for a time and for our salvation, real human weakness; and as being in his dying moments forsaken by God (Matt. 27: 46), and powerless in the hands of his enemies. The ridicule of the chief priests mocking him and the scribes and the elders—"He saved others; himself he cannot save" (Matt. 27: 42)—is solemn truth. So in the garden the only way of deliverance is prayer to the Father—"If thou be willing, remove this cup from me." (Luke 22: 41. 42.) Thus in all things he was made like unto his brethren. (Heb. 2: 17.)]

yet he liveth through the power of God.—By the power of God he was raised from the dead and liveth at God's right hand. [The resurrection is ever attributed to the power of God. (4: 14; 1 Cor. 15: 15; Rom. 4: 24; 6: 4; 8: 11; 1 Pet. 1: 21.) He who was so weak that he could not save himself from the cross now lives by the outstretched arm of Jehovah.

prove your own selves. Or know ye not as to your ownselves, that Jesus
Christ is in you? unless indeed ye be reprobate. 6 But I hope that ye shall
know that we are not reprobate. 7 Now we pray to God that ye do no evil;

And the power thus manifested is proof that (verse 3) Christ
is powerful in his church to save and to punish.]

**For we also are weak in him, but we shall live with him
through the power of God toward you.**—So Paul was weak,
patient under sufferings and wrongs inflicted upon him, but
by the power God gave him he lived toward them in correcting their wrongs, and punishing their sins. What and how
the punishment was which he threatened to inflict on the false
teachers is not clear. Some think he proposed by the exercise
of miraculous power to punish them with bodily affliction as
he did Bar-Jesus. (Acts 13: 6-12.) Others think he intended
to humiliate them by the exhibition of spiritual powers, and
expose them before the multitude, and exclude them from the
association of these in Christ. Whatever it was, the patience
of Paul in bearing with their wrong course when present with
them and his efforts then and through his epistles to turn
them away from evil are manifest.

5 **Try your own selves, whether ye are in the faith; prove
your own selves.**—They had demanded proof that Paul was
an apostle. He had furnished it, and he now admonishes
them to try themselves so as to make sure that they are in the
faith. He had already said unto them: "If any man thinketh
himself to be a prophet, or spiritual, let him take knowledge
of the things which I write unto you, that they are the commandment of the Lord." (1 Cor. 14: 37.) That is, they were
to test their lives, with an earnest desire to conform themselves unto its directions. To be in the faith is to be faithful
to the Lord.

**Or know ye not as to your own selves, that Jesus Christ is
in you? unless indeed ye be reprobate.**—Jesus Christ was in
them if they did his will; and he was in them unless they had
turned away from the faith and become reprobates.

6 **But I hope that ye shall know that we are not reprobate.**
—His power and faithfulness would be tested, as well as

not that we may appear approved, but that ye may do that which is honorable, [11]though we be as reprobate 8 For we can do nothing against the truth, but for the truth. 9 For we rejoice, when we are weak, and ye are strong: this we also pray for, even your perfecting. 10 For this cause I write these things while absent, that I may not when present deal sharply, according to

[11]Gr. *and that.*

---

theirs, and he hoped that they would know that he would stand the test and not become a reprobate.

7 Now we pray to God that ye do no evil;—He seems to apprehend that they might think his anxiety for their faithfulness was that they might approve him.

not that we may appear approved, but that ye may do that which is honorable, though we be as reprobate.—So while he prays that they do no evil, not that he should appear approved, but that they might be approved of God, even should he be condemned. Their salvation was his object, not the approval of himself.

8 For we can do nothing against the truth,—As an apostle of Christ, it was impossible for him to desire or wish to find any occasion for punishing them merely to demonstrate his own authority and power. To rejoice in evil because it gave him an advantage of any kind would have been impossible for him.

but for the truth.—[Should those who had fallen away "from the simplicity and the purity that is toward Christ" (11: 3) return, should those who had violated the obligations of love (12: 20) and purity (12: 21) repent, the cause of truth would thus be reestablished and his power of chastening would be nullified, because it is, in its very nature, being applied only for and never against the truth.]

9 For we rejoice, when we are weak, and ye are strong: this we also pray for, even your perfecting.—He was not only willing to have no opportunity of displaying his power in inflicting punishment, but he delighted in such a condition, for it meant that they were strong in their spiritual life, and in their steadfastness in the faith.

10 For this cause I write these things while absent, that I may not when present deal sharply,—While he was absent he

the authority which the Lord gave me for building up, and not for casting down.

wrote these things, lest, when he comes, he should find them in an evil way which would require him to use with severity the power the Lord had given him to build up and strengthen them.

according to the authority which the Lord gave me for building up, and not for casting down.—The powers were given for their good, but if they refused to place themselves in such condition that they could be used for their good, then the powers would be used for their destruction. This refers to spiritual powers. Jesus came to save. But those who refused to be saved by him were condemned the more deeply. The gospel is "to the one a savor from death unto death; to the other a savor from life unto life." (2: 15, 16.) What blesses the obedient punishes the disobedient. [If he should be compelled to act sharply, it would be more like pulling down than building up, and so at least an apparent contravention of the spirit of that authority with which he had been entrusted by Christ.]

8. CONCLUSION.
13: 11-14.

11 Finally, brethren, [12]farewell. Be perfected; be comforted; be of the

[12]Or, *rejoice: be perfected*

11 **Finally,**—[The conclusion is brief and in a mild tone. There are no words wasted; no personal greetings; no names are mentioned. But it is not lacking in friendliness and affection. It is a fitting close.]

brethren,—[The term is used only four times in this epistle (1: 8; 8: 1, 23; 13: 11), indicating here the importance of what he was saying and the affectionate spirit in which he spoke.]

farewell.—[Literally rejoice, or, joy to you. On account of what follows the word here, it is better to take it as an exhortation to spiritual joy. Rejoicing in our union and communion with the Lord is one of our highest duties. Blessings so

same mind; live in peace: and the God of love and peace shall be with you.
12 Salute one another with a holy kiss.

---

infinite as these should not be received with indifference. Joy
is the atmosphere of heaven, and the more we have of it on
earth, the more heavenly shall we be in character and temper.]

Be perfected;—Strive to be perfect before God. [There
was much to be amended; many grave faults had been committed; there were many deficiencies to be made good.]

be comforted;—[Be consoled by the promises and supports
of the gospel. To receive consolation by exhortation.]

be of the same mind;—Be of one mind by walking by the
same rule.

live in peace:—Be at peace by each seeking the good of others, and all seeking to walk by the directions of the word of
God. [He seeks the restoration of unity of purpose, and with
that of inward and outward peace. If these conditions should
be fulfilled, the God of love and peace would assuredly be
with them, for peace rests upon the sons of peace. (Luke 10:
6.]

and the God of love and peace shall be with you.—The God
that is full of love and peace will dwell with them and fill
their hearts with the same love and peace that he possesses.

12 Salute one another with a holy kiss.—I think, beyond all
doubt, that the object of the Holy Spirit in referring to the
kiss was to regulate a social custom, and not to institute an
ordinance. It was customary to greet with a kiss, and the
Holy Spirit said it should be a holy one. The ordinances were
instituted and observed by Jesus and recorded in his life and
teachings as part of his work. Note how baptism and the
Lord's Supper were ordained by Jesus, practiced by the apostles and churches as set forth in Acts of Apostles, and then
urged in the epistles by specific direction for observing them.
Jesus said nothing of it, never kissed or was kissed, save by
Judas, so far as we are told. There is no account in Acts of
any such custom by the apostles or churches, and it is only
mentioned in the concluding salutations of four epistles. (Rom.

13 All the saints salute you.
14 The grace of the Lord Jesus Christ, and the love of God, and the communion of the Holy Spirit, be with you all.

16: 16; 1 Cor. 16: 20; 2 Cor. 13: 12; 1 Thess. 5: 26.) Institutions and practices ordained by God, to be observed by his people, are never treated in this way. It was mentioned only when the apostle was sending salutations to others, being thereby reminded of their method of salutation. If it was intended as an ordinance of God, I do not see why it was treated so differently from his other ordinances and commands.

13 **All the saints salute you.**—The saints joining in the salutation can only mean those who were present with Paul in Macedonia at the time of writing.

14 **The grace of the Lord Jesus Christ,**—[Paul said to the Corinthians: "Ye know the grace of our Lord Jesus Christ, that, though he was rich yet for your sakes he became poor, that ye through his poverty might become rich." (8: 9.) His grace was a devotion to the good of man which knew no thought for self, which counted no sacrifice too great to attain it, not even the death of the cross. Grace, then, is an attribute of God seen in Jesus Christ who died for man. "God commendeth his own love toward us, in that, while we were yet sinners, Christ died for us." (Rom. 5: 8.) It was by the grace of God that Jesus tasted death for every man, and it is to the same grace every man owes his salvation. It begins in grace, is continued in grace, and perfected in grace. But grace passes from an attribute of the divine character to an active energy in the soul. At "the throne of grace, that we may receive mercy, and may find grace to help us in time of need" (Heb. 4: 16). The heart is "established by grace" (Heb. 13: 9), and by grace "offer service well-pleasing to God" (Heb. 12: 28). It is "in the grace that is in Christ Jesus" that we find our strength, and we are assured of its sufficiency for endurance as well as for service. "My grace is sufficient for thee." (12: 9.) We are commanded to "grow in the grace and knowledge of our Lord and Saviour Jesus Christ." (2 Pet. 3: 18.) These passages all speak of the divine influence in the

soul as the operation of grace, and regard that which has its source in the grace of God as the working power of salvation. Grace pardons the guilty, restores the fallen, delivers the captive, sanctifies the sinner, sustains and supports the believer.]

and the love of God,—[The fountain from which grace flows is the love of the Father, for it is said: "Every good gift and every perfect gift is from above, coming down from the Father of lights, with whom can be no variation, neither shadow that is cast by turning." (James 1: 17.) This love for man becomes through faith and obedience the joyful sense of comfort that we are his children, and that one day "we shall be like him; for we shall see him even as he is." (1 John : 2.)]

and the communion of the Holy Spirit, be with you all.— The fellowship or companionship which the Spirit of the Lord (3: 17, 18) makes possible for Christians to have with God, with Christ, and with his fellow Christans; hence, Christian fellowship. The "unity of the Spirit" (Eph. 4: 3) is the unity of fellowship which binds the church as the body of Christ.

COMMENTARY ON THE EPISTLE
TO THE GALATIANS

CONTENTS

SECTION THREE

HORTATORY ENFORCEMENT OF DUTIES CONNECTED
WITH THE POSSESSION OF CHRISTIAN FREEDOM
(5: 1 to 6: 18) 257

INTRODUCTION TO GALATIANS.

I. GALATIA AND THE GALATIANS.

These terms are used in two senses, one official and one popular. The Galatians proper originally belonged to migratory Celtic tribes, which early in the third century B.C. invaded Greece from the north. A considerable number of these separated from the main body, crosed the Bosphorus, and penetrated into the region which afterward bore their name. At the outset they were a movable army, encamping, marching, and plundering at will. The surrounding monarchs gradually curtailed their power and repressed them within narrow limits. For a time their kings were recognized by the Romans; but in the reign of Augustus Caesar this district was made a part of the Roman Empire, reaching from the borders of Asia and Bithynia to Iconium, Lystra, and Derbe. This was the political condition when Paul visited that district on his second and third missionary journeys. The southern part of the Roman province was the more populous, it long had colonies of Greeks and Jews; commerce and emigration were encouraged by the safety of the great Roman roads which ran through the cities just named.

The ambiguity of the terms—Galatia and Galatians—makes it difficult to determine the destination of the epistle. If Paul used the term Galatia in the popular sense, he must have intended the epistle for churches of some unnamed cities, perhaps Ancyra, Pessimus, and Tarvium; this is the "North Galatian" theory. If, however, he used it in the official sense —as the designation of the Roman province—he addressed the churches in Antioch of Pisidia, Iconium, Lystra, and Derbe; this is the "South Galatian" theory.

In favor of the former it is contended that all the "Church Fathers" refer it to the northern cities; but, even so, the existence of churches in them is merely conjectural. There is not a single name of a person or a place, or incident of any kind connected with Paul's preaching in Galatia, mentioned in Acts or the epistle that fits into the theory. And yet the work there was of a strikingly successful character. Those who advocate this theory find room for a visit to these cities in Acts 16: 6, and for a second visit implied in Gal. 4: 13; Acts 18: 23. But the way from Syrian Antioch through Galatia and Phrygia to Ephesus does not seem to lie through North Galatia, but by "the upper country." (Acts 19: 1.)

The other theory is that Paul, being a Roman citizen, would use the official designation of the countries to which he makes reference. And it is gathered from the epistle itself that the churches addressed were in the main Gentiles, though there was a Jewish element among them. According to Luke's account the churches of Antioch of Pisidia (Acts 13: 43, 48), Iconium (14: 1), and Lystra and Derbe, "and the region round about" (14: 6, 7; 16: 1-5) were composed of Jews and Gentiles. Antioch and Iconium had synagogues (13: 14), and there is other testimony to the presence of Jews in South Galatia. On the other hand, there is no testimony that there were any considerable settlements in North Galatia.

II. OCCASION OF WRITING THE EPISTLE.

Judaizing teachers had made their appearance among the Galatian churches after Paul, and with their attacks upon his apostolic authority (1: 11; 2: 14), and of their assertion of the necessity of circumcision for Gentile Christians (5: 2, 11; 6: 12) which involved as a necessary consequence the obligation of the whole law, had found but too ready a hearing, so that the Judaizing tendency was on the point of getting the upper hand (1: 6; 3: 1, 3; 4: 11-21; 5: 2-7). It is evident that Paul realized the church had been perverted; he is surprised and greatly grieved at what had taken place. Nevertheless it is evident (1: 9; 5: 3; 4: 16) that he had already spoken personally in Galatia against the Judaizing perversions and that with great earnestness. From this we learn that when he was among the Galatians the second time, the danger was not only threatening, but there already existed an inclination to yield to it, and his language against it was consequently of a warning and a precautionary nature. It was only after his departure that the false teachers set to work with their perversions;

and although they did not get so far as circumcision, still they met with so much success, and caused so much disturbance (5: 15), that the accounts came upon him with such surprise that he cried: "O foolish Galatians, who did bewitch you?" (3: 1), and "I marvel that ye are so quickly removng from him that called you in the grace of Christ unto a different gospel" (1: 6).

In accordance with this state of things which gave occasion to the writing of the epistle, it was the object of Paul to defend in it his apostolic commission and authority, and to bring his readers to a triumphant conviction of the freedom of the Christian from circumcision and the Mosaic law through the justification arising from God's grace through faith in Jesus Christ.

III. TIME AND PLACE OF WRITING.

By comparing this epistle with Second Corinthians and Romans, it is clearly seen that they bear such a striking resemblance to each other that they must be assigned to the same period in Paul's life. Second Corinthians reveals a similar state of feeling, and was written from Macedonia, on the way to Corinth, in the summer of 57; Romans discusses the same doctrines, but more calmly, fully, and maturely, and we know it was written at Corinth, just before starting on his last journey to Jerusalem, early in the year 58. So we may with some degree of certainty place the writing of Galatians, shortly after Second Corinthians, as having been at Corinth, just before Romans, in the year 57 or 58.

COMMENTARY ON THE EPISTLE TO THE GALATIANS.

SECTION ONE.
PAUL'S DEFENSE OF HIS APOSTOLIC INDEPEND-ENCE AND AUTHORITY.
1:1 to 2:21.

1. APOSTOLIC ADDRESS AND GREETING.
1:1-5.

1 Paul, an apostle (not from men, neither through ¹man, but through

¹Or, *a man*

---

1 **Paul, an apostle**—Those who taught that the Gentiles should be circumcised because Paul opposed it, called in question his apostleship, especially disparaged him as not equal to Peter, and on this relied upon his never having seen Jesus in the flesh, hence, could not be sent of him.

(not from men, neither through man,—During his personal ministry Jesus selected and qualified certain ones to bear witness of both what he did and taught to the world. Hence when he sent them out to do this work they were called apostles. Paul was not one of the original twelve, but he firmly asserts that he was an apostle.

but through Jesus Christ,—Jesus appeared unto Saul when on his way to Damascus and said unto him: "Arise, and stand upon thy feet: for to this end have I appeared unto thee, to appoint thee a minister and a witness both of the things wherein thou hast seen me, and of the things wherein I will appear unto thee; delivering thee from the people, and from the Gentiles, unto whom I send thee, to open their eyes, that they may turn from darkness to light and from the power of Satan unto God, that they may receive remission of sins and an inheritance among them that are sanctified by faith in me." (Acts 26:16-18.) This call was to do exactly the things that he had qualified and sent the twelve to do, and he had given him precisely the same commission. Hence, Paul said that he

Jesus Christ, and God the father, who raised him from the dead), 2 and all
the brethren that are with me, unto the churches of Galatia: 3 Grace to you

---

was an apostle, sent not of men, nor through men, but sent
through Jesus Christ.

[Christ was in this act the mediator, declaring the supreme
will. In another place Paul styles himself "an apostle of
Christ Jesus through the will of God." (Eph. 1: 1.) His appointment took place by a divine intervention, in which the
ordinary sequence of events was broken through. Long after
the Savior in his bodily presence had ascended to heaven,
when in the order of nature it was impossible that another
apostle should be elected, and when the administration of his
church had for several years been carried on by human hands,
he appeared once more on earth for the purpose of making a
minister and a witness. This interposition gives to Paul's
ministry an exceptional character. While the mode of his
election was in one respect humiliating, and put him in the
position of "the child untimely born," the least of the apostles
(1 Cor. 15: 8, 9), whose appearance in that capacity was un-
looked for and necessarily open to suspicion; on the other
hand, it was glorious and exalting, since it so richly displayed
the divine mercy and the transforming power of grace.]

and God the Father, who raised him from the dead),—[It
was the *risen Jesus* that he saw, and that he was conscious of
seeing in the moment of vision. The revelation that arrested
him near Damascus in the same moment convinced him that
Jesus was risen, and that he himself was called to be his servant. These two convictions were inseparably linked in
Paul's memory. As surely as God the Father had raised Jesus
from the dead and given him glory, so surely had the glorified
Jesus revealed himself to him, his persecutor, to make him his
apostle. He was not less truly than Peter and John a witness
of his resurrection. The message of the resurrection was the
burden of the apostleship.]

2 and all the brethren that are with me,—The brethren who
were with him joined in this letter so far as to approve its end
and purpose. Those with him were doubtless his fellow la-

and peace [2]from God the Father, and our Lord Jesus Christ, 4 who gave

[2]Some ancient authorities read *from God our Father, and the Lord Jesus Christ.*

---

borers who accompanied him in his work. [Not that Paul's authority rested upon its recognition even by these good men. His reference to them merely suggests that they who reject it separate themselves from this band of noble workers.]

unto the churches of Galatia:—Galatia was an extensive territory, with a number of cities in which Paul had preached and established churches.

3 **Grace to you**—This is a prayer that the favor of God may attend them, with which Paul introduces his letters generally. It is an expression of kindness to the Christians to whom he was writing, and that God would regard them with favor and compassion.

and peace from God the Father,—Reconciliation and harmony with God and with all that are in peace and harmony with him.

and our Lord Jesus Christ,—The mission of Jesus Christ is to bring "peace among men in whom he is well pleased." (Luke 2: 14.) To the faithful Philippians it was promised. "And the peace of God, which passeth all understanding, shall guard your hearts and your thoughts in Christ Jesus." (Phil. 4: 7.) The harmony, union, and peace with God brings a peace and quietness of mind in the midst of all the trials and disappointments of earth. Just before his violent death on the cross, Jesus said to his sorrowing disciples: "Peace I leave with you; my peace I give unto you: not as the world giveth, give I unto you. Let not your heart be troubled, neither let it be fearful." (John 14: 27.) Jesus had a peace and quiet of soul arising from his union with God and his trust and confidence in him that nothing could disturb. The same he bestowed upon his disciples that their hearts might not be troubled and filled with fear. This peace from God our Father and the Lord Jesus Christ lifts the disciples above the trials and disappointments of this life and enables them to abide serenely in all the promises of God. Every Christian may attain

himself for our sins, that he might deliver us out of this present evil ³world,

---

³Or, *age*

---

this soul-satisfying comfort by an earnest trust in and faithful walk with God.

4 who gave himself for our sins,—Jesus gave himself up to a life of toil, tears, privation, sorrow, and death to obtain the forgiveness of sins, that he might deliver us from the evils of this world—a deliverance from the power and control of evil, raising us above the evils while we are yet in the world. Jesus said: "I pray not that thou shouldest take them from the world, but that thou shouldest keep them from the evil one." (John 17: 15.)

that he might deliver us out of this present evil world,—[A world of bad passions, corrupt desires; a world full of ambition, of the love of pleasure; and love of riches; a world where God is not loved and obeyed; a world where men are regardless of right and truth and duty—where they live for themselves, and not for God; in short, that great community which in the scriptures is called *the world* in contradistinction from the kingdom of God. It follows, therefore, that his followers constitute "a people for his own possession" (Titus 2: 14), not predominated by the feelings of the world. If there is not a separation, then the purpose of the Redeemer's death in regard to us has not been affected, and we are still a part of that great and ungodly community.] There is no deliverance from the evils of the world until we are delivered from our sins. Sin is the cause of the evil of the world.

according to the will of our God and Father:—Christ came to deliver from sin that we might be delivered from evil in accordance with the will of God the Father. "God so loved the world, that he gave his only begotten Son, that whosoever believeth on him should not perish, but have eternal life." (John 3: 16.) This is all spoken to show that Paul was sent by Jesus, and Jesus was sent of the Father. So he was an apostle of Jesus Christ and God his Father.

according to the will of ⁴our God and Father: 5 to whom *be* the glory ⁵for
ever and ever. Amen.

⁴Or, *God and our Father*
⁵Gr. *unto the ages of the ages.*

5 to whom be the glory for ever and ever. Amen.—He as-
cribes to Jesus, the Redeemer, glory for ever and ever, as the
author of the whole plan of salvation of which Paul was an
apostle. The self-sacrifice and self-denial of Jesus to save
man will bring to him glory and honor forever.

2. ENERGETIC REBUKE OF THE GALATIANS ON ACCOUNT OF THEIR ABANDONMENT OF THE TRUTH.
1 : 6-10.

6 I marvel that ye are so quickly removing from him that called you in

6 I marvel—The change which is taking place among the
Galatian Christians is so utterly inconceivable to Paul that he
marvels. [The whole truth concerning the gospel plan of salvation had been so clearly set before them, their reception of
the truth had been so hearty, his own personal influence over
them had been so strong, that the change seemed like some
unaccountable fascination. (3 : 1.)]

that ye are so quickly removing—Their defection from the
truth was not yet complete and would continue, unless they
were brought to a better state of mind by this epistle.
Whether or not this was the case it is not known. The word
quickly may mean either that their action had been hasty,
taken without due consideration, or but little time had elapsed
between the acceptance of the gospel and their defection. On
the whole, it seems the more probable that the reference is to
the time rather than the manner of their defection; then soon
after the arrival of the false teachers is more likely than so
soon after their conversion. Paul may have intended to hint
that he had not found them so ready to accept the true gospel
as the false teachers had found them ready to accept a perversion of it.

from him that called you—From God to whom Paul attributes the call to salvation. (1 Thess. 13 : 14.) In harmony with

the grace of Christ unto a different ⁶gospel; 7 ⁷which is not another *gospel:*

⁶Gr. *good tidings.* See marginal note on Mt. 4. 23.
⁷Or, *which is nothing else save that there &c.*

the words of the Lord Jesus (John 6: 44, 65) the calling of men out of darkness is always referred to God the Father (Rom. 8: 28-30). These words reveal the gravity of the situation in which they were placing themselves.

in the grace of Christ—The grace of Christ is the instrument of the divine calling inasmuch as it is through the preaching his love and the gift that the unbeliever is at first attracted and won over to the faith. The grace of Christ is expressed in these words: "For ye know the grace of our Lord Jesus Christ, that, though he was rich, yet for your sakes he became poor, that ye through his poverty might become rich."(2 Cor. 8: 9.) His grace is'his voluntary self-surrender to humiliation and death, from no other prompting than his own love for man.

unto a different gospel;—It seems that the Judaizers explained that theirs was a gospel with a difference.

7 which is not another gospel:—Paul replied that what they preached differed so greatly from the true gospel that it was no gospel at all. He could not even allow them the name gospel. [Paul preached salvation by grace through faith (Eph. 2: 8), they preached salvation by the law through works, saying, It is needful to circumcise them, and to charge them to keep the law of Moses or they cannot be saved (Acts 15: 1, 5); the two are incompatible, and are antagonistic to that end (Rom. 11: 6). Thus at the very beginning he closes the door against compromise, and throughout the epistle this attitude is maintained. Obedience to their teaching puts in bondage (2: 4) and entanglement (5: 1), and could not result in justification (2: 16), or freedom (5: 1); it made Christ to be of no profit (5: 2), and the death of Christ, which is the essence of the gospel, a superfluous thing of no account (2: 21); and so far from bringing blessing it puts him under a curse (3: 10); and all who accepted it fell away from grace (5: 4).]

only there are some that trouble you, and would pervert the gospel of Christ.—Those who troubled them with false teach-

only there are some that trouble you, and would prevent the ⁶gospel of
Christ. 8 But though we, or an angel from heaven, should ⁸preach ⁹unto you
any gospel ¹⁰other than that which we ⁸preached unto you, let him be anathema. 9 As we have said before, so say I now again, If any man ⁸preacheth
unto you any gospel ¹⁰other than that which ye received, let him be anathema.
10 For am I now seeking the favor of men, or of God? or am I striving to

⁸See marginal note on Mt. 11. 5.
⁹Some ancient authorities omit *unto you.*
¹⁰Or, *contrary to that*

ings perverted the gospel of Christ. Christ died to redeem all
nations from sin. It was a perversion of the gospel to claim
that they could not be saved by Christ save through keeping
the Jewish law. It was turning them from a sole reliance in
Christ back to the Jewish law.

8 **But though we, or an angel from heaven, should preach
unto you any gospel other than that which we preached unto
you, let him be anathema.**—Paul's claim was that the gospel
as he had preached it was complete, absolute, and final, and if
he himself, or even an angel from heaven, should preach another gospel than that he had preached, let him be anathema
—accursed.

9 **As we have said before, so say I now again, If any man
preacheth unto you any gospel other than that which ye received, let him be anathema.**—He repeats it to emphasize its
truth and importance. To insist that a man must be circumcised and keep the law of Moses was such a perversion of the
gospel as to destroy its nature, and to call down upon him
doing it the condemnation of God.

10 **For am I now seeking the favor of men, or of God? or
am I striving to please men?**—It seems that he had been accused of being a timeserver who sought to ingratiate himself
by becoming "all things to all men" (1 Cor. 9: 22) ; in proof of
this accusation they could point to the circumcision of Timothy as an effort to gain Jewish favor, and to his repudiation of
the law as an attempt to conciliate the Gentiles, in admitting
them to salvation in Christ without circumcision.

**if I were still pleasing men, I should not be a servant of
Christ.**—In this he reaffirms a truth set forth by Jesus: "How
can ye believe, who receive glory one of another, and the

please men? if I were still pleasing men, I should not be a ¹¹servant of
Christ.

¹¹Gr. *bondservant.*

---

glory that cometh from the ónly God ye seek not?" (John 5:
44.) This clearly teaches that they who seek honor from men
cannot believe in Jesus. Men seeking to be popular with the
world cannot be true faithful believers in, and servants of,
Jesus Christ. [That popularity with men and the service of
Christ are incompatible Paul knew from actual experience immediately after he entered the service of Christ, for his former
friends took counsel to kill him (Acts 9: 23), and even at the
time of writing persecution had not ceased (5: 11).]

3. HISTORIC EVIDENCE OF HIS INDEPENDENCE OF MEN AS TO HIS APOSTOLIC COMMISSION AND HIS KNOWLEDGE OF THE GOSPEL.
1: 11-24.

11 For I make known to you, brethren, as touching the ⁶gospel which was
⁸preached by me, that it is not after man. 12 For neither did I receive it

---

11 **For I make known to you, brethren, as touching the gospel which was preached by me,**—[This was the turning point
in Paul's life. If the Galatians were to understand his teaching, they must know why he became a Christian, how he had
received the message of the gospel which he brought to them.
He felt sure that they would enter more sympathetically into
the gospel he preached if they were better acquainted with
how he received it. They would see how well-justified was
the authority, how needful the severity with which he wrote.
Accordingly he begins with a brief relation of the circumstances of his call to the service of Christ, and his career from
the days of his Judaistic zeal, when he made havoc of the
faith, till the well-known occasion on which he withstood
Peter, the chief of the twelve, to the face because he separated
himself from the Gentile Christians, "fearing them that were
of the circumcision." (2: 11-14.) His object in this recital
seems to be threefold: to refute the misrepresentations of the
Judaizers, to vindicate his independent authority as an apostle

from man, nor was I taught it, but *it came to me* through revelation of

---

of Christ, and to unfold the nature and terms of the gospel, so as to pave the way for the argument which follows, and which forms the body of this epistle.]

that it is not after man.—[Not according to man, but it was revealed to him by Jesus Christ. This initial revelation made to him was of inestimable importance to him. It made him an apostle in the august sense in which he claimed the title (1: 1.) This accounts for the vehemence with which he defends his teaching and for the awful sentence which he has passed upon his impugners. The divine authorship of the gospel he preached made it impossible for him to temporize with perverters, or to be influenced by human favor or disfavor in its administration. Had his teaching been "according to man," he might have consented to compromise; he mighty reasonably have tried to humor and accommodate Jewish prejudices. But the case is far otherwise.]

12 For neither did I receive it from man,—[The pronoun *I* is emphatic, suggesting a contrast with the Judaizers, who most likely claimed to come from the apostles who had "companied" with the Lord and had been directly commissioned by him before his ascension. But while Paul thus glorifies his ministry (Rom. 11: 13), when speaking of himself personally he uses very different language: "I am the least of the apostles, that am not meet to be called an apostle, because I persecuted the church of God." (1 Cor. 15: 9.)]

nor was I taught it,—He continues to clear the ground of all possible alternatives before declaring the means whereby he learned the facts and truths of the gospel and their meaning as applied to the needs of man.

but it came to me through revelation of Jesus Christ.—He received and was taught by a direct communication of the mind of God through Jesus Christ. When on his way to Damascus Jesus Christ appeared unto him, and arrested him by the brightness above the brightness of the noonday sun, and said unto him: "I am Jesus whom thou persecutest;" and that he had appeared unto him to make him a minister and a wit-

Jesus Christ.   13 For ye have heard of my manner of life in time past in the
Jews' religion, how that beyond measure I persecuted the church of God, and

---

ness of the things which he saw, and the things in which he
would appear unto him. Showing that he yet intended to appear unto him in fitting him for the work in which he had
called him. From Christ and by that revelation, and others in
which he appeared unto him, he received the gospel which he
preached. The enemies of Paul, because he had not seen
Christ in the flesh, denied that he was a true apostle, and that
he received his knowledge secondhand, in a corrupted and
perverted state, therefore he was not to be trusted as an apostle.

13 **For ye have heard of my manner of life in time past**—
They had most likely heard from Paul when he first preached
the gospel to them. The reason why he now refers to his past
life is to show that he had not obtained his knowledge of the
gospel from any instruction which he had received in his early
life, or any acquaintance he had formed with the apostles.

in the Jews' religion—[This refers not to the religious
beliefs, but to religious practices and to those not as they were
instituted by God, but to the system of Jewish faith and worship in its perverted form as one of blind attachment to rites
and traditions, bigotry, and self-righteousness. To what extent the religion of the Jews partook of this character in the
time of Christ appears not only from his constant exposure of
their formalism and assumption, but especially in the fact that
it occurs more frequently than otherwise as synonymous with
opposers of Christ and of his teachings. Of the spirit of Judaism, Paul, before his conversion, was a signal example. He
declares that his persecution of the church was a fruit of this
spirit, and that in the violence of his zeal he outstripped all
his associates as a zealot for the traditions of the fathers.]

**how that beyond measure I persecuted the church of God,
and have havoc of it:**—He refers to his fierce and bitter persecution of the church of God, of which Luke says: "Saul, yet
breathing threatening and slaughter against the disciples of
the Lord" (Acts 9: 1), followed them to strange cities and de-

made havoc of it: 14 and I advanced in the Jews' religion beyond many of
mine own age [12]among my countrymen, being more exceedingly zealous for
the traditions of my fathers. 15 But when it was the good pleasure of God,
who separated me, *even* from my mother's womb, and called me through his

[12]Gr. *in my race.* Comp. 2 Cor. 11. 26.

---

stroyed them so far as lay in his power. Before the mob in
Jerusalem who were seeking his life he said: "I persecuted
this Way unto the death, binding and delivering into prison
both men and woman." (Acts 22 : 4.)

**14 and I advanced in the Jews' religion beyond many of
mine own age among my countrymen,**—He was diligent and
faithful in the service, and was promoted in its positions of
honor more readily than his equals in ability and family relations. He is said to have been a member of the Sanhedrin
when yet young. If so he was advanced for ability and zeal
to the work that pertained to those of advanced years.

**being more exceedingly zealous for the traditions of my fa-
thers.**—He was entrusted with important labors because he
was diligent, faithful, and zealous in the traditions of his fathers.

15 But when it was the good pleasure of God,—God had
respect for Paul on account of his sincerity, earnestness, and
his conscientious zeal in doing what he thought was the service of God. He persecuted the church, but he did it believing he was doing God's service.

who separated me, even from my mother's womb,—Even
from his birth Paul was set apart by God for the work to
which he was appointed. The same is said of Isaiah (49: 1):
"Jehovah hath called me from the womb; from the bowels of
my mother hath he made mention of my name;" of Jeremiah
(1: 5); and of John the Baptist (Luke 1: 15). Paul uses similar language regarding himself. (Rom. 1: 1.) It is an essential
part of his argument here that from his birth it was God's
choice that made him an apostle.

and called me through his grace,—God did not save him
while persecuting his people, but revealed to him the divine
truth that he might deliver him from his sin. Jesus appeared

grace, 16 to reveal his Son in me, that I might [8]preach him among the Gentiles; straightway I conferred not with flesh and blood: 17 neither went I up

---

to him and convinced him of his wrong course and put him in the right way. Paul with a grateful heart accepted it as a kindness from the Lord. He recognized that he was a sinner, the chief of sinners, in bitterly persecuting the church of Christ, and thus he obtained pardon because he did it ignorantly in unbelief.

16 to reveal his Son in me, that I might preach him among the Gentiles;—God calls his servants to reveal in their lives the life of his Son. Paul especially became a self-denying follower of Jesus, and like his Master did suffer all things to make known Christ Jesus to the world. Christ thus was revealed in him, and he was imbued with this spirit, by which he could preach Christ to the world. This is the construction placed on this passage by some expositors, but Macknight translates it: "To reveal his Son to me, that I might preach him to the Gentiles." This was the purpose for which Jesus told Paul that he appeared to him: "For to this end have I appeared unto thee, to appoint thee a minister and a witness both of the things wherein thou hast seen me, and of the things wherein I will appear unto thee; delivering thee from the people, and from the Gentiles, unto whom I send thee, to open their eyes, that they may turn from darkness to light and from the power of Satan unto God, that they may receive remission of sins and an inheritance among them that are sanctified by faith in me." (26: 16-18.) To Ananias he said: "Go thy way: for he is a chosen vessel unto me, to bear my name before the Gentiles and kings, and the children of Israel: for I will show him how many things he must suffer for my name's sake." (Acts 9: 15, 16.)

straightway I conferred not with flesh and blood:—He neither consulted his own fleshly feelings or ties, nor with kindred or others, but at once without reference to any earthly interest or feeling began the work to which he was called.

to Jerusalem to them that were apostles before me: but I went away into

---

17 neither went I up to Jerusalem—The usual term, as Jerusalem was not only the religious capital of the Jews, but situated on high hills so that travelers from every direction, except from Bethlehem, had to ascend.

to them that were apostles before me:—He asserts his direct call from God, and he had no need to go to those who were apostles before him. He went about his work under the direction given by God. "And straightway in the synagogues he proclaimed Jesus, that he is the Son of God." (Acts 9: 20.)

but I went away into Arabia;—This was a country of the Gentiles contiguous to the east of Damascus; here, doubtless, he preached as before and after (Acts 9: 20-22) at Damascus. Thus he shows the independence of his apostolic commission.

[Some expositors claim that the purpose of Paul's sojourn in Arabia was not for the purpose of preaching, but that he might have time for meditation on his new relation to Christ, which appears to be so utterly at variance with his restless activity and zeal as to be wholly incredible. The addition to this conjecture, that he went as far as Mount Sinai, more than four hundred miles away, whither Elijah had retired before him, instead of confirming this conjecture, weakens it; for Paul knew that Jehovah had said to him, "What doest thou here, Elijah?" and that he had ordered him back to his work. (1 Kings 19: 9-18.) In the absence of all evidence for this conjecture, we should be governed in judging of the purpose of the pilgrimage by what we know of Paul's habits during the remainder of his life; and by that standard we should conclude that he was the last man to waste any precious moments, not to speak of a year or two in meditation in the desert, while the cause to which he had been called was now struggling for its very existence.]

and again I returned unto Damascus.—[He did not go to Jerusalem to consult the apostles after his visit to Arabia, but returned to the place where he first saw the light, and preached there, showing that he had not received his commission from the other apostles.]

Arabia; and again I returned unto Damascus.

18 Then after three years I went up to Jerusalem to [13]visit Cephas, and tarried with him fifteen days. 19 But other of the apostles saw I none, [14]save

[13]Or, *become acquainted with*
[14]Or, *but only*

---

18 Then after three years—The date is probably to be reckoned from the great turning point in his life—his conversion. If the visit to Arabia was short, most of this time would be spent at Damascus, probably after his return there. Luke says: "When many days were fulfilled, the Jews took counsel together to kill him: but their plot became known to Saul. And they watched the gates also day and night that they might kill him: but his disciples took him by night, and let him down through the wall, lowering him in a basket." (Acts 9: 23-25.) "After many days" corresponds to "after three years," which evidently means three years after his conversion.

I went up to Jerusalem to visit Cephas,—It was quite natural that he should wish to form the personal acquaintance of Peter, to whom the Lord had given "the keys of the kingdom." Paul's object was to show that he was independent of human instruction and direction and fully equal to the older apostles. It was in this, his first visit to Jerusalem after his conversion, that "he assayed to join himself to the disciples: and they were all afraid of him, not believing that he was a disciple. But Barnabas took him, and brought him to the apostles, and declared unto them how he had seen the Lord in the way, and that he had spoken to him, and how at Damascus he had preached boldly in the name of Jesus." (Acts 9: 26, 27.) It is probable that Barnabas was acquainted with him prior to his conversion.

and tarried with him fifteen days.—He was hurried away by a message from the Lord, who said to him: "Make haste, and get thee quickly out of Jerusalem; because they will not receive of thee testimony concerning me." (Acts 22: 18.) The mention of the brief duration of the stay is intended, especially in contrast with the three years of absence from Jerusa-

[15]James the Lord's brother. 20 Now touching the things which I write unto you, behold, before God, I lie not. 21 Then I came into the regions of Syria and Cilicia. 22 And I was still unknown by face unto the churches of Ju-

[15]Or, *Jacob*

---

lem, to show how impossible it was to regard him a disciple of the twelve, learning all that he knew of the gospel from them.

19 **But other of the apostles saw I none,**—On this visit to Jerusalem, he saw none of the apostles besides Peter.

save James the Lord's brother.—[This James is called "the Lord's brother" to distinguish him from the two apostles of the same name. "Brother" is not "cousin," but a younger son of Mary and Joseph. Compare the words, "and knew her not till she had brought forth a son" (Matt. 1: 25); "and she brought forth her firstborn son." (Luke 2: 7.) The cousin theory of the Roman Catholic Church is exegetically untenable, and was suggested chiefly by the doctrinal ascetic bias in favor of the perpetual virginity of Mary and Joseph.]

20 **Now touching the things which I write unto you, behold, before God, I lie not.**—He avers with earnestness that the things in these matters are true. Sometimes we wonder at the earnestness of Paul in these seemingly unimportant details as to his movements. But the point made against him was that he was not an apostle, but had received what he knew and taught from the twelve. He is showing that he had no opportunty to learn from them, that he had only a few days' interview with Peter during the eighteen or twenty years of his early labors, but was entirely under the immediate direction of the Lord who sent him.

21 **Then I came into the regions of Syria and Cilicia.**—We learn from the parallel narrative that he was first conveyed secretly by the disciples to Cæsarea; there he took ship and sailed for Tarsus. (Acts 9: 30.) He here was found somewhat later by Barnabas and taken to Antioch, where he remained a year. (Acts 11: 25, 26.) Antioch was the chief city of Syria, which became the center of his operations among the Gentiles. (Acts 13: 1-3; 14: 26; 15: 35-41; 18: 22.)

dæa which were in Christ: 23 but they only heard say, He that once persecuted us now [8]preacheth the faith of which he once made havoc; 24 and they
glorified God in me.

---

22 **And I was still unknown by face**—In Jerusalem itself
Paul had not time to receive instruction from anyone, still less
was this the case with the other Christian communities in
Judea. At the same time, so far were they from manifesting
any opposition to his teaching that their one thought was joy
to hear of his conversion.

unto the churches of Judaea—Judea is here distinguished
from Jerusalem. The phrase is noticeable as pointing to the
spread and early establishment of the church at a date not
more than ten years from the ascension of Jesus. Until this
time the churches in Judea did not know Paul by sight.

which were in Christ:—The churches in different sections
had a common faith, and were called by a common name, and
stood in the same direct and personal relation to Christ as
their head. It was his presence diffused among them which
gave them unity.

23 **but they only heard say, He that once persecuted us now
preacheth the faith of which he once made havoc;**—He who
had so violently persecuted them was now preaching the faith
in Christ, which he once sought to destroy.

24 **and they glorified God in me.**—Praised and honored God
because he had changed the bitter persecutor into an earnest,
self-denying apostle of the gospel of Jesus Christ. They
claimed no part in the conversion, but glorified God for it.

4. THE RECOGNITION OF HIS INDEPENDENT APOSTLESHIP
AND THE GOSPEL OF FREEDOM BY THE OTHER APOS-
TLES IN CONFERENCE AT JERUSALEM.
2: 1-10.

1 Then after the space of fourteen years I went up again to Jerusalem

---

1 **Then after the space of fourteen years I went up again to
Jerusalem**—This visit to Jerusalem was to have the question
of circumcising the Gentile converts, as a condition of their
acceptance with God, settled by the apostles. [Since for the

with Barnabas, taking Titus also with me.   2 And I went up by revelation;

---

purpose of his argument that he had not been dependent on
the other apostles (1 : 12, 17), that is in contact with them, it
is pertinent to mention the fact that throughout the period of
which he is speaking Jerusalem was the headquarters of the
apostles. And this being the case the denial, by implication,
was the strongest possible way of denying communication
with them. It follows also that, had there been other visits to
Jerusalem in this period, he must have mentioned them, unless indeed they had been made under conditions which excluded communication with the apostles, and this fact had
been well known to his readers. Even in that case he would
naturally have spoken of them, and appealed to the well-
known absence of the apostles or spoken, not of going to Jerusalem, but of seeing those who were apostles before him. The
argument is strengthened by the use of the word "after,"
which suggests that the period of fourteen years constituted a
period of noncommunication with the apostles.]

with Barnabas,—As the prophets and teachers at Antioch
ministered to the Lord, the Holy Spirit said, "Separate me
Barnabas and Saul for the work whereunto I have called
them," and they sent them away, and they went through Cyprus, the home of Barnabas; and then through the provinces
of Asia Minor, proclaiming the word of God, and returning to
Antioch, and called the church together, and rehearsed all
things that God had done with them; and that he had opened
a door of faith unto the Gentiles. "And certain men came
down from Judaea and taught the brethren, saying, Except ye
be circumcised after the custom of Moses, ye cannot be saved.
And when Paul and Barnabas had no small dissension and
questioning with them, the brethren appointed that Paul and
Barnabas, and certain other of them, should go up to Jerusalem
unto the apostles and elders about this question." (Acts 15 : 1,
2.)

taking Titus also with me.—[It should be noted carefully
that it does not say that Paul took Barnabas as well as Titus,
for the church at Antioch had appointed that Barnabas equally

and I laid before them the ¹gospel which I preach among the Gentiles but

¹See marginal note on ch. 1. 6.

with Paul should go to Jerusalem. Nor was it Titus as well as others—for there were others appointed by the church to go (Acts 15: 2), but Paul makes no reference to them. The *also* calls attention to the fact of Paul's taking Titus in view of the sequel, as though he had said: "I not only went up to Jerusalem at this particular time under divine direction, but I took with me Titus *besides.*" *With* refers to Paul himself— "Titus who was with *me.*" (Verse 3.) From this it appears that Paul wished him to go, as an uncircumcised disciple, doubtless to have a practical example of what they would require in the case. This question was one that reached and became a disturbing element in every church among the Gentiles.]

2 **And I went up by revelation;**—Paul was directed by the Holy Spirit to go up to Jerusalem and let the apostles decide the question. The Holy Spirit had decided it for Paul, and he taught the decision to the people; but the disaffected portion of the disciples denied his apostleship, and ability to decide such questions. [We can well conceive that amid the disputes at Antioch Paul sought counsel from God, and received a special reply, which moved him to undertake the journey. This revelation, guiding Paul's movements, attests his close relation to God. In Luke's account (Acts 13: 1, 2) of this he tells of the appointment of Paul and Barnabas to go to Jerusalem in order to promote the settlement of the anxious controversy.]

and I laid before them the gospel which I preach among the Gentiles—[The persons to whom this communication was made were the disciples in Jerusalem. Perhaps we can more clearly understand what is meant here by referring to Acts 25: 14-21. There we are told that Festus laid Paul's case before Agrippa with the view of careful consultation concerning it. So here Paul, in harmony with the purpose for which he had gone to Jerusalem, laid before the brethren the gospel he was preaching to the Gentiles—the conditions of salvation and

privately before them who ²were of repute, lest by any means I should be
running, or had run, in vain. 3 But not even Titus who was with me, being
a Greek, was compelled to be circumcised: 4 ³and that because of the false
brethren privily brought in, who came in privily to spy out our liberty which
we have in Christ Jesus, that they might bring us into bondage: 5 to whom

²Or, *are*
³Or, *but* it was *because of*

the obligations of believers. It should be noted that the word
preach is in the present tense, which asserts the continuity
and consistency of his preaching, even to the moment of writing this epistle.]

but privately—He did this privately because he had been
more or less misrepresented by his detractors. These private
consultations were a wise precaution to avoid minunderstand-
ing. Such private conferences are usually held in connection
with public assemblies for the purpose of preparing and ma-
turing business for final action.

before them who were of repute,—James, Cephas, and John,
and others who were reputed leaders of the church in Jerusalem.

lest by any means I should be running, or had run, in vain.
—[The whole phrase implies that Paul saw in the existing situation a danger that his work on behalf of the Gentiles, both
past and future, might be rendered ineffectual by the opposition of the Jerusalem church, or of certain men in it, and the
disapproval of the apostles, and fearing this, he sought to
avert it.]

3 But not even Titus who was with me, being a Greek, was
compelled to be circumcised:—Certain false brethren of the
Judaizing party brought him into the conference unawares to
Paul and the apostles, and demanded that he should be circumcised.

4 and that because of the false brethren privily brought in,
who came in privily to spy out our liberty which we have in
Christ Jesus,—The freedom of which the apostle speaks is, of
course, the freedom of the Christian from the bondage to the
law, which would have been surrendered in principle and
practice if the Gentile Christians had been compelled to be cir-

we gave place in the way of subjection, no, not for an hour; that the truth of
the ¹gospel might continue with you. 6 But from those who ²were reputed to

cumcised. (4: 8-31; 5: 1-3, 13.) [That he calls it "our liberty"
shows that, although the obligation of the Gentiles to be circumcised was the particular question at issue, this was in
Paul's mind only a part of a larger question, which concerned
both Jewish and Gentile Christians. The Antioch incident
(verses 11-21) shows how closely the question of freedom of
the Jews was connected with that of the liberty of the Gentile
Christians.]

   that they might bring us into bondage:—That is, to the law,
implying an already possessed freedom. This language refers
to Christians in general, not to the Gentiles exclusively. Paul
distinctly charges that these men entered the church for a prop-
agandist purpose, in order to make a legalistic body of it.

   5 to whom we gave place in the way of subjection, no, not
for an hour;—He clearly saw that to yield to false brethren
would be in effect to surrender the gospel of Christ. This he
positively refused to do. [In antithesis to the possibility of
his work proving fruitless (by reason of the opposition of the
Jerusalem church and the apostles) Paul here sets forth the
fact that on this very occasion and in a test case his decision
prevailed. The fact of the presence of Titus with Paul had already been mentioned in the preceding sentence. Its repetition here is evidently, therefore, for an argumentative purpose, and doubtless as emphasizing the significance of the fact
that he was not circumcised. It is upon this element that *not
even* throws its emphasis. The opponents of Paul, the "false
brethren," desired, of course, the circumcision of all Gentile
Christians. But so far were they from carrying through their
demand that not even Titus, who was there on the ground at
the time, and to whom the demand would first of all apply,
was not circumcised. The noncircumcision of Titus, therefore, was in reality a decision of the principle.]

   that the truth of the gospel might continue with you.—He
did this that the truth of the gospel might continue with the

be somewhat (⁴whatsoever they were, it maketh no matter to me: God accepteth not man's person)—they, I say, who were of repute imparted nothing to me: 7 but contrariwise, when they saw that I had been intrusted with the ¹gospel of the uncircumcision, even as Peter with *the* ¹*gospel* of the circumci-

⁴Or, *what they once were*

Gentiles, which could not be if they observed the law of Moses. (5 : 2, 3.)

6 **But from those who were reputed to be somewhat**—So far from Paul receiving the gospel from the apostles, those who in conference seemed to be the most important, most referred to, added nothing to him, taught him nothing that had not already been revealed to him, showing that God had as fully entrusted his will to Paul as to the chiefest of the apostles.

(whatsoever they were, it maketh no matter to me: God accepteth not man's person)—they, I say, who were of repute imparted nothing to me:—In this parenthesis he evidently refers not to personal character but to standing, which the three here referred to had by reason of their personal relation to Jesus while he was in the flesh, in the case of James as his brother, in that of Peter and John as his personal followers. This fact of their history was undoubtedly referred to by the opponents of Paul as giving them standing and authority wholly superior to any that he could claim. (cf. 2 Cor. 5: 16; 10: 7.) Paul answers that the facts of this sort do not concern him, have no significance. Apostleship rests on a present relation to the glorified Christ, open to him equally with them.

7 **but contrariwise, when they saw that I had been intrusted with the gospel of the uncircumcision, even as Peter with the gospel of the circumcision**—So far from giving to him fresh ideas and thoughts, they recognized that God had committed to him the gospel of the uncircumcision, as he had the gospel of the circumcision to Peter. That is, God had as fully inspired Paul to preach to the Gentiles as he had Peter to the Jews. For he that enabled Peter to work as an apostle effectually to the Jews was equally gracious to Paul in enabling him to work among the Gentiles. [The gospel is the same, but the sphere of labor is different. Paul was directed to the field of his labor among the Gentiles at his conversion (Acts

sion 8 (for he that wrought for Peter unto the apostleship of the circumcision wrought for me also unto the Gentiles) ; 9 and when they perceived the
grace that was given unto me, [5]James and Cephas and John, they who [2]were
reputed to be pillars, gave to me and Barnabas the right hands of fellowship,

[5]Or, Jacob

9: 15), and more clearly by a special revelation in the temple
at Jerusalem (Acts 22: 17-20). Yet the division of labor was
not absolute and exclusive. Paul generally commenced his
work in the various places he visited in the synagogue because it furnished the most convenient locality and the natural
historical connection for the beginning of gospel work, and
because it was resorted to by the numerous proselytes who
formed the most favorable access to the heathen. On the
other hand, Peter opened the door for the conversion of the
Gentiles by the conversion and baptism of Cornelius.]

8 (for he that wrought for Peter unto the apostleship of the
circumcision wrought for me also unto the Gentiles) ;—Paul
was as fully enabled to work miracles among the Gentiles as
Peter was among the Jews. This was recognized as the manifestation of the divine presence and of apostolic power and authority.

9 and when they perceived the grace that was given unto
me,—The grace that was given unto Paul sums up the facts of
his having been put in trust of the gospel of the uncircumcision, and of God's having wrought on his behalf in his discharge of that trust.

James and Cephas and John, they who were reputed to be
pillars,—Pillars or supports, leading men, chief champions in
the church. The expression is used in all languages, especially among the Jews of the great teachers of the law. [Paul
does not deny his colleagues to be the leading apostles among
the Jews; they were so still in fact as he was the pillar in the
church among the Gentiles; but the Judaizers used the expression in a partisan sense and with a view to deprecate
Paul.]

gave to me and Barnabas the right hands of fellowship,—
This was done to express their approval of the work in which
they were engaged. The work of Paul and Barnabas among

that we should go unto the Gentiles, and they unto the circumcision ; 10 only *they would* that we should remember the poor ; which very thing I was also zealous to do.

---

the Gentiles had been called in question, and they had been discouraged by many ; these apostles, to encourage them and to show to all gainsayers that they regarded Paul and Barnabas on an equal footing with the very chiefest apostles.

that we should go unto the Gentiles, and they unto the circumcision ;—Thus Paul shows that the very apostles in praise of whom these people denied his apostleship had endorsed Paul and Barnabas as apostles. [The mutual recognition of the different spheres in which each was called to preach does not mean that Paul and Barnabas were precluded from preaching to the Jews, or the others to the Gentiles. The one message of salvation was to be offered to men, as they were, whether circumcised or uncircumcised. The whole evidence, therefore, clearly indicates that the meaning of the agreement was that Paul and Barnabas were to preach the gospel in Gentile lands, and the other apostles in Jewish lands.]

10 only—[They had but one stipulation to make, and that did not touch the matter of preaching at all—so little foundation was there for the charge that Paul was indebted to the original apostles, either for the matter of the gospel he preached or for the authority to preach it.]

they would that we should remember the poor ;—Remember the poor saints in Judæa. This would not only afford temporal relief to the needy, but be a bond of union between the Jewish and Gentile believers, and furnish a proof of the gratitude of the Gentiles, to the Jews for the unspeakable gift of the blessings of the gospel which came through them. Such a collection was raised during the great famine in the reign of Claudius Caesar, by the church at Antioch, as early as A.D. 41, and sent to the elders by the hand of Barnabas and Saul. (Acts 11 : 28-30.) On his third missionary tour Paul raised a large contribution in the Gentile churches for this purpose, and accompanied by messengers of the churches took it to Jerusalem. That he had respected the wish of the church at Jerusalem in the matter was well known to the Galatians, before whom he had laid the claims of the Jewish brethren. (1 Cor. 16: 1; Rom. 15: 25-27; 2 Cor. 8: 8, 9; Acts 24: 17.)

Paul did this no doubt out of kindness for them in their sufferings, and also as a means of breaking down the feelings of enmity between the Jews and Gentiles. When the Gentiles gave to the Jews, it eradicated in their hearts all feelings of bitterness against the Jews, and it had a tendency to subdue the feelings of enmity on the part of the Jews toward the Gentiles.

which very thing I was also zealous to do.—In this he intimates that he did not need the admonition the apostles gave him, and his practice vindicated his claim.

5. FINAL PROOF OF HIS APOSTOLIC INDEPENDENCE INCIDENTALLY INVOLVING ANTICIPATION OF HIS POLEMIC AGAINST LEGALISM.
2: 11-21.

11 But when Cephas came to Antioch, I resisted him to the face, because

---

11 But when Cephas came to Antioch,—Paul sojourned at Antioch both before and after he had brought the decrees of the apostles at Jerusalem on the subject of circumcision. While he was in Antioch, Peter came to the city. There has been differences among Bible students as to whether this visit was before or after the conference. From the interviews Paul reports in this epistle of his having with Peter up to the time of the conference, I am confident that it could not have been before. [The most judicious commentators claim that this visit of Peter to Antioch took place soon after the return of Paul and Barnabas from Jerusalem, in the interval described in Acts 15: 35, shortly before the separation of Paul and Barnabas, and the departure of Paul on his second missionary journey.]

I resisted him to the face,—[This instance is one of faithful public reproof; and every circumstance in it is worthy of special attention, as it furnishes a most important illustration of the manner in which such reproof should be conducted—it was done openly and frankly and addressed to the offender

he stood condemned. 12 For before that certain came from James, he ate
with the Gentiles; but when they came, he drew back and separated himself,
fearing them that were of the circumcision. 13 And the rest of the Jews

himself. This was a case so public and well known that Paul
administered the reproof before the whole church.]

because he stood condemned.—[He was condemned by his
own inconsistency. By first eating with the Gentiles and then
pressing upon them observance of the very principle he had
violated.] Some think that Peter could not have been guilty
of such a course after he had aided in reaching the decision at
the conference; but he had been instrumental in introducing
the Gentiles into the church, at the house of Cornelius, some
ten years before this, and knew that God had accepted them.
His course was not the result of ignorance, but of fear of offending the Jewish prejudice. His wrong would have been as
great before as after the conference.

12 **For before that certain came from James, he ate with the
Gentiles;**—[The visit to which reference is made took place
soon after the return of Paul and Barnabas from Jerusalem, in
the interval described in Acts 15: 35, shortly before the separation of Paul and Barnabas, and the departure of Paul on his
second missionary journey.] While on this visit, with Paul
and Barnabas, he ate with the Gentile brethren.

**but when they came, he drew back and separated himself,
fearing them that were of the circumcision.**—Some came from
James at Jerusalem, stirred up the prejudice on the subject,
and Peter withdrew from this association with the Gentiles,
fearing the Jews. [It would be wrong to charge that James
so instructed the men who came, for we are warned against
this by the fact that the men from Jerusalem who stirred up
the first strife in Antioch received no commandment at all.
(Acts 15: 24.)]

13 **And the rest of the Jews dissembled likewise with him;**
—The other Jews dissembled and acted the hypocrite with
Peter. [The men who had hitherto eaten with the uncircumcised and now withdrew because they shrank from giving offense were, in fact, affecting religious scruples which they did

dissembled likewise with him; insomuch that even Barnabas was carried
away with their dissimulation. 14 But when I saw that they walked not
uprightly according to the truth of the ¹gospel, I said unto Cephas before
them all, If thou, being a Jew, livest as do the Gentiles, and not as do the
Jews, how compellest thou the Gentiles to live as do the Jews? 15 We being

---

not feel, and Paul does not hesitate to denounce such insincerity by saying they acted hypocritically.]

**insomuch that even Barnabas was carried away with their
dissimulation.**—The current became so strong that Barnabas,
who had been reared in Cyprus among Gentiles, and had labored among the Gentiles, was swept into the current of dissimulation, and withdrew with the others from association
with them.

**14 But when I saw that they walked not uprightly accord-
ing to the truth of the gospel, I said unto Cephas before them
all,**—When Paul saw that they walked not according to the
way of truth, he rebuked Peter as the leading apostle and
most blameworthy of all, before all, that all might be rebuked.
[For only in this public way the censure could have its desired effect upon the body of Jewish Christians.]

**If thou, being a Jew, livest as do the Gentiles, and not as do
the Jews,**—[Peter had lived as a Gentile in the house of Cornelius, in Cæsarea, and had done the same for a time in Antioch.]

how compellest thou the Gentiles to live as do the Jews?—
[Now, by withdrawing from the Gentiles, he was virtually saying to the Gentiles that they must live like the Jews or they
could not have social intercourse with him.] Peter sought
salvation not according to the Mosaic law, but through faith
in Jesus Christ, which admitted persons not as Jews, but as
men. This caused Peter to illustrate a truth we weldom recognize, that is, that the miraculous gift of the Holy Spirit did
not save, as it gave them the knowledge of the truth. It revealed the truth to them, then kept them under that truth to
struggle with the temptations to do wrong as other men. The
Jews reared in Gentile lands of necessity did not imbibe the
strong prejudices against association with the Gentiles as the
Jews of Judæa cherished. Paul, then, was not the subject of

Jews by nature, and sinners of the Gentiles, 16 yet knowing that a man is not ⁶justified by the works of the law but through faith in Jesus Christ, even

⁶Or, *accounted righteous: and so elsewhere.* Comp Rom. 2. 13.

---

so strong prejudices as Peter, the chief of the apostles, for his course. We are not told, but Peter must have knowledged his wrong under this reproof and changed his course. Not to have done so, when his sin was thus pointed out, would have intensified it. For him to acknowledge his wrong would have been another acknowledgment of Paul's superiority to him. The facts of the case show this whether Peter owned it or not. It is introduced as a crowning truth to his claims to be the equal of the foremost apostle. God, Jesus Christ, the Holy Spirit, and all the apostles own him as an apostle. Why should these Galatians, his own children in the gospel, call it in question?

15 **We being Jews by nature,**—[The outspoken protest against an insidious attempt to force on Gentiles the Jewish law leads naturally to an inquiry what this law has done for men who are Jews by birth. Did it justify them before God? They knew it did not. They had to turn to Christ for the peace with God which the law could not give.]

and not sinners of the Gentiles,—[This expresses the insolent contempt of Judaizers for Gentiles, who did not belong to the holy nation nor inherit the law and the covenants. Yet in spite of these arrogant pretensions to superior sanctity they were driven by their own consciousness of being sinners to embrace the faith in Christ because they knew that no flesh could possibly be so perfect in obedience to law as to be thereby justified.]

16 **yet knowing that a man is not justified by the works of the law but through faith in Jesus Christ,**—Those who came into Christ from the Jews knew that a man is not justified by the works of the Jewish law, but through faith in Jesus Christ.

even we believed on Christ Jesus, that we might be justified by faith in Christ,—Even Paul and Peter sought justification through Christ instead of depending on the works of the law

we believed on Christ Jesus, that we might be justified by faith in Christ, and
not by the works of the law: because by the works of the law shall no flesh

---

to justify them. In doing this they ignored or turned from
that which made them Jews, and identified themselves in so
doing with sinners needing a Savior. [We cannot doubt that
Peter, before Andrew led him to Jesus, and Paul, before he
went to Damascus, had sought the favor of God by obedience
to the law; and that the failure of their search had taught
them that thus it cannot be obtained. Indeed without this
preparation the words of Jesus to Peter (Matt. 16: 19), and
afterwards to Paul (Acts 26: 19), would have been ineffective.
Until we find that our good works cannot save us, we cannot
trust for salvation to the word of Christ. Consequently these
words are true of all who venture to repose faith in Christ,
and they were a powerful appeal to Peter's remembrance of
his own life. For he was now practically setting up a condition, and in this sense a means, which, when he first came to
Christ, he had forsaken because he had found from it salvation
could not be obtained. In Paul's address to Peter he appeals
to him to take their own case. Although they were born Jews
and not the offspring of idolaters and sharers of the awful im-
morality of heathenism, yet, inasmuch as they found by experience that no justification comes from works done in obedience to the law, but only through faith in Christ, even we
born Jews and as compared with other moral men put faith in
Christ in order that in him we might have a justification not
to be derived from works of law.]

and not by the works of the law:—The works here referred
to are the works of Moses which the Jews trusted in for salvation. In coming to Christ they turned from all that was dis-
tinctively Jewish.

because by the works of the law shall no flesh be justified.
—It is true that no man could be justified by the law because
no man left to himself could obey the law without fault, and
only perfect obedience could bring justification through law,
but Paul is not dealing in abstractions here. He is contrasting the salvation through works of the Jewish law, which the

be justified. 17 But if, while we sought to be justified in Christ, we ourselves also were found sinners, is Christ a minister of sin? God forbid. 18
For if I build up again those things which I destroyed, I prove myself a

---

Jews sought and the salvation through Christ. The same
thing is taught in the following: "For what the law could not
do, in that it was weak through the flesh, God, sending his
own Son in the likeness of sinful flesh and for sin, condemned
sin in the flesh." (Rom. 8: 3.) The law of Moses had failed to
keep the Jews from sin, and it was taken out of the way and
faith in Christ Jesus is presented as leading to salvation.

17 But if, while we sought to be justified in Christ,—The
word *sought* suggests that they who followed after a low of
righteousness did not arrive at that law (Rom. 9: 30, 31) and
had then turned themselves to Christ for the satisfaction
which the law had not afforded them.

we ourselves also were found sinners,—They discovered
themselves to be sinners, suggesting the surprise of the Jew
who learned for the first time that before God he had no moral
superiority over the Gentiles whom he contemptuously called
sinners, while he esteemed himself to be righteous (verse 15;
Rom. 7: 10), and now in the light of the life and death of
Jesus Christ the Jew discovered himself to be exactly in the
same condition (Rom. 3: 9).

is Christ a minister of sin?—Did Christ make them sinners
when through his gospel he revealed to them their sinful condition, and they learned that they all with their legal righteousness were under sin (Rom. 3: 9), and that "by the works of
the law shall no flesh be justified"?

God forbid.—An expression of strong denial and aversion,
rebutting an unjustifiable inference from his teaching.

18 For if I build up again those things which I destroyed,
—He had preached Christ as to the end of the law. It was
their tutor to bring them to Christ that they might be justified
through faith in Christ, but when faith came they were no
longer under law. (3: 24, 25.) Then if he by observing the law
built up what he had pulled down, he made himself a trans-

transgressor. 19 For I through the law died unto the law, that I might live
unto God. 20 I have been crucified with Christ; and it is no longer I that

---

gressor. He and all who had preached Christ had preached
that the law was fulfilled, taken out of the way, nailed to the
cross. For him to observe the law and teach others to observe it was to nullify the death of Jesus and to take away the
results of his death.

I prove myself a transgressor.—[If Peter did right in refusing to eat with the Gentiles, he had done wrong in associating
with them earlier; if he had done right to obey the vision from
heaven, he was a transgressor in disobeying it now.]

19 For I through the law died unto the law,—Paul was
brought by the law to Christ. Jesus said: "Ye search the
scriptures, because ye think that in them ye have eternal
life; and these are they which bear witness of me." And,
"For if ye believed Moses, ye would believe me; for he
wrote of me." (John 5: 39, 46.) Of Timothy it is said: "From
a babe thou hast known the sacred writings which are able to
make thee wise unto salvation through faith which is in
Christ Jesus." (2 Tim. 3: 15.) [To die to a thing is to cease
to have any relation to it, so that it has no further claim upon
or control over one. (Rom. 6: 2, 10, 11; 7: 6.) That to which
reference is here made is evidently the law as a legalistic system, a body of statutes legalistically interpreted. It was on
the basis of the law in this sense that it was demanded that
the Gentile believers should be circumcised and keep the law
of Moses. It was under this that Paul had lived as a Pharisee, and under which he had ceased to live—died to it. How
the necessity of abandoning the law was made evident to him
by law, Paul does not here state, but it is most probable that
he had in mind his experience under the law, which he describes in Romans 7: 7-25, where he tells us that his own experience under it taught him his own inability to meets its requirements and its own ability to make him righteous, and
thus led him finally to abandon it, and seek salvation through
Christ. (Phil. 3: 5-9.)]

that I might live unto God.—In entering into Christ he died

live, but Christ liveth in me: and that *life* which I now live in the flesh I

---

unto the law, that in Christ he might live unto God. [This implies that subjection to the law in reality prevented the unre-
served devotion of the life to God—this is one vice of legalism, that it comes between the soul and God—and that it had
to be abandoned if the life was really to be given to God.]

20 **I have been crucified with Christ;**—Christ was crucified,
died to the law. Paul was crucified with Christ and so died to
the law. Having died to the law, he was made alive in Christ.
[Christ, though he had fully dispatched every obligation imposed by the law, endured the extreme penalty prescribed for
"every transgression and disobedience." (Heb. 2: 2.) When
one, therefore, believes with the heart that Jesus is "the
Christ, the Son of the living God" (Matt. 16: 16), he acknowl-
edges the judgment of God against sin to be just, and accepts
the death of Christ as the execution of that judgment upon
him for his own guilt. In thus believing he becomes identified
with Christ in his death, and since death nullifies all claims and
obligations is "made dead to the law" (Rom. 7: 4) and ceases
to be under the jurisdiction of the law. The idea of the believer's death reappears in Rom. 6: 3, 4; Col. 2: 11, 12. The
reference to this mode of execution, with its association with
shame, heightens the contrast between the fancied law keeping of his opponents and the actual fact of their absolute
failure to attain to righteousness thereby. The shame of the
cross was not his who died upon it, but theirs whose transgression and disobedience made the cross necessary.]

and it is no longer **I that live, but Christ liveth in me:**—
Christ lived in Paul. He, through faith in Christ, was made
alive in him. The life of Christ was reproduced in him.
[Christ lived in him by his Spirit. "If any man hath not the
Spirit of Christ, he is none of his. And if Christ is in you, the
body is dead because of sin; but the spirit is life because of
righteousness." (Rom. 8: 9, 10.) Christ in his glorified body
is in heaven, but he is represented here by the Holy Spirit.
(John 14: 17; Rom. 8: 11.) When Paul sought to establish
his own righteousness, everything depended upon vigilance

live in faith, *the faith* which is in the Son of God, who loved me, and gave himself up for me. 21 I do not make void the grace of God: for if righteousness is through the law, then Christ dies for nought.

and energy, but when he realized the failure of his best efforts, and trusted in Christ for directions as to how to live, he became conscious of a new power working within him.]

and that life which I now live in the flesh I live in faith,— [The believer is said to have died with Christ, and also to have been raised together with him through faith (Col. 3: 1), and it is this life of the spirit in association with Christ to which reference is here made.] The new life is received through faith (3: 27), and is maintained by the exercise of faith (2 Cor. 7: 7), which is the characteristic function of the new life.

the faith which is in the Son of God,—Christ is presented here as the proper object of the believer's confidence. What Christ has done for man is the guarantee of his will and of his power to continue and to complete the work of salvation.

who loved me, and gave himself up for me.—The love wherewith he loved Paul inspired a responsive love in his heart for Christ, and loving him he kept his commandments. Keeping the commandments of Jesus makes us like him. [In his love for the church (Eph. 5: 25) Christ does not lose sight of the individual believer. Each member of his body is the direct object of his love, and it is as true that he died for each as it is that he died for all. Hence, the individual believer appropriates to himself that which is the possession of all.]

21 I do not make void the grace of God:—In trusting God, walking by faith in Jesus Christ and seeking salvation through him, and turning from the law he did not frustrate or make vain the grace of God. [The teaching of the Judaizers certainly did set it aside, for if salvation is by grace it is no more of works, and conversely, if it is of works it is no more of grace; works and grace are incompatible, they are mutually exclusive. (Rom. 11: 6.)]

for if righteousness is through the law, then Christ died for nought.—God seeks to make man righteous, and if righteousness could have been attained through the law of Moses, there would have been no need of the death of Christ. Hence his mission and death were meaningless, fruitless, without good to man. It was a vain and profitless mission and sacrifice that Christ made if man could have gained through the law, and without Christ all that was gained through him. Christ came to save man from his sins and make him righteous before God and to fit him to dwell with him. If the law could have fitted him for this divine companionship, the death of Christ was meaningless and vain. If man can be made righteous by any means out of Christ, it is equally true that Christ died for nought.

Thus he has vindicated, without dispute, his apostleship, and that the law was dead, and that life and salvation are to be found through Christ, and he urges the folly of leaving the gospel, and turning to the law of Moses or to any theory of man.

SECTION TWO.

THE ALL-SUFFICIENCY OF THE GOSPEL AND THE UTTER INSUFFICIENCY OF THE LAW FOR THE JUSTIFICATION OF MEN.
3: 1 to 4: 31.

1. FERVID REMONSTRANCE WITH THE GALATIANS FOR THEIR INCONSIDERATE ABANDONMENT OF THE ONLY MEANS OF SALVATION.
3: 1-10.

1 O foolish Galatians, who did bewitch you, before whose eyes Jesus Christ was openly set forth crucified? 2 This only would I learn from you,

---

1 **O foolish Galatians, who did bewitch you,**—[The Galatians were not naturally stupid, but they had not used their senses, else they would never have allowed themselves to be led into the absurd position in which they were found. The tone is not that of contempt, nor is it so much of indignation as of reproach. They had been subjected to an evil influence; a deadly fascination, like that of the "evil eye" had fastened on their minds. Behind the spite of the Judaizers Paul recognized a malice and cunning like that with which "the serpent beguiled Eve." (2 Cor. 11:3.)]

before whose eyes Jesus Christ was openly set forth crucified?—His crucifixion had been clearly set forth before them. Paul well knew this as he had first preached among them, and here, as at Corinth, he says: "I determined not to know anything among you, save Jesus Christ, and him crucified." (1 Cor. 2: 2.) Paul had fully and clearly set forth the death of Christ as the one hope of the world; that he died for our sins and rose again for our justification.

2 **This only would I learn from you,**—The churches generally had spiritual gifts bestowed on them to guide and instruct them until the revelation of God's will was completed and collected for their guidance. These Galatians, I take it from what he says, had received these miraculous gifts.

Received ye the Spirit by the works of the law, or by the hearing of faith?—That is, through the provisions of the Jew-

Received ye the Spirit by the works of the law, or by the [7]hearing of faith?
3 Are you so foolish? having begun in the Spirit, [8]are ye now perfected in
the flesh? [4]Did ye suffer so many things in vain? if it be indeed in vain. 5

[7]Or, *message*
[8]Or, *do ye now make an end in the flesh?*

---

ish law or the faith in Jesus. It never occurred to Paul that
the Spirit could be received through any other means than either the obedience to the Jewish law or by receiving the word
of the Spirit into the heart. God has chosen the word as the
means through which he works. It is the seed of the kingdom. The things addressed to the eyes of the heart (Eph. 1:
18), to be accepted and obeyed, constituted the hearing of
faith. He knew they had received these gifts through obedience of the gospel. Jesus said: "If ye love me, ye will keep
my commandments. And I will pray the Father, and he shall
give you another Comforter, that he may be with you for ever,
even the Spirit of truth." (John 14: 15-17.) The Holy Spirit
was sent in the first place to the disciples who obeyed him and
to none others, and the gifts and powers of the Spirit were
distributed on the same conditions. Hence the question
showed the folly of their course.

3 **Are ye so foolish? having begun in the Spirit, are ye now
perfected in the flesh?**—They had trusted in Christ and received the benefits and manifestations in the Spirit and were
foolishly turning from "the law of the Spirit of life in Christ
Jesus" to the Jewish law with its "carnal ordinances, imposed
until a time of reformation." (Heb. 9: 10). The religion of
Judaism depended upon the fleshly relations and fleshly ordinances and services, that of Christ on the Spirit.

4 **Did ye suffer so many things in vain?**—They in common
with all Christians had suffered most severely for their faith
in Christ. If they now turn to Judaism, they give up all that
for which they suffered and say that the sufferings were needless and vain. The chief persecution against Paul was because he forsook Judaism. The Jews scattered throughout
Gentile lands persecuted those who followed Christ. When
Paul was arrested in Jerusalem and sent to Rome, it was at
the instigation of the Jews. Luke says: "The Jews from Asia,

He therefore that supplieth to you the Spirit, and worketh ⁹miracles ¹⁰among

⁹Gr. *powers.*
¹⁰Or, in

when they saw him in the temple, stirred up all the multitude and laid hands on him, crying out, Men of Israel, help: This is the man that teacheth all men everywhere against the people, and the law, and this place." (Acts 21: 27, 28.) And Paul says: "If I still preach circumcision, why am I still persecuted?" (5: 11.) The offending of the Jewish law was the cause of the persecution. [These persecutions had failed to move them from their faith in Christ. Would they now succumb before the subtler methods of the Judaizers?]

if it be indeed in vain.—[In this he shows that he is unwilling to believe that they had actually turned away from the faith, and that he hopes they will yet shake themselves free from the trammels of the false teachers.

The question addressed to the Galatians addresses itself to the churches untrue to the spiritual principles that gave them birth. The faith of the apostolic church that endured so faithfully the severe persecutions finally yielded its purity to the blandishments of wicked and designing men. The pioneers of the restoration movement of the nineteenth century staked their lives on a "thus saith the Lord in faith and practice." For this glorious principle they suffered bitter persecution and ostracism; and now that the victory is won, there are those among their children who scout the very idea of such a struggle and even ostracize those who "contend earnestly for the faith which was once for all delivered unto the saints." (Jude 3.) And now that the victory is won, there are those of their children who are wholly indifferent and care nothing for the principles for which their fathers so nobly fought and suffered. Out of indifference and worldly pride they have abandoned the spiritual heritage bequeathed to them. Did their fathers suffer so many things in vain? Was it an illusion that sustained these faithful heroic souls, who through faith "wrought righteousness, obtained promises, stopped the mouths of lions?" Was it for nought that so many of Christ's

you, *doeth he it* by the works of the law, or by the ⁷hearing of faith? 6
Even as Abraham ¹¹believed God, and it was reckoned unto him for righ-

¹¹Gen. xv. 6.

---

faithful servants suffered the loss of all things rather than
yield by subjection to a usurping and worldly clergy? And
can we who reap the fruits of their faith and courage afford, in
these perilous times, to surrender the principles whose maintenance cost our fathers so dear a price?]

5 **He therefore that supplieth to you the Spirit,**—Paul himself, no doubt, had been the person who ministered the Spirit
to them. At Ephesus, a city in a neighboring province, he had
laid hands on the twelve and they received the Holy Spirit.
(Acts 19: 1-16.) He asked them: "Did ye receive the Holy
Spirit when ye believed?" which would indicate that it was
common during the period before the New Testament scriptures were completed and collected, when persons were converted, to bestow upon them such gifts as were needed to
bring to their minds the instructions given by inspired teachers. Paul bestowed gifts on these Galatian disciples.

and worketh miracles among you,—This was a strong re-
minder that he who opposed the turning to the law of Moses
possessed the Spirit, ministered or distributed gifts of the
Spirit, and wrought miracles in their midst.

**doeth he it by the works of the law, or by the hearing of
faith?**—All the manifestations of the divine presence were
connected with the hearing of faith, not with the works of the
law, and came through those who opposed a turning to the
Jewish law. These were God's testimonies in the behalf of
faith.

6 **Even as Abraham believed God,**—He goes back to Abraham to show that he was justified by faith and not by works
of the Jewish law. God dealt with Abraham on the same
principle that he deals with men under Christ. He accepted no
service from Abraham unless he did it through faith. Faith, as
used in distinction from the works of the law, does not mean
faith distinct from the works of the faith, or the obedience that
pertains to faith. But it is a distinction between the system of

teousness. 7 ¹Know therefore that they that are of faith, the same are sons of Abraham. 8 And the scripture, foreseeing that God ²would justify the

¹Or, *Ye perceive*
²Gr. *justifieth.*

which faith is the leading, pervading principle, and the system of Moses in which certain works with faith secured the blessing.

and it was reckoned unto him for righteousness.—Abraham's faith was accounted to him for righteousness only after it had led him to give up the home of his childhood, his kindred, and friends to follow God, not knowing whither he went. In other words, it was faith perfected by works, the work of faith.

7 **Know therefore that they that are of faith, the same are sons of Abraham.**—The Jews thought they were sure of salvation because they were Abraham's children after the flesh. John warned them: "Think not to say within yourselves, We have Abraham to our father: for I say unto you, that God is able of these stones to raise up children unto Abraham." (Matt. 3: 9.) Jesus said unto them: "If ye were Abraham's children, ye would do the works of Abraham." (John 8: 39.) Paul said: "He is not a Jew who is one outwardly; neither is that circumcision which is outward in the flesh: but he is a Jew who is one inwardly; and circumcision is that of the heart, in the spirit not in the letter; whose praise is not of men, but of God." (Rom. 2: 28, 39.) These scriptures teach that Abraham's blood in the veins was of no avail in the way of salvation unless accompanied by Abraham's faith in the heart. Under the reign of Christ, all who walk by faith are the true children of Abraham, and not those who are born of the flesh, and seek blessings by fleshly relations to Abraham. Many at the present day think that to be a member of the church will save them; but without the faith of the gospel, membership in the church cannot save. Faithful obedience to the gospel alone can save.

8 **And the scripture,**—What God has promised is ascribed to the scripture itself, not simply because it is related in the scripture, but because the scripture, as inspired of God, is con-

[3]Gentiles by faith, preached the gospel beforehand unto Abraham, *saying,* [4]*In thee shall all the nations be blessed.* 9 So then they that are of faith are

[3]Gr. *nations.*
[4]Gen. xii. 3.

ceived as the organ of the Spirit of God. The same then is true of God's foreknowledge, from which the promise proceeded.

foreseeing that God would justify the Gentiles by faith,— [The present tense is used because this is the sole ground upon which God accepts any person at any time, and hence when he came to deal with Gentiles for their salvation he would take no other. From the scripture Paul has shown that Abraham had been justified by faith, and if their forefather according to the flesh, then surely the Jews likewise. But what of the Gentiles? He quotes scripture again to show that the Gentiles are to be accepted in the same way. He shall justify the circumcision by faith, and the uncircumcision through faith. (Rom. 3: 20.) The change in the prepositions here is made to suit the different relation in which Jew and Gentile stood with God. The Jew had the divine law; if he could not be justified on the ground of his obedience to that, on what ground could he be justified? On the ground of faith; by a personal appropriation of the promises of God. The Gentiles, on the other hand, had no point of contact with God. By what means, then, could the Gentiles be justified? By the means of faith, for in due time the gospel would be preached to them also.]

preached the gospel beforehand unto Abraham,—[The words that follow, spoken to Abraham, anticipated the gospel, which is now preached as an accomplished fact. (Rom. 1: 2.) In Abraham the family and nation were founded from which the promised Deliverer came; in Abraham also began a line of spiritual men whose characteristic is *faith in God,* and who are drawn from "every nation and tribe and tongue and people." (Rev. 14: 6.) These and not those who merely trace to him their descent "after the flesh" are the true sons of Abraham.]

blessed with the faithful Abraham. 10 For as many as are of the works of
the law are under a curse: for it is written ⁵Cursed is every one who contin-

⁵Dt. xxvii. 26.

---

saying, In thee shall all the nations be blessed.—This was
the promise of a coming Savior in Abraham's seed that would
bless all nations. [The Gentiles as well as the Jews. When
this declaration of the purpose of God to bless mankind was
first made in the form of a promise to Abraham, the human
race had but recently begun to divide into separate groups,
tribal and national, and the nation Israel had no existence.
The developments among men in Gen. 11: 1-9 were part of the
purpose of God (Deut. 32: 8); along these lines he had designed that we should be prepared for the coming of his Son,
and for the salvation promised. To Abraham God imparted a
knowledge of his purpose, and, indeed, of the agent of its accomplishment. (John 8: 56.) When at length the nation Israel
was brought into being; it became possible for him to reveal
his mind to them with increasing distinctness. To Israel were
the promises given, and to them "were entrusted the oracles
of God" (Rom. 3: 2), in which the promises were enshrined.
But that "all nations," and not Israel only, were in the mind
of God for salvation is plain from each grand division of the
scriptures—the Law, the Prophets, and the Psalms. (Rom. 9:
25-27; 10: 18-21; 15: 9-12.)]

9 **So then they that are of faith are blessed with the faithful
Abraham.**—As Abraham secured the blessing through faith,
all who believe as he did, whether Jews or Gentiles, will be
blessed with him.

10 **For as many as are of the works of the law are under a
curse:**—The sacrifices on the altar could make none of the sinners coming thereunto perfect as pertaining to the conscience.
The sacrifices had no virtue to secure the forgiveness of
sins. "For it is impossible that the blood of bulls and goats
should take away sins." For "in those sacrifices there is a remembrance made of sins year by year." (Heb. 10: 3, 4.) The
same sins were remembered and atoned for ever year, and the
sacrifices could not take them away, but rolled them forward

ueth not in all things that are written in the book of the law, to do them. 11 Now that no man is justifed [6]by the law before God, is evident; for, [7]The

[6]Gr. *in.*
[7]Hab. ii. 4.

from year to year; but finally "Christ having come a high priest of the good things to come, through the greater and more perfect tabernacle, not made with hands, that is to say, not of this creation, nor yet through the blood of goats and calves, but through his own blood, entered in once for all into the holy place, having obtained eternal redemption." (Heb. 9: 11, 12.) Those then who are of the works of the law, who only depended upon these, were not freed finally from sin, even while the law was in force. Much less are they freed from sin by the law after it had been taken out of the way and superseded by Christ. Not being made free from sin, they are under the curse and condemnation of the law.

for it is written, Cursed is every one who continueth not in all things that are written in the book of the law, to do them. —None kept the law perfectly, hence all who were under the works of the law were under a curse.

2. FURTHER EVIDENCE OF THE INCOMPETENCY OF THE LAW FOR THE JUSTIFICATION OF MEN.
3: 11-19.

righteous shall live by faith; 12 and the law is not of faith; but, [8]He that

[8]Lev. xviii. 5.

11 Now that no man is justified by the law before God, is evident:—This principle is continually repeated in the New Testament. And in the law they were justified, not by faith, but by doing the things commanded by the law. As there could be no justification without faith, there can be no justification by the law.

for, The righteous shall live by faith:—This is frequently interpreted to mean that the justified shall live by faith only, but it does not mean that they shall live through believing separate from the obedience to which faith leads.

doeth them shall live in them. 13 Christ redeemed us from the curse of the
law, having became a curse for us; for it is written, ⁹Cursed is every one

⁹Dt. xxi. 23.

**12 and the law is not of faith; but, He that doeth them shall
live in them.**—Faith in God leads a man to obey the things
commanded of God, and in doing these things he is blessed of
God.

**13 Christ redeemed us from the curse of the law, having be-
come a curse for us;**—As all under the law are under condemnation of the law for violating it, and as the blood of bulls and
goats could never take away sin, but only rolled them forward
and suspended the condemnation of the law from year to year
until Christ came and suffered under the law and to finally
take away their sins. [Christ's death was that of the most
abandoned criminals. By the combined verdict of Jew and
Gentile, of civil and religious authority, endorsed by the voice
of the populace, he was pronounced a malefactor and blas-
phemer. But this was not all. The hatred and injustice of
men are hard to bear; yet many a sensitive man has borne
them in a worthy cause without shrinking. It was a darker
dread, an infliction far more crushing, that compelled the cry:
"My God, my God, why hast thou forsaken me?" (Matt. 27:
46.) Against the maledictions of men Jesus might surely at the
worst have counted on the Father's good pleasure. But even
that failed him. There fell upon his soul the death of death,
the very curse of sin—*abandonment of God!* Men "did esteem
him stricken, smitten of God." (Isa. 53: 4.) He hung on
the cross abhorred of men, forsaken of his God; earth all hate,
heaven all blackness to his view. Are Paul's words too
strong? God did in truth make him a curse for us. "By the
determinate counsel and foreknowledge of God" (Acts 2: 23),
Jesus was set in the place of condemned sinners, and allowed
the curse of the wicked world to claim him for its victim.
The Jewish Sanhedrin fell upon him for the purpose of declaring him accursed, they thus stigmatized him. They made the
Roman governor and the heathen soldiers their instrument in
crucifying their Messiah. Pilate in his extremity cried out:

that hangeth on a tree: 14 that upon the Gentiles might come the blessing of

---

"Shall I crucify your King?" (John 19: 15). "But they cried out exceedingly, Crucify him." (Mark 15: 14.) It was the desire of the Sanhedrin to lay on the hated Nazarene an everlasting curse.]

for it is written, Cursed is every one that hangeth on a tree: —This saying attached in the Jewish mind a peculiar loathing to the person of the dead thus exposed. Once crucified they thought the name of Jesus would surely perish from the minds and lips of men; no Jew would hereafter dare to confess faith in him. His cause could never surmount this ignominy. [This sentence of execration Paul has woven into a crown of glory. Paul freely admits that Jesus was hanged on a tree, crushed with reproach, and accursed, as his enemies said, but he was the long-expected Messiah and Savior. But the curse he bore was *ours*. His death, unmerited by him, was the price of our redemption to ransom us from the curse of sin and death. We know that we were condemned by the law; that the sinless Christ came under the law's curse, and taking the place of sinners, he was "made to be sin on our behalf; that we might become the righteousness of God in him." (2 Cor. 5: 21.) He bore the inflictions incurred by our sins, and due to ourselves. Paul says, "Christ redeemed *us*," thinking of his Jewish kindred, on whom the law weighed so heavily—it was offered "to the Jew first," but not to him alone, nor as a Jew. The time of release had come for all men.]

14 that upon the Gentiles might come the blessing of Abraham in Christ Jesus;—The Jews were taken from the law and, like Abraham, were to walk by faith. They were placed upon the same plane with the Gentiles. Jesus Christ was the seed of Abraham in whom all nations were to be blessed and that the Gentiles might become heirs of the blessings of Abraham by entering into Christ.

that we—The *we* here refers to the children of Abraham *through faith,* whether Jew or Gentile. Christ coming and redeeming those were under the law, and bearing their sins for them, was the occasion of the blessings of Abraham being

Abraham in Christ Jesus; that we might receive the promise of the Spirit
through faith.

---

opened to the Gentiles as well as to the Jews. "For he is our
peace, who made both one, and brake down the middle wall of
partition, having abolished in his flesh the enmity, even the
law of commandments contained in ordinances; that he might
create in himself of the two one new man, so making peace;
and might reconcile them both in one body unto God through
the cross, having slain the enmity thereby: and he came and
preached peace to you that were far off, and peace to them
that were nigh: for through him we both have our access in
one Spirit unto the Father." (Eph. 2: 14-17.)

might receive the promise of the Spirit through faith.—
With the coming of Christ had been promised the free and
full outpouring of the Holy Spirit to lead men, as the following clearly shows: "And it shall come to pass afterward, that
I will pour out my Spirit upon all flesh; and your sons and
your daughters shall prophesy, your old men shall dream
dreams, your young men shall see visions: and also upon the
servants and upon the handmaids in those days will I pour
out my Spirit." (Joel 2: 28, 29.) This promise of the Spirit,
Jesus repeated to his disciples: "If ye love me, ye will keep
my commandments. And I will pray the Father, and he shall
give you another Comforter, that he may be with you for ever,
even the Spirit of truth." (John 14: 15-17.) "Nevertheless I
tell you the truth.": It is expedient for you that I go away; for
if I go not away, the Comforter will not come unto you; but if
I go, I will send him unto you. And he, when he is come, will
convict the world in respect of sin, and of righteousness, and of
judgment: of sin, because they believe not on me; of righteousness, because I go to the Father, and ye behold me no
more; of judgment, because the prince of this world hath been
judged. . . . Howbeit when he, the Spirit of truth, is come,
he shall guide you into all the truth." (John 16: 7-13.) Joel's
prophecy was quoted by Peter on the day of Pentecost as on
that day fulfilled. (Acts 2: 16-21.)

15 Brethren, I speak after the manner of men: Though it be but a man's covenant, yet when it hath been confirmed, no one maketh it void, or addeth thereto. 16 Now to Abraham were the promises spoken, and to his seed.

---

15 Brethren, I speak after the manner of men:—He speaks of what is regarded as sacred among men to illustrate the certainty and sanctity of God's covenant with Abraham.

Though it be but a man's covenant, yet when it hath been confirmed, no one maketh it void, or addeth thereto.—If a covenant be but of man, if it be confirmed, no man adds to or takes therefrom. Much more, the conclusion is, if God makes a covenant and confirms it, it will stand unchanged. Now such a covenant was made by God with Abraham: "For when God made promise to Abraham, since he could swear by none greater, he sware by himself, saying, Surely blessing I will bless thee, and multiplying I will multiply thee. And thus, having patiently endured, he obtained the promise. For men swear by the greater: and in every dispute of theirs the oath is final for confirmation. Wherein God, being minded to show more abundantly unto the heirs of the promise the immutability of his counsel, interposed with an oath; that by two immutable things, in which it is impossible for God to lie, we may have a strong encouragement, who have fled for refuge to lay hold of the hope set before us." (Heb. 6: 13-18.) Now God had confirmed the covenant with Abraham by his own oath and it could not be added to or taken from.

16 Now to Abraham were the promises spoken, and to his seed.—The promise made to Abraham and his seed was the basis of the covenant that God made with Abraham and his seed, and confirmed with an oath.

He saith not, And to seeds, as of many; but as of one, And to thy seed, which is Christ.—The promise was: "And the angel of Jehovah called unto Abraham a second time out of heaven, and said, By myself have I sworn, saith Jehovah, because thou hast done this thing, and hast not witheld thy son, thine only son, that in blessing I will bless thee, and in multiplying I will mutiply thy seed as the stars of the heavens, and as the sand which is upon the sea-shore; and thy seed shall

He saith not, And to seeds, as of many; but as of one, [10]And to thy seed,

[10]Gen. xiii. 15; xvii. 8.

possess the gate of his enemies; and in thy seed shall all the nations of the earth be blessed; because thou hast obeyed my voice." (Gen. 22: 15-18.) The promise was of the increase of the family referred to all his seed. But the final outcome of the promise—"In thy seed shall all the nations of the earth be blessed"—was the spiritual and everlasting blessing and referred to Christ alone, and then through him to all the spiritual family of Abraham who shall be blessed in him. Abraham did not understand the meaning and reach of these promises. He expected temporal blessings to all his family. When God restricted these promises to the promised child of Sarah, "Abraham said unto God, Oh that Ishmael might live before thee! And God said, Nay, but Sarah thy wife shall bear a son; and thou shalt call his name Isaac: and I will establish my covenant with him for an everlasting covenant for his seed after him. And as for Ishmael, I have heard thee: behold, I have blessed him, and will make him fruitful, and will multiply him exceedingly; twelve princes shall he beget, and I will make him a great nation." (Gen. 17: 18-20.) God promised a large family and temporal blessings to Ishmael, but the everlasting covenant was made with Isaac and his seed. (Gen. 26: 3.) He repeats the promises of Abraham to Isaac. (Gen. 28: 13, 14.) This everlasting promise was repeated to Jacob and his seed after him, excluding Esau, then to David's line. The promise was restricted as time progressed until possibly for the first time it is told by Paul that the promise continued in one seed, not seeds as of many, but one —Jesus Christ. And in him all the families of the earth may find a blessing.

This much may be said of all the promises of God. When they fail as pertaining to earthly and temporal blessings, they find full and everlasting fulfillment in the spiritual blessings. Canaan was to be the earthly inheritance to the children of Israel. This promise failed as a temporal good because they sinned and transgressed the covenant they made with God.

which is Christ. 17 Now this I say: A covenant confirmed beforehand by
God, the law, which came four hundred and thirty years after, doth not disannul, so as to make the promise of none effect. 18 For if the inheritance is

---

But fleshly Israel and earthly Canaan typified spiritual Israel
and heavenly Canaan. So this promise finds its complete and
everlasting fulfillment in these great spiritual antitypes. So
the real covenant with Abraham is fulfilled in Christ.

17 **Now this I say: A Covenant confirmed beforehand by
God,**—This covenant was confirmed by God to Abraham to be
fulfilled in Christ. This covenant or promise was first made
with Abraham when he was yet in Ur of the Chaldees. (Gen.
12: 1-4.)

the law, which came four hundred and thirty years after,—
The law was given by Moses four hundred and thirty years
after this promise was made to Abraham. (Ex. 12: 40.) Many
interpret this to mean that they sojourned in Egypt four
hundred and thirty years. But they dwelt in tents and had no
permanent habitation during their sojourn in Canaan and
Egypt and in the wilderness from the call in Ur until the entrance into Canaan after the Egyptian bondage.

doth not disannul, so as to make the promise of none effect.
—This law could not annul or make void the promise made
four hundred and thirty years before it was given. The law
of Moses did not confer blessings on all nations. It brought
blessings only to the fleshly children of Abraham, or those
who would enter the family as children of Abraham. It prepared the children of Israel for bringing forth Jesus, and for
presenting through him the blessing to the world; but the
blessing could be bestowed upon all nations only through the
taking out of the way of the law of Moses.

8 **For if the inheritance is of the law, it is no more of promise:**—If the inheritance covenanted to all nations, in the promise to Abraham, came through the law of Moses, that rendered the prior promises of none effect. [The fulfillment of
the promise is unaffected by the law. For it is not dependent
upon the law, or upon the law and the promise combined—the
law modifying the promise—but upon the promise alone. The

of the law, it is no more of promise: but God hath granted it to Abraham by promise. 19 What then is the law? It was added because of transgressions,

---

law does not come in at all. Law and promise are incompatible ideas.]

but God hath granted it to Abraham by promise.—The land of Canaan was promised to Abraham as a free gift, and as a free gift the spiritual Canaan is thrown open to his spiritual descendants.

3. THE DESIGN AND SIGNIFICANCE OF THE LAW.
3: 19-29.

till the seed should come to whom the promise hath been made; *and it was* ordained through angels by the hand of a mediator. 20 Now a mediator is

---

19 When then is the law?—If the promised blessing to all nations could not come through the law of Moses, what end or purpose did the law serve?

It was added because of transgressions,—It was because the children of Israel transgressed the will of God and sinned that the law of Moses was added.

till the seed should come to whom the promise hath been made;—It was added because of the sins of the people, to train and fit and qualify them to receive the seed to whom the promise was made—Jesus Christ. This is exemplified in the travels of the children of Israel from Egypt to Canaan. They were brought to the border of Canaan. Had they been prepared to enter, they could have done so at once. By transgression they were unfitted to enter. A sojourn in the wilderness of forty years was added to fit and prepare them to enter. They were not fitted for the blessing, so the law was added, that in obeying it they might be trained for the coming seed. This may carry the idea that had Abraham's seed being faithful the promised seed would have appeared sooner. The transgression rendered them unfit to receive him, so his coming was postponed and the law was added to train and fit them for his coming.

not *a mediator* of one; but God is one. 21 Is the law then against the promises of God? God forbid: for if there had been a law given which could

---

**and it was ordained through angels by the hand of a media-
tor.**—Stephen said to the Sanhedrin: "Ye who received the
law as it was ordained by angels, and kept it not." (Acts 7:
53.) And again, it is said: "For if the word spoken through
angels proved stedfast, and every transgression and disobedience received a just recompense of reward." (Heb. 2: 2.)
These passages show that according to apostolic interpretation God gave the law to Moses, not by speaking in his own
person, but by speaking through angels whom he sent to
Moses.

20 **Now a mediator is not a mediator of one; but God is one.**
—A mediator does not mediate with one, but stands between
two parties. God was one of the parties and the Jews the
other between whom Moses was mediator.

21 **Is the law then against the promises of God? God forbid:**
—Because the promises cannot be fulfilled through the law of
Moses, does the law militate against the fulfillment of the
promises? By no means. Very frequently a thing that cannot accomplish an end may be helpful to place in a position
that it can be reached. Take Paul's illustration. Primary
schools that teach no Latin, Greek, or higher mathematics can
never teach those branches, yet they are necessary to prepare
for the school that can teach them. So the law could not
bring righteousness, but it could discipline and educate and fit
them for the school that could make them righteous and receive final forgiveness.

**for if there had been a law given which could make alive,
verily righteousness would have been of the law.**—If law
could give life, righteouness would come by that law.
Because there can be no life without righteousness, sin and
death are indissolubly joined together, and righteousness and
life in the nature and being of God. Hence, Christ came that
he might save men from their sins, that he might save them
from death. So eternal life was not promised under the law of
Moses, because it could no free from sin and hence could not

make alive, verily righteousness would have been of the law. 22 But the scripture shut up all things under sin, that the promise by faith in Jesus Christ might be given to them that believe.

23 But before faith came, we were kept in ward under the law, shut up

---

give life. The blood of bulls and goats could never free from sin, could only roll forward the exemption until Christ came and by his blood took it away, so that there is no more remembrance of sin.

22 **But the scripture shut up all things under sin,**—The scripture then regarded both Jew and Gentile as under sin. All sinned, the Jew under the law, the Gentile from under it, that all as sinners might come through faith to Jesus and receive the forgiveness of sins, or might receive through faith the promises made to Abraham.

that the promise by faith in Jesus Christ might be given to them that believe.—Because they were to be fulfilled and could be enjoyed only in Christ Jesus. So the Jews and the Gentiles could alike come to these promises through faith in Christ.

23 **But before faith came, we were kept in ward under the law,**—Faith came with Christ. God dealt with Abraham by the law of faith; on account of sins he substituted the law of works through Moses. The law remained in force till Christ came and through him the law of faith was again restored as a means of justification. But before faith came in Christ Jesus, "we [Jews] were kept in ward under the law"—kept under it as a child is kept under a tutor, directed and trained by him, fitted for the faith should afterward be revealed in Christ. So the law of Moses served as a tutor to fit and train the Jewish people, or those who kept it, for Christ. This was the mission of the law. The Jews transgressed, fell away from God, and became so given over to the flesh and to the hardness of heart that they could not act from faith; but without faith the heart could not be purified nor the soul trust in God, so God placed them under the law of Moses to train them to obedience through the law of works, which required fleshly obedience to

unto the faith which should afterwards be revealed. 24 So that the law is
become our tutor *to bring us* unto Christ, that we might be justified by faith.
25 But now that faith come, we are no longer under a tutor. 26 For ye
are all sons of God, through faith, in Christ Jesus. 27 For as many of you

---

a law that controlled the actions of the body for temporal
ends, but through this discipline gradually fitted men to exercise faith in Jesus Christ, and to lift up the spirit and prepare
it to act on eternal motives in accord with spiritual laws.

shut up unto the faith which should afterwards be revealed.
—The law of works, while it served this purpose to the Jews
to bring them to Christ, the same scriptures now help us as
examples, and by the application in the Old Testament, to understand the operation and application of the law of faith.

24 **So that the law is become our tutor to bring us unto
Christ, that we might be justified by faith.**—So the law served
as a tutor to train the Jews for Christ, that coming to him
they might be justified, by faith in Jesus, and conform the life
to the law of faith, given through Christ.

25 **But now that faith is come, we are no longer under a tutor.**—But after they had been prepared to believe in Jesus
Christ, and had come to faith through him, for they were no
longer under the tutor that trained them for faith.

26 **For ye are all sons of God,**—Having come into Christ,
they are now the sons of God through faith in Jesus Christ, not
through the works of the Jewish law. [The "ye are all" carries the emphasis of the sentence, and is directed against the
distinction made by the Judaizing teachers between those believers who had received circumcision and those who had not.
The Jews stood in covenant relation with God before Christ
came, the Gentiles did not; but whatever their former condition, now all who trusted in Christ had been brought into a
relationship with God far superior even to that of Israel before Christ came.]

through faith, in Christ Jesus.—[The point Paul is seeking
to establish, and the idea is, sons of God in Christ Jesus, and
made such, not by circumcision, but by faith.]

as were baptized into Christ did put on Christ. 28 There can be neither Jew
nor Greek, there can be neither bond nor free, there can be no male and

---

27 For as many of you as were baptized into Christ did put
on Christ.—This explains how faith made them the sons of
God. Faith had led them to follow Jesus—to put themselves
under his leadership. In the commission, Jesus said to his disciples: "All authority hath been given unto me in heaven and
on earth. Go ye therefore, and make disciples of all the nations, baptizing them into the name of the Father and of the
Son and of the Holy Spirit." (Matt. 28: 18, 19.) To be thus
baptized is to be baptized into Christ. In the passage before
us, baptism is set forth as a part of the law of faith, and so far
as being regarded by Paul as work that is condemned, it is put
in contrast with the works of the law. He is contrasting the
law of works under the Mosaic code with the law of faith.

28 There can be neither Jew nor Greek,—There is no difference between Jew and Greek coming into Christ. They all
stand on an equal footing before God, and they must enter
into Christ on the same terms.

there can be neither bond nor free,—[Social distinctions do
not obtain in Christ; the rich and the poor, the master and the
slave, the wise and simple meet together in Christ to share a
common salvation.] But entering into Christ did not destroy
the distinction between master and slave. Each had duties
growing out of his position and relation peculiar to himself
after becoming Christians. (Col. 3: 22; 4: 1.)

there can be no male and female;—Male and female are
equally accepted in Christ, and without reference to that
which distinguishes each, may enjoy the mercies and blessings
of God in Christ. This had not been so under the Jewish dispensation. It does not mean that all could indiscriminately
perform.all the work and duties in the church. All men cannot occupy the same or similar positions. The husband is to
be the head of the wife, and the wife is to be subject to him.
(Eph. 5: 23, 24; 1 Pet. 3.) Saying that husband and wife are
one does not mean that there are no duties peculiar to each in

female; for ye all are one *man* in Christ Jesus. 29 And if ye are Christ's, then are ye Abraham's seed, heirs according to promise.

the marriage relation. The wife is to bear children, guide the house, be a worker at home; the husband and father provides for, and is the head of, the family. Men have obligations as men, from which women are exempted, and women, as women, that do not pertain to men.

for ye all are one man in Christ Jesus.—All with the peculiarities that pertain to each are admitted into Christ on the same terms. [These distinctions of individuals outside of Christ appear as nonexistent, completely merged in that higher unity to which they were all raised in virtue of their fellowship in Christ, but in the definite sense of their relation as Christians, inasmuch as this unity was wholly dependent upon Christ, to all believers live and belong. (2: 20; 2 Cor. 5: 15; Rom. 14: 18.)]

29 **And if ye are Christ's, then are ye Abraham's seed, heirs according to promise.**—If they were in Christ, they were made so by faith, and by faith they were Abraham's children. [The final conclusion of this profound, comprehensive varied, and terse reasoning, in proof of the assertion in verse 7, that the believers are the true children of Abraham, and consequently heirs by promise. (We must keep in mind that Christ is expressly declared to be the seed of Abraham, verse 16.) Union with Christ constitutes the true spiritual descent from Abraham, and secures the inheritance of all the Messianic blessings by *promise,* as against *inheritance by law.*]

4. THE DIFFERENCE BETWEEN MAN'S MINORITY UNDER
LEGAL AND OTHER PREPARATORY DISCIPLINE, ON THE
ONE HAND, AND THE FULLNESS OF HIS PRIVI-
LEGES UNDER GRACE ON THE OTHER.
4: 1-11.

1 But I say that so long as the heir is a child, he differeth nothing from a
bondservant though he is lord of all; 2 but is under guardians and stewards
until the day appointed of the father. 3 So we also, when we were children,
were held in bondage under the [1]rudiments of the world: 4 but when the

[1]Or, elements   2 Pet. 3. 10, 12.

---

1 But I say that so long as the heir is a child, he differeth
nothing from a bondservant though he is lord of all;—Paul illustrates the condition of the Jews under the law, and their
deliverance from the law through the gospel of Christ by the
child, who is kept under tutors and guardians, although he is
heir of the throne, until he becomes of age, when he enters
into the rule of his possessions.

2 but is under guardians and stewards until the day appointed of the father.—Children look to present gratification
and not to future good. Just as the child, though heir of great
riches, is kept under tutors and governors until he is qualified
to freely follow right, and to manage his possessions looking
to future good, and walking by principles of right rather than
the present gratifications.

3 So we also, when we were children,—Even when they
were children, incapable of being moved by promises of future
good, God kept them for a time under the law of Moses before
he granted to them the high honors and privileges of the gospel of Christ. This family through which the seed was to
come he kept under the law, training and qualifying them to
enjoy the privileges of the promises through Christ.

were held in bondage under the rudiments—Paul represents
the Jewish system as an elementary religion of childhood, full
of external rites and ceremonies, pointing beyond themselves
to an age of manhood in Christ. The whole Old Testament
dispensation was an elementary or a preparatory school for
the gospel, a religion of types and shadows, of hope and promise, destined to lose itself in Christ as its substance and fulfillment.

fulness of the time came, God sent forth his Son, born of a woman, born
under the law, 5 that he might redeem them that were under the law, that

---

of the world:—[Not the physical universe, but mankind
which needed such a training for the coming Messiah. It
may be that the expression comprehends the heathens as well
as the Jews. But the Jews were in fact the religious repre-
sentatives of the whole race of mankind in the motion towards
Christ.]

4 but when the fulness of the time came,—When the time
came that they could walk by faith in God and look to the future rewards and punishments. [This period was fixed in the
counsel of God with reference to the development of the race.
The words "fulness of the time" express the whole philosophy
of history before Christ, and the central position of the birth
of Christ. The ancient history of Jews and Gentiles was a
preparation for the coming of Christ, and Christ is the turning
point of history, the end of the old world and the beginning of
the new. Jesus himself began his preaching with the declaration: "The time is fulfilled, and the kingdom of God is at
hand." (Mark 1: 15.) The Savior could not appear in any
other country, nor at any other time, nor in any other nation,
according to the order of the divine government, and prear-
ranged history.]

God sent forth his Son,—He certainly existed before his
birth in Bethlehem, in heavenly glory, with the Father.

born of a woman,—He was born of a woman that he might
sympathize with humanity. [This expresses the realness of
the humanity of Jesus Christ.]

born under the law,—That he might fulfill the law, take it
out of the way, and deliver his people from the bondage of the
law. [These words bring the Lord Jesus into relation with
the Jewish nation. (cp. Rom. 15: 8; Heb. 2: 14-18.) He thus
took upon himself the obligations imposed by God upon the
Jews in the law given at Sinai. The fulfillment of this law by
the Lord was the outward and evident token of his acceptance
with God, and of his competence for the work he had undertaken to do.]

we might receive the adoption of sons. 6 And because ye are sons, God sent

---

5 **that he might redeem them that were under the law,—**
[Neither his coming in the flesh nor his keeping the law in the
days of his flesh availed, in whole or in part, for the redemption of men. He he not been clothed in flesh, death would
have been impossible for him; hence this was the condition
necessary for the accomplishment of the redemption, but was
itself no part of that redemption. His redemptive work proper
began and ended on the cross; accordingly the statement
of the Savior's relation to sin is invariably made in terms that
confine that relationship to his death. Hence it is nowhere
stated in the New Testament that Christ kept the law for us.
Only his death is vicarious. He is not said to have borne sin
during any part of his life; it was on the cross that he became
the *sin bearer*. (1 Cor. 15: 3; Gal. 1: 4; Heb. 9: 28; 1 Pet. 1:
24; Rev. 1: 5.) Jesus declared that the purpose of his life was
"not to be ministered unto, but to minister, and to give his life
a ransom for many." (Mark 10: 45.) His death was in complete harmony with his life, and was its fitting climax, but the
two are here distinguished by the Lord himself, and his distinction is observed by each of the New Testament writers.
Inasmuch as it was necessary that the Jews might be redeemed from under the law, much more must the Gentiles not
allow themselves to be brought under it when they become
believers in him who died to accomplish that redemption.
The death of Christ secures for the believers freedom from the
curse (3: 13), and from the bondage of the law (4: 3; Rom. 6:
14.)]
that we might receive the adoption of sons.—To adopt is to
receive the child of another as one's own and to bestow upon
it the affection, treatment, and privileges as one's own child.
Christians are spoken of by God as his adopted children.
They are his by adoption. This would indicate that they are
not his naturally—they are not born by natural birth into his
family. Man was in the beginning a child of God. God
created him as his own child, and as his child placed him to
reign over the world. The genealogy of the human family,

forth the Spirit of His Son into our hearts, crying, Abba, Father. 7 So that

as given in the New Testament, traces all back to "Adam, the son of God." He was created by God as a member of his family. But now the children of Adam are not by virtue of their birth in the family of God. Adam sinned against God, accepted the devil as his ruler, and thus alienated himself and the world from the family of God. In order that man might be reinstated in God's favor, God proposes to readopt him into his family, or so many of the children of men as will trust and follow him. As preparatory to being received as sons, the Spirit of adoption must be in their hearts, a desire to become members of his family. This desire is imparted through faith in God. When the person has been fitted in heart and life by faith and repentance towards God, for the enjoyment of the privileges of the family of God, he is then by a burial out of his old family relations and a resurrection in the new ones adopted into the family of God. Baptism is the act of adoption by which we pass out of one family, and are brought into the new one with God as our Father, and Jesus Christ as our elder brother, and by which we acquire the right to the blessings and favors of the family of God. After we have been legally adopted into the family of God, we must drink more and more into the spirit of the family that we may not lose our fitness for its privileges and forfeit our rights to its inheritance. The adoption does not help us unless it is legally perfected.

6 **And because ye are sons, God sent forth the Spirit of his Son into our hearts,**—This has no reference to the time or the manner of receiving the Spirit of God. It is a contrast between the law of Moses and the law of Christ. Under the law of Moses they were servants; under the law of Christ they are sons. Because they are sons, not servants, God sent the spirit of a son into their hearts. Taken in connection with corresponding passages, this scripture settles the point that the spirit of a son is put into the heart by writing the law in his heart. The promise was: "I will put my law in their inward parts, and in their heart will I write it; and I will be their

thou art no longer a bondservant, but a son; and if a son, then an heir
through God.

God, and they shall be my people." (Jer. 31: 33.) When
Christ came the new covenant was made, the law was written
in their hearts; they were no longer servants with a spirit of
fear, but sons with a spirit of love. Writing the law in their
hearts and sending the spirit of a son are the same thing, because the word is the seed of the kingdom, in which the Spirit,
which gives life, dwells. The scriptures show that the Spirit
of God dwells in the word of God. (Luke 8: 11; John 6: 63;
Rom. 8: 9-11; 1 Cor. 4: 15; 2 Cor. 3: 16; James 1: 18; 1 Pet. 1:
22, 23.) I do not know a single scripture, taken in its connection, that does not teach the same thing. All scripture, with
the facts and analogies of nature, teaches that the spirit of
him who begets passes to him that is begotten in the act of
begetting. It passes in the seed that begets. This law was
stamped upon creation—vegetable, animal, and spiritual.
Every tree, every animal, every being was created, yielding
fruit after his kind. It is a contradiction of the law of God in
nature and in grace to say that the spirit of the father is imparted to the child after birth. The person who believes is
just as much begotten by the Father, the child of God, before
it is baptized as it is afterwards. The difference is: one is a
born child, the other an unborn child. Unless the unborn
child is brought by the birth into a state suited for developing
life, it will perish. The spirit is imparted in the begetting, the
spirit enters with the seed. The word of God is the seed of
the kingdom. The Spirit enters the heart with the word of
God; it grows with the growth of the word of God in the
heart and life of man. If a man ever becomes a truly spiritual
man, it must be by taking the word of God fully into his heart
and bringing his life into harmony with God's laws.

crying, Abba, Father.—The Spirit was given unto them by
which they could regard and call on God as Father. They felt
not as servants, but as children. [Abba, the Chaldean or Aramaic word for father, was a word used by Jesus. (Mark 14:
36.) No one had hitherto approached God as Jesus did. His

8 Howbeit at that time, not knowing God, ye were in bondage to them

---

utterance of this word, expressing the attitude of his life of prayer and breathing the whole attitude of his life, profoundly affected his disciples. So that word became a watchword of the early church, being the proper name of the God and Father of our Lord Jesus Christ. Gentile believers used it conscious that in doing so they were joined in spirit to the Lord who said: "I ascend unto my Father and your Father, and my God and your God." (John 20: 17.) Greek-speaking Christians supplemented it by their own equivalent as we by the English *Father*. This precious word is carried down the ages and around the whole world in the mother tongue of Jesus, a memorial of the hour when through him men learned to call God *Father*.]

7 **So that thou art no longer a bondservant, but a son;**—Under the Jewish law they had felt that they were slaves or servants. Now through faith they can feel that they are sons—children. A son obeys from love, a servant from fear. Now they are no longer servants, but sons, and the son is the heir of the heritage of the father.

and if a son, then an heir through God.—Then as son an heir of the Father, and that kinship comes through Jesus Christ. He is the Son of God. He redeemed them, he purchased them, he pardoned them. They entered into him through faith, and in him they became heirs with him of his Father and their Father. Their Father because Jesus is his Son, and they are in him.

8 **Howbeit at that time, not knowing God, ye were in bondage to them that by nature are no gods:**—This seems more especially spoken to the Gentile converts among the Galatian Christians. They had known God only a short while, and before they knew him they had worshipped idols which are no gods. They are in their very nature devoid of all qualities of God. The Jews were liable to this same charge, for they had, in time past, while claiming to believe in God, gone into the worship of idols.

that by nature are no gods: 9 but now that ye have come to know God, or rather to be known by God, how turn ye back again to the weak and beggarly ¹rudiments, whereunto ye desire to be in bondage over again? 10 Ye observe days, and months, and seasons, and years. 11 I am afraid of you,

¹Or, *elements* See ver. 3.

---

9 but now that ye have come to know God, or rather to be known by God,—But having learned of the true God, or what is more important, God having owned them as his children by the gift of his Spirit.

how turn ye back again to the weak and beggarly rudiments,—How could they, the apostle asks, turn from the rich spiritual services, promises, and rewards of eternal life to these weak and beggarly elements? To serve in them was a bondage of slavery, and how could they return to them?

whereunto ye desire to be in bondage over again?—[Relapsing into bondage, to begin anew its rudiments in the form of Judaism, instead of the former heathenism. The Galatians had never been under the Mosaic yoke; yet they had been under the elements of the world—the common designation for Jewish and Gentile systems in contrast with the gospel. Both consisted in outward, sensuous worship, and were in bondage to the elements of sense as though these could give justification and sanctification, which the power of God through Jesus Christ alone could give.]

10 Ye observe days, and months, and seasons, and years.— They kept these Jewish feasts and observances which all found fulfillment in Christ. God, in the Mosaic law, had appointed the daily offering, the feast of the new moon, the feast of the Passover, the feast of weeks, the feast of trumpets, the feast of ingathering, and quite a number of others. They had all found their fulfillment in Christ, and the law of Moses was done away. [While it is probable that these were the occasions in the mind of Paul when he wrote, still they need not be taken too literally, as though the Galatians had already actually observed all these, and had been observing the year of jubilee. If they observed the least of them they acknowledged the principle. It was as though they observed all. Heretofore he had mentioned circumcision only as indicative

lest by any means I have bestowed labor upon you in vain.

---

of the declension of these believers, but of course they could
now draw the line at that; once they put themselves under the
law, they became debtors to do all the law enjoined (5: 3).]

**11 I am afraid of you, lest by any means I have bestowed
labor upon you in vain.**—The zeal for these things was an in-
dication of waning faith. and interest in the law of Christ, and
filled Paul with fear lest the labor he had bestowed on them
had failed to bear fruit. Fondness for observing these days
was regarded as indicative of indifference to Christ.

It is true that those churches which lay most stress on the
observance of the days not authorized in the scriptures pay
least regard to the observances ordained by God. The
churches that observe Easter, and other days ordained by men,
pay the least regard to the scriptural observance of the first
day of the week. Paul discusses the observance of days in
worship to God not especially required by the Scriptures
(Rom. 15: 4, 5), and says if a man wishes to observe a day,
and is satisfied in his own mind, let him do it; let him have his
faith to himself; but he is to do it as an individual, so as not
to impose it on others. When a church has a special Easter
service or any such service, it imposes its service on every
member of the congregation. This Paul clearly condemns.
Sometimes things harmless in themselves becomes harmful
from the use made of them. Jesus illustrates this by the
washing of hands, harmless in itself, but when done as a religious ceremony, Jesus says it is sin. (Matt. 15: 2.) God condemns those whose fear of him is a commandment of men,
which has been taught them. (Isa. 29: 13.) Then a service
that may be right under some circumstances, when done as a
religious service because taught by man, becomes sin. The
Christians ought to be careful to do all they do, in the name of
the Lord, and only what he commands. When men start out
to do those things not required by the scriptures, where will it
end? One step leads to another, till the service of God is lost
sight of in the multiplicity of human observances. To observe
Easter now is to honor the Roman Catholic Church, not
Christ; for it, not he, ordained the service.

5. AFFECTIONATE APPEAL FOR AN EARNEST HEARING BASED ON PAST ASSOCIATION AND FELLOWSHIP.
4: 12-20.

12 I beseech you, brethren, become as I *am*, for I also *am become* as ye *are*. Ye did me no wrong: 13 but ye know that because of an infirmity of

---

12 I beseech you, brethren,—This is the expression of a painfully agitated, affectionate, and loving heart.

become as I am,—His object was to persuade them to abandon the Jewish rites and customs. He appealed to them, therefore, by his own example, for he had laid aside its supposed advantages, and his lifelong prejudice (Phil. 3: 7) in order to take his place beside the Gentiles. Now he entreats those who put themselves under the law, or who contemplate doing so, to take their place beside him—be as free as he was free.

for I also am become as ye are,—He had conformed to their customs in many things; had abandoned his own peculiarities; had given up his customs as far as possible to benefit and save them. He was a Jew of the Jews. Of himself he said: "Though I myself might have confidence even in the flesh: if any other man thinketh to have confidence in the flesh, I yet more: circumcised the eighth day, of the stock of Israel, of the tribe of Benjamin, a Hebrew of Hebrews; as touching the law, a Pharisee; as touching zeal, persecuting the church; as touching the righteousness which is in the law, found blameless." (Phil. 3: 4-6.) He had all the Jewish feelings and regard for Jewish services that they could possibly have, yet he had given them all up for Christ. He appeals to them to do as he had done.

Ye did me no wrong:—Many expositors understand this to mean that they did him no personal injury in turning to Judaism, for his interest in them was that they might be saved; others connect it with the following verse, and make it refer to the treatment they gave him while he was among them.

13 but ye know that because of an infirmity of the flesh I preached the gospel unto you the first time:—They did not while he was among them injure or annoy him, but in infir-

the flesh I ²preached the gospel unto you the ³first time: 14 and that which
was a temptation to you in my flesh ye despised not, nor ⁴rejected; but ye
received me as an angel of God, *even* as Christ Jesus. 15 Where then is that

²See marginal note on ch. 1. 8.
³Gr. *former.*
⁴Gr. *spat out.*

mity of the flesh he preached to them and they kindly received
him, more than kindly received him, as the following verses
show.   He at his first coming among them preached with
some fleshly infirmity.   That infirmity is referred to on several occasions, but no clue is given by which to determine
what it was.   Of it Paul says: "And by reason of the exceeding greatness of the revelations, that I should not be exalted
overmuch, there was given to me a thorn in the flesh, a messenger of Satan to buffet me, that I should not be exalted
overmuch. Concerning this thing I besought the Lord thrice,
that it might depart from me. And he hath said unto me, My
grace is sufficient for thee: for my power is made perfect in
weakness.   Most gladly therefore will I rather glory in my
weaknesses, that the power of Christ may rest upon me." (2
Cor. 12: 7-9.)   I take it that this refers to some fleshly weakness of Paul.

**14 and that which was a temptation to you in my flesh ye
despised not, nor rejected;**—There seems to have been a
temptation which grew out of the infirmity.   It was of a character that they could see and understand.

but ye received me as an angel of God, even as Christ Jesus.
—He seems to have thought they would despise and reject
him, but says, as something to their credit, that they received
him as though he had been an angel from heaven, and more
than an angel, as Jesus Christ himself. [Out of the most un-
propitious circumstances under which he had ever introduced
the gospel to a new community, there sprang up the sweetest
fruits of all his labors; for there are no other churches of
whose devotion to him he speaks in similar terms. Such experience as this illustrated to him the Lord's meaning, when
he said unto him, in answer to his prayer about the thorn in
the flesh, "My grace is sufficient for thee: for my power is

gratulation ⁵of yourselves? for I bear you witness, that, if possible, ye would have plucked out your eyes and given them to me. 16 So then am I become your enemy, ⁶by telling you the truth? 17 They zealously seek you in no

⁵Or, *of yours*
⁶Or, *by dealing truly with you.*

---

made perfect in weakness," and it was experience like this which enabled him at length to say: "Most gladly therefore will I rather glory in my weaknesses, that the power of Christ may rest upon me. Wherefore I take pleasure in weaknesses, in injuries, in necessities, in persecutions, in distresses, for Christ's sake: for when I am weak, then am I strong." (2 Cor. 12: 9, 10.)]

15 **Where then is that gratulation of yourselves?**—If they received him "even as Christ Jesus," they rejoiced greatly in his presence and spoke of it. [What had become of that spirit which animated them not so long ago? (1: 6.)]

for I bear you witness, that, if possible, ye would have plucked out your eyes and given them to me.—The manifestation of feeling toward him was such that he testified, if it had been in their power, they would have plucked out their eyes and given them to him. The Galatians were of the same nation as the French, noted for their excitability and intensity of feeling. Such people are liable to run from one extreme to another. So they had run to the extreme of denying that Paul was an apostle sent by Jesus.

16 **So then am I become your enemy,**—He had told them the truth in reference to their determination to turn to the Jewish law, and they had become offended, and had manifested feeling against him.

by telling you the truth?—Truth alone can help man. It is sometimes disagreeable, contrary to his feelings and wishes. It is nonetheless good for him because disagreeable, but he is very prone to regard him who tells him disagreeable truths as any enemy. He who tells one the truth ought to do it in a kind manner, but we should regard him who tells us the truth as a friend because truth alone can benefit man.

good way; nay, they desire to shut you out, that ye may seek them. 18 But it is good to be zealously sought in a good matter at all times, and not only when I am present with you. 19 My little children, of whom I am again in travail until Christ be formed in you—20 but I could wish to be present with

17 **They zealously seek you in no good way;**—These Judaizers who turned them to Moses and turned their feelings against Paul, aroused their zeal, but not in a proper direction nor from a proper motive.

nay, they desire to shut you out, that ye may seek them.— They would lead them away from Christ that they might serve their selfish ends. Paul denounces unsparingly those who sought to subvert the faith of Christians. (2 Cor. 11: 4-14.) [If the Judaizing teachers could persuade those who had been taught that faith and obedience to the gospel alone were necessary to salvation, that circumcision and submission to the law of Moses were also essential, the effect would invariably be just what Paul describes. They must turn to their new teachers for that assurance of salvation, which, they would suppose, the gospel as preached by Paul could not supply.]

18 **But it is good to be zealously sought in a good matter at all times, and not only when I am present with you.**—It is well to be excited to zeal in a good thing. He assures them that the zeal they showed for God under his teaching was a worthy zeal in a good cause, and he desired that they should continue that zeal for Jesus Christ and not be diverted from it as well when he was absent as when he was present with them. They were of that class of people easily led by plausible men who might be present with them. This class of people are common, and have no convictions of their own, but are led by every wind of doctrine.

19 **My little children,**—Paul spoke of those whom he had been instrumental in converting as begotten of him. "In Christ Jesus I begat you through the gospel." (1 Cor. 4: 15.)

of whom I am again in travail until Christ be formed in you—He had once begotten them, and they were turning from Christ to Judaism, and he is now striving with anxiety to bring them back to Christ; calling this a travailing with them in birth again until Christ be formed in them. To restore

you now and to change my tone; for I am perplexed about you.

them to a true faith in Christ was to have Christ formed in
them again. [Just as the undeveloped embryo by degrees
takes the shape of man, so the undeveloped Christian by degrees takes the likeness of Christ. As he grows in grace that
likeness becomes more and more defined, till at last he reaches
"unto the measure of the stature of the fulness of Christ."
(Eph. 4: 13.)]

20—but I could wish to be present with you now,—[To
adapt his speech more fully to their present condition and
wants, in this critical juncture in their spiritual history when
the future of the work of the gospel in Galatia hangs in the
balance, to use severity or gentle persuasion as may be best. (1
Cor. 4: 21.)]

and to change my tone; [He longed to speak to them with
confidence in their fidelity to the true gospel of Christ instead
of with the mingled apprehension, expostulation, and appeal
of this letter. This he could do only if they should turn from
the Judaizing teachers. He longed to be able to say to them
as he was able to say to those at Corinth: "I rejoice that in
everything I am of good courage concerning you." (2 Cor. 7:
16.)]

for I am perplexed about you.—He is absent from them;
and he is perplexed as to what he ought to think of them, and
what he ought to say to them.

6. THE LAW AND THE GOSPEL IN ALLEGORY.
4: 21-31.

21 Tell me, ye that desire to be under the law, do ye not hear the law?

21 Tell me, ye that desire to be under the law,—This is addressed to those who were inclined to follow the Judaizing
teachers, and make legal observance as well as faith in Christ
the ground of acceptance with God.

do ye not hear the law?—The law of Moses is, of course, in
this argument, the great embodiment of the principle of law.
Moreover it had a divine sanction which belongs to none

22 For it is written, [7]that Abraham had two sons, one by the handmaid, and
one by the freewoman.   23 [8]Howbeit the *son* by the handmaid is born after

[7]Gen. xvi. 15.
[8]Gen. xxi. 2.

other. It is immaterial whether we restrict the word law to
the Pentateuch, or regard it as synonymous with the Old Testament generally.

22 For it is written,—These words generally introduce a
quotation from the Old Testament; here they introduce a
brief summary of Old Testament history, and take the Judaizers on their own ground.

that Abraham had two sons,—Ishmael and Isaac.

one by the handmaid,—Hagar, an Egyptian servant, servant
to Sarah and mother of Ishmael.

and one by the freewoman.—Sarah, Abraham's wife (Gen.
20: 12), and mother of Isaac. [The article is attached to each
of these words as to persons whose history was well known to
Jews and Christians in Galatia.]

23 Howbeit the son by the handmaid is born after the flesh;
—Notwithstanding the fact that they were the children of one
father, there was a further difference between them beyond
that consequent on the different states of their respective
mothers. Abraham and Hagar were united in accordance
with natural counsels and with results after the order of nature. Sarah was aware, indeed, of the promise of God to
Abraham that he should have a son, but her own name had
not yet been mentioned in connection therewith, and assuming
that the promise was impossible of fulfillment through herself,
she planned to bring it about through Hagar, her handmaid.
(Gen. 16: 1, 2.) To Sarah's device Paul refers. From it
sprang evils innumerable, first for Abraham and Sarah, then
for Isaac, then for the people of Israel at large. God's word is
settled forever in heaven, and cannot fail of its fulfillment; but
God is not to be hindered or hurried in any. [Whoever attempts one of the other dooms himself to disaster. Scheming
and faith are mutually exclusive. He who trusts God will not

the flesh; but the *son* by the freewoman *is born* through promise. 24 Which things contain an allegory: for these *women* are two covenants; one from mount Sinai, bearing children unto bondage, which is Hagar. 25 ⁹Now this Hagar is mount Sinai in Arabia and answereth to the Jerusalem that now is: for she is in bondage with her children. 26 But the Jerusalem that is

⁹Many ancient authorities read *For Sinai is a mountain in Arabia.*

---

scheme; he who schemes makes its manifest that he does not trust God.]

but the son by the freewoman is born through promise.— Isaac was the child of promise, was conceived after both parents were past age, and his conception was of the direct power of God—not after the fleshly desires.

24 Which things contain an allegory:—Allegory means a description of one thing under the figure of another, so that the real or intended meaning differs from the obvious sense of the words.

for these women are two covenants;—They represent the two covenants.

one from mount Sinai, bearing children unto bondage, which is Hagar.—Hagar represents the covenant and law of mount Sinai.

25 Now this Hagar is mount Sinai in Arabia, and answereth to the Jerusalem that now is: for she is in bondage with her children.—Hagar answers to the Jerusalem that now is, or the present fleshly Israel, bearing children in bondage. Ishmael was born of the impulses of the flesh, while Abraham impatiently waited and lost faith in the child of promise; just as the law was added, while the child of promise delayed his coming, and served as the tutor to bring them to Christ. [We should not overlook the distinction that Paul draws between the two Israels, a spiritual Israel which embraces all obedient believers in Christ, whether of the circumcision or of the uncircumcision, and is the true heir of the promise, and the carnal Israel, which has only the circumcision of the flesh, and not of the heart, which is of the blood, but not of the faith of Abraham, and is cast out like Hagar and Ishmael. (Rom. 4: 12-17; 9: 6-9.)]

above is free, which is our mother. 27 For it is written,

---

26 **But the Jerusalem that is above is free,**—Sarah, the freewoman, mount Zion, or the Jerusalem which is above—the
church of God. [Sarah, with Isaac, born in fulfillment of a
promise, points to the heavenly, the ideal Jerusalem with its
inhabitants, under no control of this world; and these in turn
point to those Jews and Gentiles who have trusted Christ and
who are free from the law in him; for the law of the Spirit of
life in Christ Jesus makes free from the law of sin and of
death. (Rom. 8 : 2.)]

which is our mother.—She, this church of God, is the
mother of all true Christians. [This language is, of course,
figurative, and forms a basis for what is said of Abraham,
when it is declared that "he looked for the city which hath the
foundations, whose builder and maker is God." (Heb. 11 : 10,
16.) And it is further declared that believers in Christ "are
come unto mount Zion, and unto the city of the living God,
the heavenly Jerusalem." But while, spiritually and poten-
tially, obedient believers have already come to that city, yet,
and indeed, on this account, they have here no permanent
dwelling place, they "seek after the city which is to come."
(13 : 14.) To the church in Philadelphia the Lord said: "He
that overcometh, I will make him a pillar in the temple of my
God, and he shall go out thence no more: and I will write
upon him the name of my God, and the name of the city of my
God, the new Jerusalem, which cometh down out of heaven
from my God, and mine own new name." (Rev. 3 : 12, 13.)
And before the close of the vision, John sees the city descending, and is invited to a closer view of it under the guidance of
the angel. (21 : 2, 9, 10.) The city exhibits the hosts of the
redeemed in the renewed conditions of life when the purposes
of God have been accomplished and all things have been made
new. (21 : 5.) To this figure of an ideal city the language of
Paul conforms: "For our citizenship is in heaven; whence also
we wait for a Saviour, the Lord Jesus Christ: who shall fashion anew the body of our humiliation, that it may be conformed to the body of his glory, according to the working

¹⁰Rejoice, thou barren that bearest not;
Break forth and cry, thou that travailest not:
For more are the children of the desolate than of her that hath the
    husband.
28 Now ¹¹we, brethren, as Isaac was, are children of promise. 29 But as

---

¹⁰Is. liv. 1.
¹¹Many ancient authorities read *ye*.

---

whereby he is able even to subject all things unto himself."
(Phil. 3: 20, 21.) That city of God is dominated by the powers of the age to come, the same powers that work in the believer now for his establishment in holiness and love.]

**27 For it is written, Rejoice, thou barren that bearest not;
Break forth and cry, thou that travailest not: For more are
the children of the desolate than of her that hath the husband.**
—Isaiah (54: 1) had foretold this state, that she who first was
barren, brought forth no children, would rejoice in the number of her children, for she would have more children than the
one that bore children. Sarah, the lawful wife, childless until
the child of promise came, had more children than Hagar,
who early bore children of the flesh. So the church of promise, or the promise through the seed of promise, had in these
last days burst forth and bore children not only among the
fleshly children of Abraham, but among the Gentiles not married to Christ. And there were many more converts among
the Gentiles who had not been in covenant relation with God
than among the Jews who had been.

28 Now we, brethren, as Isaac was, are children of promise.
—The Christians, as Isaac, are the children of promise. The
Jews are the children of Abraham according to the flesh.
They are the children of Hagar, not of Sarah. [Whatever privileges the Judaizers could claim as descendants of Abraham,
whatever they might hold out to others on condition of being
circumcised and keeping the law of Moses, Paul also could
claim the same. (2 Cor. 11: 22; Phil. 3: 5.) The Galatians,
being Gentiles, of course, could claim none of them. But Paul
knew that neither did his natural descent confer any advantage upon him, nor did theirs disqualify them. He, though
Jew he was, must be justified by faith, not by works of the
law, or on account of his fleshly relationship to Abraham.

then he that was born after the flesh persecuted him *that was born* after the
Spirit, so also it is now. 30 Howbeit what saith the scripture? [12]Cast out
the handmaid and her son: for the son of the handmaid shall not inherit with
the son of the freewoman. 31 Wherefore, brethren, we are not children of a
handmaid, but of the freewoman.

[12]Gen. xxi. 10, 12.

They, Gentiles, though they were, could be justified through
faith, impossible as it was claimed by the Judaizers. (Rom.
3 : 30.) Thus he and they alike were children of God in virtue
of the promise to Abraham, which promise had received its
pledge of fulfillment in the brith of Isaac. (3 : 6, 7.)]

29 **But as then he that was born after the flesh persecuted
him that was born after the Spirit, so also it is now.**—Ishmael
persecuted Isaac. (Gen. 21 : 9.) It is likely that Ishmael denied the birthright, Isaac claimed that he himself was the
first-born, Sarah saw and heard it and said to Abraham: "Cast
out this handmaid and her son: for the son of this handmaid
shall not be heir with my son, even with Isaac." (Gen. 21 : 10.)
While Ishmael was the older, he, as not the child of promise,
was not the lawful child.

30 **Howbeit what saith the scripture? Cast out the handmaid and her son: for the son of the handmaid shall not inherit with the son of the freewoman.**—The slave woman must
be cast out to give place to the lawful wife. The covenant of
Sinai must be done away, taken out of the way to give place
to the covenant made with Abraham and his seed, which the
law, given afterward, could not annul, and which had its fulfillment in Christ. Which means that the law of Sinai, the
law of works, the law written on the tables of stone were
taken out of the way and superseded by the law of faith, the
law written in the tables of the heart, that are spiritual and
eternal in their character.

31 **Wherefore, brethren, we are not children of a handmaid,**
—The apostle having fully established the difference between
the law and grace, flesh and spirit, bondage and freedom, and
their incompatibility one with another, now makes direct application of the inference drawn from the allegory, which is
that the inheritance is given by promise, to faith, and cannot
be obtained by work done in obedience to the law.

but of the freewoman.—There may be many slaves, but one true wife, one freewoman. So there are many ways along which men seek acceptance with God, there is but one of his appointment, and by it alone men may draw near to him.

SECTION THREE.

HORTATORY ENFORCEMENT OF DUTIES CONNECTED WITH THE POSSESSION OF CHRISTIAN FREEDOM.
5: 1 to 6: 18.

1. ENSLAVEMENT TO THE LAW THROUGH CIRCUMCISION INVOLVES A PRACTICAL ABANDONMENT OF CHRIST AND THE GOSPEL.
5: 1-12.

1 For freedom did Christ set us free: stand fast therefore, and be not entangled again in a yoke of bondage.

---

1 **For freedom did Christ set us free:**—Paul has shown that the services of the law were a system of bondage, of slavery, and that in and by Christ they were freed from that bondage. He therefore admonishes them to stand fast in the liberty or freedom from the Jewish law which Christ had fulfilled and taken out of the way. So they were freed from obligations to observe that law.

stand fast therefore, and be not entangled again in a yoke of bondage.—The Judaizers sought to induce them to turn to the law and observe its requirements. Paul exhorts them to stand fast in Christ, not to turn to the law, for it was a "yoke of bondage." Peter on the occasion of the apostles' deciding the question of requiring the Gentiles to be circumcised asked: "Now therefore why make ye trial of God, that ye should put a yoke upon the neck of the disciples which neither our fathers nor we were able to bear?" (Acts 15: 10.) It was against the danger of returning to this yoke of the law of Moses that Paul warned them to be firm and steadfast. Many misapply this language and warm against rigid obedience to the laws of the New Testament. Certainly Jesus did not die to release men from the laws that he sealed as laws at his death. . The laws of Jesus are adapted to children, not slaves. A child ought to be more zealous of the observance of the laws of his father than a slave of the laws of his master. One acts from love, the other from fear. The service of love is a joyful service; the heart, the feelings are in it. The service of

2 Behold, I Paul say unto you, that, if ye receive circumcision, Christ will profit you nothing. 3 Yea, I testify again to every man that receiveth circumcision, that he is a debtor to do the whole law. 4 Ye are [18]severed from Christ, ye who would be justified by the law; ye are fallen away from grace.

[18]Gr. *brought to naught.* Comp. Rom. 7. 2, 6 (in the Gr.).

---

fear is a burdensome, unwilling service. The child that does not render faithful service to the father is more reprehensible than the slave that fails to render faithful service to the master. This passage is no wise releases from the implicit obedience to the law of faith. It frees from the law of Moses that we may with a more undivided fealty obey "the law of the Spirit of life in Christ Jesus."

2 **Behold, I Paul say unto you, that, if ye receive circumcision, Christ will profit you nothing.**—This does not mean that it was wrong for a Jew to circumcise his children. If circumcision had been forbidden to the Jew when he became a Christian, the question of circumcising the Gentiles could not have been raised. Had it been forbidden to the Jews, nobody could have believed it was required of the Gentiles. Then, too, Paul took Timothy and circumcised him. (Acts 16:3.) But circumcision was the sign between the Jewish people and God. It was the pledge of the Jews to observe the law of Moses. When the Jew was delivered from the law of Moses it might be perpetuated as a national mark; but for a Gentile to be circumcised was a pledge that he would obey the law of Moses, and through that law look for divine blessings. To a man who did this, Christ could bring no blessing. He blessed by taking the law out of the way and putting them under the grace of God. (Titus 2:11, 12.)

3 **Yea, I testify again to every man that receiveth circumcision, that he is a debtor to do the whole law.**—In being circumcised they took upon themselves the obligation to observe the whole law of Moses. Circumcision was the seal or pledge that bound them to the whole law.

4 **Ye are severed from Christ, ye who would be justified by the law;**—If they did the works of the law of Moses to be justified thereby, they gave up Christ, who came to deliver from the law and give justification through faith.

5 For we through the Spirit by faith wait for the hope of righteousness. 6
For in Christ Jesus neither circumcision availeth anything, nor uncircumci-

---

ye are fallen away from grace.—To turn to the law is to give up Christ and all that came through him—is to give up justification through faith. Salvation through Christ is salvation by grace. The grace, the favor, the love of God caused Jesus to suffer and die for sinful men. The salvation that came through Christ is salvation by grace in contrast with the works they came through the Jewish law. Grace means the favor, mercy, love exemplified in the salvation brought to man through Jesus Christ. Christ is called the grace of God, as embodying his mercy to man. "For the grace of God hath appeared, bringing salvation to all men, instructing us, to the intent that, denying ungodliness and worldly lusts, we should live soberly and righteously and godly in this present world." (Titus 2: 11, 12.) To turn from the gracious plan of redemption brought to light through Christ, to the law of Moses, was to fall from grace.

5 For we through the Spirit by faith wait for the hope of righteousness.—A Christian guided and led and strengthened by the Spirit waits for the things hoped for, or promised to the righteousness that comes by faith, not for that which comes through the works of the law of Moses. The righteousness that comes by faith is the righteousness to which faith in Jesus Christ leads. Faith in Christ works by love, and leads to trusting obedience to his will. In that *trusting obedience* we are in heart, life, and character made like unto Christ, so that the righteousness through faith becomes our righteousness.

6 For in Christ Jesus neither circumcision availeth anything, nor uncircumcision;—Neither being circumcised or uncircumcised helps those in Christ. A Jew that has that faith that works by love is blessed of God. The uncircumcised Gentile that has that faith that works by love is accepted equally with the circumcised Jew, neither was in Christ.

but faith working through love.—To work through love is to work from a principle of love. If we love God, we seek to

sion; but faith ¹⁴working through love. 7 Ye were running well; who hindered you that ye should not obey the truth? 8 This persuasion *came* not of him that calleth you. 9 A little leaven leaveneth the whole lump. 10 I have

¹⁴Or, *wrought*

---

please him, do his will. The faith in God leads to the love of God because he loved us. Love to man leads us to do good to man. A faith that works by love leads one to do the will of God, and to do good to his fellow men. These two principles are conjoined by God and must not be put asunder by man.

7 **Ye were running well;**—They had made a good start, but suddenly had changed their course.

who hindered you that ye should not obey the truth?— They had received gifts of the Spirit, had miracles wrought among them; and gifts of the Spirit, enabling them to work miracles, were distributed among them. (3:2-5.) These were tangible manifestations of the divine approval.

8 **This persuasion came not of him that calleth you.**—This refers to Paul as the one through whom God called them. (1:6-11.) He modestly reminds them that he, for whom they would have plucked out their eyes, had it been possible did not persuade them to turn from the begun pathway. Paul has vindicated his apostleship, reminds them of what he had done for them; how deep their gratitude had been to him, and now he reminds them that it was others who were endeavoring to get them to turn aside from the gospel to Judaism.

9 **A little leaven leaveneth the whole lump.**—An active working principle of God will leaven the whole lump and make all good. As Jesus taught, an active working principle of error and evil will work ruin to a church. This is the lesson here taught. A few evil persons in the churches of Galatia had wrought this evil in turning them away from Christ to the law of Moses. [Evil spreads surely and rapidly, and must be opposed in its beginning it if is to be opposed successfully. It is a serious mistake to despise the day of small things whether of good or evil. (Zech. 4:11.) Just as one plague-infected person may bring devastation upon a city, so may one teacher of doctrine subversive of the gospel corrupt a whole community of believers.]

confidence to you-ward in the Lord, that ye will be none otherwise minded:
but he that troubleth you shall bear his judgment, whosoever he be.   11 But
I, brethren, if I still preach circumcision, why am I still persecuted? then
hath the stumbling-block of the cross been done away.   12 I would that they

---

10 **I have confidence to you-ward in the Lord, that ye will
be none otherwise minded:**—He affirms his confidence that
these brethren will not be otherwise minded than he has here
taught. They will accept these teachings and walk in them.

**but he that troubleth you shall bear his judgment, who-
soever he be.**—But he who had introduced the discord, turned
them from the truth, shall bear his judgment, no matter what
he may claim for himself. These perverters claimed to be superior to Paul. It is singular, or would be if it were not uni-
versally manifest, how easy it is to pervert men and churches
from the truth. From the beginning, earnest and true men
have preached the truth, built up churches, selfish place seek-
ers have come and speedily perverted them from the truth. It
is so easily done. They so soon forget their teachers and fathers in the gospel. But God intends that all men of every
generation shall be tried. None but those who can withstand
the influence to lead them away from God will be accepted.
It is true that in every age many are called, but few are chosen.

11 **But I, brethren, if I still preach circumcision,**—The persecutions which Paul endured were instigated by the Jews,
greatly because he refused to require the Gentiles to be circumcised. This is especially true of the persecutions which
arose against him in the Gentile countries. There is some ob-
scurity as to the bearing of this. Many think that these false
teachers had accused Paul of inconsistency in circumcising
Timothy and not forbidding the Jews to circumcise their children, so that he taught one way with the Jews, another with
the Gentiles, seeking to please both.

**why am I still persecuted? then hath the stumbling-block
of the cross been done away.**—If this be so—if Christ be
preached and at the same time circumcision be taught—the
preaching of the cross has ceased to be an offense ; because, as

that unsettle you would even ¹go beyond circumcision.

¹Gr. *mutilate themselves.*

said before, the chief ground of offense to the Jews was that
Paul preached that the law was done away in Christ.

**12 I would that they that unsettle you would even go be-
yond circumcision.**—It is something of a play on the idea.
They insisted in cutting off the foreskin. He would that they,
as the useless foreskin, were cut off from them. The punishment spoken of (verse 10) may refer to the action of the congregation in withdrawing fellowship from them, as well as the
approval of this act of the church by God in punishing them
for dwindling his people. No greater sin than this does God
recognize. Paul desired that those who troubled the church
in turning away from the truth should be cut off, turned over
to Satan.

2. LIBERTY IN CHRIST NOT TO BE PERVERTED INTO LICEN-
TIOUSNESS, BUT MAINTAINED THROUGH WALKING
BY THE SPIRIT AND CRUCIFYING THE FLESH.
5 : 13-26.

13 For ye, brethren, were called for freedom; only *use* not your freedom
for an occasion to the flesh, but through love be servants one to another. 14

13 For ye, brethren, were called for freedom;—He reminds
them that they had been called from under the bondage of the
law into the liberty of the children of God.

only use not your freedom for an occasion to the flesh,—
Only do not so use that liberty for the purpose of exalting the
fleshly relations of Judaism above the spiritual relations of
Christians. Or do not so use this as to give rule to the passions, lusts, and appetites of the flesh. The fleshly appetites
and feelings involve men in bitterness, wrath, and strife.
These had manifested their fruits among them in the course
pursued on the question of circumcision. Instead of following
these fleshly passions and desires, moved by love for each
other, serve and help one another.

but through love be servants one to another.—Love as a
principle seeks the good of others. In its workings it does

For the whole law is fulfilled in one word, *even* in this: [2]Thou shalt love thy neighbor as thyself. 15 But if ye bite and devour one another, take heed that ye be not consumed one of another.

[2]Lev. xix. 18.

---

good to them. Love practiced is doing the thing required in the law of God to be done. Because to do what God's law requires of us to do to man is to do to him the greatest good possible. [The love that fulfills the law is that given by the Lord: "All things therefore whatsoever ye would that men should do unto you, even so do ye also unto them: for this is the law and the prophets." (Matt. 7: 12.) This is love's law, to put oneself in another's place and to act toward him as though he were oneself. Thus will the Christian not merely work no ill to his neighbor, he will, as need arises and as opportunity offers, spend himself in his neighbor's service, for would not he have his neighbor do the like for him? This is what James calls "the perfect law, the law of liberty" (1: 25), "the royal law" (2: 8). By it is the Christian bound, and in it he finds that a life of self-renouncing love is a life of liberty.]

14 **For the whole law is fulfilled in one word, even in this:** —They desired to be under the law; here then is the sum and substance of the law, and faithfulness to the gospel would not hinder them, but on the contrary would enable them to do what the law required to be done, that is, to live according to the will of God.

Thou shalt love thy neighbor as thyself.—There are two classes of commands in the law of Moses—one embracing man's duty to God, the other to his fellow men. Man cannot discharge the duties he owes to his fellow men unless he first discharge those he owes to God; they stand first. Discharging these fits him to perform those he owes to man. Hence, he who performs the duties he owes to man must have discharged those he owes to God. The performance of these implies the performance of those. Hence, he who loves his neighbor as himself has fulfilled the whole law—these laws regulating his duties to God as well as those to man.

16 But I say, Walk by the Spirit, and ye shall not fulfil the lust of the flesh. 17 For the flesh lusteth against the Spirit, and the Spirit against the flesh; for these are contrary the one to the other; that ye may not do the

15 **But if ye bite and devour one another,**—The Galatians were of a warm temperament, quick to resent wrong and prone to imagine it. The dissension excited by the Judaizers had aroused their combative temper to a high degree, and excited a spirit of commotion and recrimination among them. [*Biting* describes the wounding and exasperating effect in which their controversies were carried on; *devour* warns them of its destructiveness. Taunts were hurled at each other; vituperation supplied the lack of argument. It bore fruit in personal thrusts and quarrels, in an angry, vindictive spirit which spread through the churches and broke out in various forms of contention.]

take heed that ye be not consumed one of another.—This state of things was incompatible with the law of love, and if continued the Galatian churches would cease to exist.

16 **But I say, Walk by the Spirit,**—The apostle here gives the general directions as to how to avoid the courses by telling them to follow the teachings of the Spirit as revealed through inspired men; cultivate in the heart the temper, the feelings that are in accord with the Spirit.

and ye shall not fulfil the lust of the flesh.—There are two distinct elements recognized as existing in man—the spirit and the flesh. The inward or spiritual man and the outward or animal man. The former connects man with God above, the latter with the brute creation below. The question is, which shall rule or control in man? The Holy Spirit through Paul says: "I delight in the law of God after the inward man: but I see a different law in my members, warring against the law of my mind, and bringing me into captivity under the law of sin which is in my members." (Rom. 7: 22, 23.)

17 **For the flesh lusteth against the Spirit, and the Spirit against the flesh; for these are contrary the one to the other;** —These two principles war against each other and without external help, the flesh overcomes the spirit, and brings it into subjection to the rule of the flesh, its lusts and passions. The

things that ye would. 18 But if ye are led by the Spirit, ye are not under

---

law of Moses failed to give the needed help to enable the
spirit to overcome the flesh. The first tabernacle could not, "as
touching the conscience, make the worshipper perfect" (Heb.
9: 9), but "what the law could not do, in that it was weak
through the flesh, God, sending his own Son in the likeness of
sinful flesh and for sin, condemned sin in the flesh," so as to
enable man to overcome it, through Christ Jesus. In Christ
the spirit of man is so helped by the Spirit of God as to enable
the spirit to overcome the flesh. "For the law of the Spirit of
life in Christ Jesus made me free from the law of sin and of
death." (Rom. 8: 2.)

that ye may not do the things that ye would.—So the flesh
hinders the spirit of man from doing what it would, save as it
is helped by the Spirit of God. There is no help for deliverance from sin save in the guidance and help of the Spirit of
God. The constant appeals of the flesh for gratification cool
the spiritual ardor and render men lukewarm in the service of
God. This cooled ardor leads to neglect of the service of God
and indifference to the salvation of souls, both of our own and
those of others; destroys our love for God and his institution
and makes us willing to substitute the institutions of men,
which we persuade ourselves are more conformable to human
wisdom, for the works of God. The tendency to grow lukewarm is universal. It was so in the apostolic age and has
been in every age and country since, and is now the besetting
sin of Christians. It is fatal in its influence in the Christian
life.

18 But if ye are led by the Spirit,—This implies an entire
surrender of the believer to the authority and guidance of the
Spirit. He is led by the Spirit through the word of truth,
which is the chart of his journey through life.

ye are not under the law.—[Not, on the one hand, because
there is now no need of its beneficial influences, nor on the
other, because it is now become an alien principle, because it
finds nothing, in the one led by the Spirit, to forbid or condemn. (Verse 23.) Legalism and carnality go together. The

the law. 19 Now the works of the flesh are manifest, which are *these*: fornication, uncleanness, lasciviousness, 20 idolatry, sorcery, enmities, strife,

---

Spirit makes free from the law of sin and death. The law was
made for the fleshly man, and fleshly works (1 Tim. 1: 9); not
for the righteous man (Rom. 6: 14, 15).]

19 Now the works of the flesh are manifest, which are these:
—They are plainly seen and may be easily recognized so
that all may know when they are following the flesh.

fornication,—Strictly speaking, fornication is illicit sexual
intercourse of unmarried persons. Adultery is a violation of
the marriage bed, or unlawful sexual intercourse with another,
whether married or unmarried. Fornication often signifies
adultery. (Matt. 19: 9.) [Fornication among the Gentiles was
practically universal in Paul's day. Sins of impurity found a
place in every picture of Gentile morals in heathen literature.
On this subject, even today, it is difficult to speak faithfully
and yet directly. Newspapers, novels, and the movies which
reek of the divorce court and trade in garbage of human
life, in things of which it is a shame to speak, are no more
fit for ordinary consumption than the air of the pesthouse
is for breathing. They are the sheer poison of the imagina-
tion, which should be fed on whatsoever things are honorable and pure and lovely and of good report. Wherever
and in whatever form, the offense exists which violates the
sexual relationship, the interdict of every Christian should be
launched upon it. The anger of Jesus Christ burned against
this sin. In the wanton look he discerned the crime of adultery. (Matt. 5: 27, 28.) The Lord is an avenger in everything that touches the honor of the human person and violates
the sanctity of the marriage relationship. (1 Thess. 4: 1-8.)
The church of Christ should wage such a relentless warfare
against all such wickedness that all such characters would
either come to repentance, or find that the church has no
fellowship for them.]

uncleanness,—Unnatural practice—self-abuse, bestiality,
and sodomy. This was common among the heathen. (Rom.
1: 24; 2 Cor. 12: 21.)

jealousies, wraths, factions, divisions, ³parties, 21 envyings, drunkenness rev-
　　³Gr. *heresies*.

---

lasciviousness,—Any kind of unchastity. There may be lascivious eyes and lascivious desires. Jesus said: "For out of
the heart come forth evil thoughts, murders, adulteries, forni-
cations, thefts, false witness, railings: these are the things
which defile the man." (Matt. 15: 19, 20.) From this we
should learn the great importance of heeding the command:
"Keep thy heart with all diligence; for out of it are the issues
of life." (Prov. 4: 23.) He thinks no evil and indulges no im-
pure and unholy feelings and keeps his life clean and pure,
righteous and holy.

20 **idolatry,**—The worship of idols, embracing the idola-
trous feasts and rites of different gods and goddesses. Paul
says: covetousness is idolatry. (Col. 3: 5.) Jesus says: "Ye
cannot serve God and mammon." (Matt. 6: 24.)

sorcery,—The use of magical enchantment, divination by
supposed assistance of evil spirits, witchcraft. The practice of
sorcery was extensive and its powers great in many places
visited by Paul. (Acts 19: 19.)

enmities,—The qualities which make enemies—hatred, ill
will. [These are private hatreds or family feuds, which break
out openly in strife.]

strife,—Acts of contention to which enmities lead. [This is
seen in church troubles, when men take opposite sides, not so
much from different convictions, as from personal dislike and
the disposition to thwart an opponent.]

jealousies,—Painful feelings, anxious fear, and unfounded
suspicions aroused in the heart over the excellences of others; unholy desires and strife to excel one another, rivalries.
Jealousies never allow one to "rejoice with them that rejoice"
(Rom. 12: 15); but, on the other hand, make one miserable.
Zeal and jealousy come from the same word, and may be used
in a good sense. "For I am jealous over you with a godly
jealousy." (2 Cor. 11: 2.)

wraths,—Wraths are the open eruption of anger, which,
when powerless to inflict injury, will find vent in furious lan-

ellings, and such like; of which I ⁴forewarn you, even as I did ⁴forewarn

⁴Or, *tell you plainly*

---

guage and menacing gestures. [There are persons in which these tempests of wrath take a demoniac form. "The face grows livid, the limbs move convulsively, the nervous organism is seized by a storm of frenzy, and until it is passed, the individual is completely beside himself."]

factions,—This implies self-interest and policy in those concerned. [It is sometimes associated with jealousy. "Where jealousy and faction are, there is confusion and every vile deed." (James 3: 16.)]

divisions,—A state in which a community is thrown by the working of the spirit of strife. [Not only is the believer to beware of causing divisions himself, he is to be on the guard against those who manifest this disposition, and to "turn away from them." (Rom. 16: 17.)]

parties,—These are due to self-will and devotion to opinions. [It does not imply of necessity any doctrinal difference as the ground of the party distinctions in question. At the same time, this expression is an advance on those foregoing, pointing to such divisions and have grown, or threaten to grow, into distinct and organized parties.]

21 envyings,—The rankling anger, the persistent ill will caused by party feuds. [Quarrels leave behind them grudges and resentments which become inveterate. Envyings, the fruit of old contentions, are in turn the seed of strife. Settled rancor is the last and worst form of contentiousness. It is so much more culpable than jealousy or wrath, as it has not the excuse of personal conflict, and it does not subside, as the fiercest of passions may, leaving room for forgiveness. It nurses its revenge, waiting for the time to come when it shall find the opportunity to give expression to its pent-up grudge.]

drunkenness,—The practice in seeking pleasure in intoxication is a remnant of savagery, which exists to a shameful extent, and is growing at an alarming rate in this country. It appears to have been prevalent among the Galatians. [A man drinks and forgets his poverty, and remembers his misery no

you, that they who practise such things shall not inherit the kingdom of God.

---

more. For the hour, while the spell is upon him, he has untold wealth—the world's wealth is his! He awakes to find that he is wretched and miserable and poor and blind and naked. With fornication at the head of this dark list, and drunkenness at its close, the description of the works of the flesh is far from being out of date. The horrible processions of sins march on before our eyes. Races of men and temperaments vary, but the ruling appetites and passions, of perverted human nature, are unchanged, and its blighting vices are with us today.]

revellings,—Revellings are excessive and boisterous festivities; carousals; taking part in or enjoying something without restraint; acting conspicuously and wantonly; giving reins to one's inclinations, propensities, or passions.

and such like;—This includes not only the things enumerated, but all of that kind. None included in this list can be omitted, and all others of the same kind are included. It is sometimes contended by worldly-minded church members that revelry does not include dancing; if not, *such like* certainly does.

of which I forewarn you, even as I did forewarn you,—He warns them now of the judgment impending over those who are guilty of such sins, and reminds them that his teaching on this subject had been the same when he was with them.

that they who practise such things shall not inherit the kingdom of God.—He acted on the principle given to the prophet of old: "Son of man, I have made thee a watchman unto the house of Israel: therefore hear the word at my mouth, and give them warning from me. When I say unto the wicked, Thou shalt surely die; and thou givest him not warning, nor speakest to warn the wicked from his wicked way, to save his life; the same wicked man shall die in his iniquity; but his blood will I require at thy hand. Yet if thou warn the wicked, and he turn not from his wickedness, nor from his wicked way, he shall die in his iniquity; but thou hast delivered thy soul." (Ezek. 3: 17-19.) Whatever may be the relation of men to the church, however their profession of faith in

22 But the fruit of the Spirit is love, joy, peace longsuffering, kindness,

Christ, they shall not, if their works are such as he has just enumerated, be admitted into the everlasting kingdom of our Lord and Savior Jesus Christ. (2 Pet. 1: 11.) Their very characters unfit them for that kingdom. Moreover they are rebels against the government of God.

22 But the fruit of the Spirit—The Spirit produces fruit by so ruling in and controlling man that it subdues and holds in restraint all the evil passions and lusts that dwell in the flesh, and develops into activity and life the germs of the spiritual life in man. There are in every human spirit the germs and capabilities of all these virtues and excellences here enumerated. They are overrun and smothered out by the gross and sensual desires of the flesh and find no development until, through Christ, the Spirit of God trains them into life and activity; restrains the passions and appetites of the flesh, and they grow and bear fruit in life and fit the character for companionship with God.

is love,—The leading principle that he puts into the heart is love, and love is, in the first instance and above all, love to God. This springs from the knowledge of God's love to man. "God is love," and "love is of God;" and "every one that loveth is begotten of God, and knoweth God." (1 John 4: 7, 8.) The man who knows this love, whose heart responds to the manifestations of God in Christ, is ready to become the abode of pure affections, and his life the exhibition of Christian virtues. For the love of the Father is revealed to him; and the love of the Son is enkindled in his soul. Love thus educated and directed by God fulfills its mission in doing what God requires to be done.

joy,—Joy lifts us above all the trials, troubles, and disappointments of time. [Love makes us capable of pain and shame; but equally of triumph and joy. Therefore the Lord Jesus, the lover of mankind, was the "man of sorrows," whose love bared his bosom to the thrusts of scorn and hate; and yet "for the joy that was set before him endured the cross, despising shame." (Heb. 12: 2.) There was no sorrow like that of

goodness, faithfulness, 23 meekness, self-control; against such there is no

Christ rejected and crucified; no joy like the joy of Christ risen from the dead and reigning. This joy, the delight of love satified in those it loves, is that whose fulfillment he promises to his disciples. (John 15: 8-11.) Such joys the selfish heart never knows; heaven's highest favors fail to bring it joy. But of all the joys love gives to life, that is the deepest which is ours when "the love of God hath been shed abroad in our hearts."]

peace,—Thus walking brings peace with God that passes all understanding. This peace we have or enjoy through Christ, because through him we obtain justification which induces it. But it is not peace in the sense of exemption from the troubles of this world; it is peace of conscience, peace of soul.

longsuffering,—Love leads the Christian to bear with the mistakes and wrongs that grow out of weaknesses, infirmities, and evil designs of others. Jesus taught that this is the pathway to happiness and true good.

kindness,—To be gentle toward all, and return good for evil. [Kindness looks to the benefits conferred, seeking to make it as full and large as possible.]

goodness,—Goodness shows a kindly activity for the true good of others. [It may be, however, that this includes the sterner qualities of doing good to others, but not by gentle means. As an illustration of this we find in the Lord Jesus when he drove the buyers and sellers out of the temple (Matt. 21: 12, 13), and his pronouncing woes upon the scribes and Pharisees (23: 13).]

faithfulness,—Trustfulness, the habit of mind which does not doubt that God is working all things together for the good of those who love and trust him (Rom. 8: 28), that seeks to realize the truth of Paul's word concerning love that it "believeth all things" (1 Cor. 13: 7). Trustfulness in our dealings with others, in opposition to suspicion and distrust. Suspicion of God, whether of his love or of his wisdom, is a work of the flesh, and so is suspicion of those around us; it darkens and

law. 24 And they that are of Christ Jesus have crucified the flesh with the passions and the lusts thereof.

---

embitters the soul, hinders efficiency in service, and makes fellowship impossible.]

23 **meekness,**—Meekness is a quiet and forbearing spirit, that suffers wrong without resentfulness; but firmness and unyielding devotion to right. From this we see that true meekness goes far deeper down than any attitude towards man. It lays hold on the sovereign will of God as our supreme good, and delights in absolutely and perfectly conforming itself thereto. Blessings and good are frequently promised to the meek in the Old Testament. Noah, Daniel, and Job are models of a meek and quiet patience and forbearance with true fidelity to God. Jesus was a perfect model of meekness, submissiveness, and forbearance yet firm for right and truth under the most trying difficulties and bitter perseuctions. (Matt. 11: 29.) It is commanded as a virtue to be cherished. (Eph. 4: 2; Col. 3: 12; 1 Pet. 3: 4, 15.) [Those who learn to control their spirits, and be meek and quiet under trial and persecutions, become like Jesus, and have the promise both of the blessings in this world and in that to come. That quiet perseverance brings success in our undertakings on earth, and fits the soul for companionship with the redeemed in heaven.]

self-control;—Self-control is the restraining of all the passions and desires within the limits that will promote the highest activity of all the faculties of body, mind, and heart.

against such there is no law.—Neither God nor man makes laws against such qualities and virtues as these, because they work good to all, and ill to none. Even wicked men make laws only against such things as work evil to them or their interests. These virtues do neither. So the qualities of the Christian are such as to lead men to be at peace, and not to oppress. Through this harmless character is brought about much of the protection from the wicked that God promises to those who love him.

24 **And they that are of Christ Jesus**—They that belong to Christ in contrast with those who are under the law of Moses.

25 If we live by the Spirit, by the Spirit let us also walk. 26 Let us not

---

They are Christ's property, the gift of the Father (John 17: 6), and redeemed by his blood (1 Pet. 1: 18, 19); they are under the law of Christ (1 Cor. 9: 21); they call him Master and Lord (Jude 4).

have crucified the flesh with the passions and the lusts thereof.—[The term crucifixion here is used figuratively and not to be taken literally, as either the flesh or its passions had been so dealt with either by God or the believer himself that they had ceased to exist. On the other hand, they are still with him and in him, and ready to spring into activity again should the restraint of faith in the will and power of Christ to overcome them be removed; the believer in Christ is to make the corresponding realities good in his own life. But just as obedience which controls the body is the only evidence of faith, so the state of the believer, as manifested by his walk before men, is the only competent evidence of his standing before God.]

25 If we live by the Spirit, by the Spirit let us also walk.— Those who claim to live in the Spirit should walk in or according to the directions of the Spirit. [The walk mentioned in verse 16 is the general manner of life of the individual believer considered in itself; here it is the manner of life in its relation with others. That is an exhortation to walk boldly and firmly as guided and enabled by the Holy Spirit through the word of truth; this is an exhortation to keep step with one another in the same strength and guidance. Submission of heart to the guidance of the Holy Spirit alone secures peace to the individual and harmony in the church. He who walks by the Spirit in his everyday life is the man who, by the same Spirit, keeps step with his brethren. The obvious way of uniformity of step is that each should keep step with Jesus Christ, the leader of all. To be in step with him is to be in step with all who walk with him. Hence, in order to attain to the unity among believers in Christ each is to watch, not his brother, but his Lord and Master.]

become vainglorious, ⁵provoking one another, envying one another.

⁵Or, *challenging*

---

26 **Let us not become vainglorious,**—Do not become proud or vain of empty advantages, as of birth, property, social standing, learning, or such like things.   It is likely that the reference here is to some supposed advantages gained thereby. The teaching of the gospel is that in great and most vital respects men are on a level; that such things constitute nothing in the way of salvation, and that Christians should esteem them of little importance, and that they should not be allowed to interfere with their fellowship, or to mar their harmony and peace.

provoking one another,—Those who are vainglorious provoke those whom they regard as inferior by a haughty carriage and a contemptuous manner toward them.   They look upon them with contempt; treat them as beneath their notice, and thus provoke them; on the other hand, there is produced resentment, hatred, and a disposiion to take revenge.   If men realized, as all Christians should, that the great interests center in Jesus Christ, where all such distinctions vanish and all stand on a level, vainglorying would cease.

envying one another.—[These words describe character in its active manifestations.   Vainglorying challenges competition to which the stronger natured respond in kind, while those who are weaker are moved to envy.   Not to be sound in the faith merely, but character counts, therefore, let those who are "sound in the faith" (Titus 1: 13) be sound "in love" also (2: 2).   Of what profit to hold a form of godliness if the power thereof be not experienced in the inner man and be not evident in the daily walk and conversation?]

3. THE SERVICE OF LOVE WHICH IS DUE TO THOSE WHO
ARE BESET WITH INFIRMITIES AND TEMPTATIONS.
6: 1-5.

The apostle having vindicated his apostleship, and shown the superiority of the gospel of Christ over the Jewish law, and the ruin that must come to those who turn back from the gospel to the law, and that the blessings of the Spirit are to be

1 Brethren, even if a man be overtaken ⁶in any trespass, ye who are spiritual, restore such a one in a spirit of gentleness; looking to thyself, lest thou

⁶Or, *by*

found in the gospel and not in the law, then the works of the flesh without the Spirit, and of the fruit of the Spirit; now he tells them how Christians under the guidance of the Spirit of God must conduct themselves toward one another; and in this section how to treat the weak and erring.

1 Brethren,—[This word, describing their mutual relationship in the Lord, provides the ground for the exhortation that follows, and is introduced here apparently with the purpose of reminding them that in all their dealings one with the other, of whatever kind, must be ruled by this fundamental fact. Those who were not brethren could not be dealt with by them at all (1 Cor. 5: 12); those who were, however grave the sin, must be dealt with as brethren, in love, or not at all.]

even if a man be overtaken in any trespass,—Trespass is used of breach of the law of God, whether that given to Adam (Rom. 5: 15), or that given through Moses (Rom. 5: 20), and of laws that regulate human intercourse (Matt. 6: 14, 15). The same things are here in view as are described as "the works of the flesh" (5: 17-21); the net is purposely cast very widely. God has so ordered it, that to sin against others or ourselves is to sin against him.

ye who are spiritual,—When the fleshly passions and lusts have overcome a man and led him into wrongdoing, those in whom the Spirit rules should restore him. [The spiritual man is one who walks by the Spirit (5: 16, 25), and who himself manifests the fruit of the Spirit in his own life. The spiritual state of the soul is normal for the believer, but to this state all believers do not attain, nor when it is attained is it always maintained. (1 Cor. 3: 1-3.) The spiritual state is reached by a diligent study of the word of God and prayer, and it is maintained by obedience. Spirituality is not a fixed or absolute condition, for the evidence of true spirituality is: "Grow in the grace and knowledge of our Lord and Saviour Jesus Christ." (2 Pet. 3: 18.)]

also be tempted. *2 Bear ye one another's burdens, and so fulfil the law of*

restore such a one in a spirit of gentleness;—To restore is to win from evil, or induce him to turn from the wrong, repent of the sin, confess it, and pray to God to forgive it. Such work is not to be lightly undertaken, nor is it even to be undertaken by anyone lacking the qualification of spirituality, for it must be done in gentleness, and there is danger of falling into a sense of superiority—"I am better than thou" spirit. But it is to be done in an humble and unpretentious and gentle spirit.

looking to thyself, lest thou also be tempted.—Christians are frequently admonished to be meek and gentle in teaching, correcting, and dealing with others, especially with the erring. Paul says: "And the Lord's servant must not strive, but be gentle towards all, apt to teach, forbearing, in meekness correcting them that oppose themselves; if peradventure God may give them repentance unto the knowledge of the truth, and they may recover themselves out of the snare of the devil, having been taken captive by him unto his will." (1 Tim. 2: 24-26.) There is danger, in the very act of correcting a wrong in another, that the Spirit of the Pharisee, thanking God that he is not as other men, may be excited, which is a great sin. Then we are frequently warned against overconfidence in ourselves: "Wherefore let him that thinketh he standeth take heed lest he fall." (1 Cor. 10: 12.) The meek, gentle, sympathizing spirit which recognizes the weakness of all will most likely reach the heart of the sinner and bring him to repentance.

2 Bear ye one another's burdens,—Here the burden is the sense of weakness and shame, the sense of dishonor done to the name of the Lord Jesus, which is the portion of a believer who has been overtaken in a trespass. It is not uncommon in such case that the rest should hasten to repudiate the fallen brother and dissociate themselves from him, lest the world should suppose they were indifferent about wrongdoing; yet it may be readily discerned that not concern for the name of the Lord, but self-righteousness prompts this course. Here,

Christ. 3 For if a man thinketh himself to be something when he is nothing, he deceiveth himself. 4 But let each man prove his own work, and then shall he have his glorying in regard of himself alone, and not of ⁷his neigh-

⁷Gr. *the other.* See Rom. 13. 8.

in marked contrast to the way of men, is the law of Christ, who was at once jealous for the honor of his Father and meek and lowly in heart. "Wherefore let him that thinketh he standeth take heed lest he fall" (1 Cor. 10: 12), and with this sense of the community of danger let him seek the restoration of his fallen brother (2 Cor. 11: 29). When we see a brother overtaken in any trespass, weak and struggling to rise again, we should with genuine sympathy render him all the assistance possible. Sympathy with a man is to suffer with and for him.

and so fulfil the law of Christ.—To fulfill the law of Christ is to "love thy neighbor as thyself." (Matt. 22: 39.) Help him as you would yourself. Jesus came to bear our burdens and sins, so we must help others.

3 For if a man thinketh himself to be something when he is nothing, he deceiveth himself.—The one who approaches an erring brother should beware lest through an overconfident spirit he also falls. Within himself he has neither wisdom nor power, but is entirely dependent upon the grace of the Lord alike for his deliverance from sin, and for his maintenance in the way of holiness.

4 But let each man prove his own work,—A man can prove his own work by bringing in the test of God's word. Let every word and act be brought to this test. [Nothing is to be taken for granted in the Christian life; the scriptures provide the standard by which the believer is to test alike what he is, what he does, and what he allows. He is to prove himself (1 Cor. 11: 28), not with the hope of any worthiness in himself, but rather to reassure himself that he is in the faith (2 Cor. 13: 5). He is to find in the needs of the poor saints the opportunity of proving the sincerity of his love. (2 Cor. 8: 8; 1 John 3: 17.) He is to avoid the way of darkness and to walk in the light and thus to learn by experience what is well-pleasing to the Lord as distinguished from his own liking (Eph. 5: 10) and as he increases in love he learns from God to judge all

bor. 5 For each man shall bear his own ⁸burden.

⁸Or, *load*

things by a spiritual standard in prospect of the day of all accounts when the Lord comes (Phil. 1: 10).]

and then shall he have his glorying in regard of himself alone,—Let him bring his character and work to the test of God's word, then he will have rejoicing in himself, not in another. [Self-examination will lead to a true estimate of oneself, ascertained not by comparison with the attainments of others, but with the requirements of the law of Christ. It may result in humiliation and shame that would lead him to glory, not in himself, but in the mercy and love of God.]

and not of his neighbor.—[He will judge his own actions by the word of God, and will find as much ground for boasting as it will give him, and no more. His standard will be absolute and not relative, and the amount of his boasting will be proportioned accordingly. He will not seek to excuse himself by dwelling upon his neighbor's weaknesses, for his exultation will frequently be turned into self-abatement.]

5 For each man shall bear his own burden.—Every man is accountable to God. As said in verse 2, one may help another out of his difficulties and so assist him in bearing his burdens, but in the end he must give an account for himself. One cannot excuse himself before God because others failed to do their duty to help him. Another can help only as he enables one to bear his burdens.

4. EXHORTATION TO THE MAINTENANCE OF CHRISTIAN TEACHERS AND TO BENEFICENCE IN GENERAL.
6: 6-10.

6 But let him that is taught in the word communicate unto him that

6 But let him that is taught in the word communicate unto him that teacheth in all good things.—Those who are taught are under obligations to help the teacher by sharing with him all good things. The necessity of helping those who teach is frequently taught in the Scriptures. Those earthly things men

teacheth in all good things. 7 Be not deceived; God is not mocked: for whatsoever a man soweth, that shall he also reap. 8 For he that soweth

---

generally need are designated and are designated "goods" or "good things." (Luke 12: 19; 16: 25.) In all these, whether money, or food, or clothing, and such necessary things, the taught are to communicate with faithful teachers, share with them, and share with their reward. [This does not exclude spiritual fellowship. The true teacher counts this far more sacred, and has this interest far more at heart than the temporal. He labors for the unity and spiritual development of the church; he strives to secure the mutual sympathy and cooperation of the church in every good word and deed. He must have the sympathy of the whole body in the work or his joy will be little and the success scant indeed. The teaching of the word of God is designed to awaken this sympathetic response, which takes expression in the rendering of whatever help the gifts and means of the taught and the needs for which occasion calls. When the sympathetic union that God requires is maintained between the taught and the teacher, the matter of the temporal support of the teacher comes in as a necessary detail to be generously and prudently arranged, but which will not be felt on either side as a burden or a difficulty. Everything depends on the fellowship of the Spirit, on the strength of the bond of love that knits together the members of the body of Christ.]

7 **Be not deceived;**—Do not deceive yourselves with the idea that you sow one thing and reap another. The special aim is to enforce the duty of liberality to the cause of Christ, and to the wants of the poor; but while that is his special object, he draws the conclusion that such is our duty towards those who teach, and towards the poor, from the universal law governing our whole life here, that what we sow that shall we also reap. This he lays down as the universal law of God's government over us.

God is not mocked:—If we should think that we can sow one thing and reap another we would be thinking that we had the power to mock God—that is, defy him by overriding his plans and arrangements.

unto his own flesh shall of the flesh reap corruption; but he that soweth unto the Spirit shall of the Spirit reap eternal life. 9 And let us not be weary in

for whatsoever a man soweth, that shall he also reap.—He who spends his means and time in gratifying the flesh sows to the flesh, and will of it reap corruption. [The present life is the seedtime, and the future the harvest. He who sows grain will reap grain, who sows tares will reap tares; who sows plentifully will reap plentifully; who sows sparingly will reap sparingly. Those who keep this great truth constantly before their eyes will redeem every hour and use every opportunity to do as God directs.]

8 **For he that soweth unto his own flesh shall of the flesh reap corruption;**—He who spends his time and means in gratifying the flesh sows to the flesh and will of it reap corruption. As used here the word corruption applies to the condition of the soul. [But if a corrupted, decayed, putrefied body is a thing to be abhorred, what must be a putrefied, corrupted soul? He who sows the actions and thoughts and money and energies of his life to the flesh shall as his harvest reap a corrupted soul. The process of decay begins already on this side of the grave; and is often made visible by appalling signs. The bloated face, the restless, vicious eye, the sullen brow indicate what is going on within. The man's soul is rotting in his body. Lust and greed are eating out of him the capacity for good. And if he passes on to the eternal harvest as he is, what can possibly await him but the awful words: "Depart from me, ye cursed, into the eternal fire which is prepared for the devil and his angels."]

but he that soweth unto the Spirit shall of the Spirit reap eternal life.—To give to those who preach the gospel, to help the sick, the poor, the needy, to use his time, talent, and means according to directions of the word of God is sowing to the Spirit, and the fruit will be life everlasting.

Men often deceive themselves, but God is never deceived as to man's character or as to his ability or as to the motives that actuate him in anything he does. Self-deception is the most common phase of deception among men. This warning grows out of man's tendency to deceive himself. Many while grati-

fying the flesh imagine they are following the Spirit. Many
preachers preach for money and ease, and imagine that they
are preaching to save souls. Men often build costly houses to
gratify their pride and persuade themselves that they are doing
it to serve God. Most of life's failures come from self-deception. The divine warning is: "Be not wise in your own conceits." (Rom. 12: 16.) That is, he is to learn to distrust his
own wisdom as folly, that he may learn the wisdom of God;
for what the world esteems wise is foolishness with God. All
the provisions of human wisdom for the advancement of the
church of Christ result in evil, and not in good. The works
that human wisdom devise for good bring evil to themselves
and to the world.

There never was a time when there were so many human
helps and so much money expended at home and abroad as at
present to hold and convert the people, and yet the churches
are growing relatively weaker and are losing ground. Which
certainly shows that the Lord has taken the wise men of the
churches in their own craftiness. They have thought that
they could improve, by their wisdom and craft, on the ways of
God, and he has shown them that they bring weakness to the
churches and drive men away from God. The church of
Christ, which is his temple, is defiled, and it is growing
weaker under the addition of these human organizations and
helps. They are parasites that sap the life from the church,
while for a time seeming to add to its verdure and life.

Yet with all these warnings of God in the scriptures confirmed by the example of the destructive effects of the human
inventions, the churches and men claiming to be sensible and
to believe in the Bible follow the same path of ruin. This is
not an evil omen for the truth. There has drifted into the
churches an amount of unbelief in the scriptures. All disposition to bring human organizations into the work and worship
of the church comes from a feeling of worldly wisdom which
is foolishness with God. It is a manifestation of unbelief, and
this must be thrust out of the churches before they can be
blessed of God. It is not often that a church organization
that starts wrong ever turns. They usually run the path of
folly and ruin. Lack of confidence in the appointments of

well-doing: for in due season we shall reap, if we faint not. 10 So then, ⁹as
we have opportunity, let us work that which is good toward all men, and

⁹Or, *while*

God is lack of faith in God. The introduction of every new
society is a new declaration of distruct in God. Be not deceived as to these; God is not mocked. When a man or a
church turns from God's appointed ways to man's he turns
from God to man. But this falling away is no new experience
in the church.

9 **And let us not be weary in well-doing;**—Well-doing is to
do the will of God. To obey the will of God and do right involves us in fewer difficulties and troubles, but is more difficult, requiring self-denial, more than to gratify the flesh.
[This suggests a happy alternative to the selfishness, which is
sowing to the flesh, and presents in concrete form the idea un-
derlying the metaphor of sowing unto the Spirit. The warning is against discouragement, the tendency to lose hope-
fulness.]

for in due season we shall reap,—The season is the time of
God's appointment, and is neither to be hastened nor delayed
by the act of any of his creatures. The reference is to the relation between the seedtime and harvest; it carries on the idea
of sowing. The reaping is related to the sowing, not only in
the quality of the seed, but also in regard to the quantity sown.
(2 Cor. 9: 6.) The reaping may in some cases, but not invariably, and then only in a limited way, be anticipated in this
life, but the promise will be completely and finally fulfilled
only at the coming of the Lord. (Rev. 22: 12.)

if we faint not.—This warning is against the relaxation of
the effort. This requires us to keep our hearts and spirits
alive to our responsibility to God, and to keep before us the
promise that we shall reap lest we faint and give up before we
reach the end.

10 **So then, as we have opportunity,**—[In view of the harvest and of the fact that the nature of the seed sown, and of
the ground in which it is sown, determine the character of the
harvest, the present life affords to the believer the one "due

especially toward them that are of the household of the faith.

season" for sowing; as the opportunity presents itself, let it be seized and used, for opportunities do not return.]

let us work that which is good toward all men,—As the occasions to do good come before the believer, he should be ready to take advantage of them. In the parable of the good Samaritan, Jesus teaches that he who is in need, with whom we come in contact, is our neighbor. In perfect harmony with this Paul gives this instruction—give counsel, sympathy, help of whatever kind is needed. Jesus went about doing good; as his servants we must follow his example.

and especially toward them that are of the household of the faith.—The believer is debtor to all men to do them good by word and deed. But in Christ he is brought into a new relationship, not indeed to all men, but with those who hold the same faith and share the same salvation, and who owe allegiance to the same Lord; to these his obligation is emphasized. He is not, however, to relax his efforts in behalf of all; he is to increase them in behalf of those who are in Christ.

5. FINAL REFERENCE TO THE JUDAIZERS.
6: 11-18.

11 See with how large letters I [10]write unto you with mine own hand. 12 As many as desire to make a fair show in the flesh, they compel you to be

[10]Or, *have written*

11 See with how large letters I write unto you with mine own hands.—At this point the apostle, who usually employed an amanuensis for the writing of his epistles (Rom. 16: 23), and had doubtless done so in the case of this epistle, also took the pen in hand to authenticate the epistle (1 Cor. 16: 21; Col. 4: 18; 2 Thess. 3: 17) and write the concluding words. [This led him to write larger characters than his amanuensis had employed; the size of the letters would have somewhat the effect of bold-face type in a modern book, and since Paul himself called attention to it, it would impress not only the one person who might be reading the epistle to a congregation, but the listeners also. Precisely how far he continued to use

circumcised; only that they may not be persecuted [11]for the cross of Christ.
13 For not even they who [12]receive circumcision do themselves keep the law;

[11]Or, *by reason of*
[12]Some ancient authorities read *have been circumcised.*

the large characters we have no certain means of ascertaining,
but probably to the close.]

12 As many as desire to make a fair show in the flesh,—
This gives the key to the character of the Judaizers. Their
aim was to get so many Gentiles circumcised, to win proselytes through the church to Judaism. Every Christian brother
persuaded to submit himself to this rite was another trophy
for them. His circumcision, apart from any moral or spiritual
considerations involved in the matter, was of itself enough to
fill these proselyters with joy. They aimed not at the glory of
God, nor at the welfare of the Galatian Christians, but solely
at securing their own glory and safety. Inevitably their selfishness must bring its own retribution; they also of the flesh
would reap corruption.

they compel you to be circumcised;—This suggests the purpose in view, but not that success would necessarily attend
their efforts. The question as yet undecided was: Would the
Judaizers succeed in the Galatian churches where they had
failed in the case of Titus? (2: 3.)

**only that they may not be persecuted for the cross of
Christ.—**They cared nothing for circumcision in itself; their
zeal was that they themselves might escape the consequences
inseparable from the preaching of the cross, which not only
pronounces man the sinner, the lawbreaker, but the religious
lawkeeper as well. The cross is thus an offense to the Jew
and Gentile alike. [The addition of something as a means to,
or a condition of, salvation, such as circumcision, to the free
unmerited grace of God manifested through faith, has proved
the most effective way of avoiding that offense. But to
preach a gospel without the cross is to preach what is not a
gospel at all.]

**13 For not even they who receive circumcision do them-
selves keep the law;—**He condemns them because they did
not even attempt to keep the law. He impugns their sincer-

but they desire to have you circumcised, that they may glory in your flesh.
14 But far be it from me to glory, save in the cross of our Lord Jesus

ity; they demanded an acknowledgment of the obligation to
keep the law without themselves showing any corresponding
zeal in their own ways. This obvious insincerity could result
only in intensified and extended hypocrisy.

**but they desire to have you circumcised, that they may
glory in your flesh.**—They desired them to be circumcised
that they might glory in their fleshly adherence to the family
of Abraham—converts to the Jewish nation. [There were
two reasons for this advocacy which he so strenuously opposed. The first was they thereby avoided persecution at the
hands of the bigoted Jews; the second was that they could
boast of their success in proselyting the Gentiles. Thus we
see that the motive which actuated them was not to further
their growth in the Christian life, but that they themselves
might gain some advantage out of them in the sight of men.]

[The policy of the Judaizers were dishonorable both in
spirit and in aim. They were false to Christ in whom they
professed to believe; and to the law which they pretended to
keep. They were facing both ways, studying the safest, not
the infallible way, anxious in truth to be friends at once with
the world and Christ. Their conduct has found many imitators
in men who make godliness a way of gain, whose religious
course is dictated by considerations of worldly self-interest.
A little persecution, or social pressure, is enough to turn them
out of the way. They cast off their allegiance to Christ as
they change their clothes to suit the fashion. Business pa-
tronage, professional advancement, a tempting family alliance,
the entrance into some select and envied circle—such are the
things for which loyalty to Christ are bartered, for which men
put their souls and children in great peril.]

**14 But far be it from me to glory, save in the cross of our
Lord Jesus Christ,**—Christ and him crucified are placed in
contrast with the circumcision of the Jewish law, just as faith
and the law of Moses are placed in contrast. (3: 23-25.)
Before Paul received the gospel and had seen the cross in the
light of revelation like other Jews he regarded it with horror.

Christ, through [13]which the world hath been crucified unto me, and I unto the world. 15 For neither is circumcision anything, nor uncircumcision, but a

[13]Or, *whom*

Its existence covered the cause of Jesus with ignominy. It marked him out as an object of divine abhorrence. But now this disgraceful cross in his eyes is the most glorious thing in the universe; and for this reason he gloried in it because it was the salvation of men. His love for men made him boast of it, no less than his zeal for God. The gospel burning in his heart and on his lips was "the power of God unto salvation to every one that believeth; to the Jew first, and also to the Greek." (Rom. 1: 16.) [He said this by the testimony of his constant experience. It was bringing men from darkness to light, raising them from the degradation of hideous vices and guilty despair, taming the fiercest passions, breaking the strongest chains of evil, driving out of the human hearts the demons of lust and hate. This message, wherever it went, was saving men, as nothing had done before, as nothing else has done since.]

through which the world hath been crucified unto me,— Through the gospel he had lost interest in worldly things. Paul and the world are dead to each other. The cross stands between them. [He had said: "I have been crucified with Christ" (2: 20), and that "they that are of Christ Jesus have crucified the flesh with the passions and the lusts thereof" (5: 24). The whole world was crucified for Paul when his Lord died upon the cross. The world that slew his Master put an end to itself so far as he was concerned. He can never take pride in it, nor do homage to it any more. It was stripped of its glory, robbed of its power to charm or govern him. The death of shame that old "evil world" inflicted upon Jesus has in Paul's mind reverted to itself; while for the Savior it was changed into a life of heavenly glory and dominion. Paul's life was withdrawn from it, to be "hid with Christ in God." (Col. 3: 3.)]

and I unto the world.—[The crucifixion was therefore mutual. *Saul the Pharisee* was a reputable, religious man of the world, recognized by it, alive to it, taking his place in its af-

new ¹creature. 16 And as many as shall walk by this rule, peace *be* upon

¹Or, *creation*

---

fairs. But that "old man" has been crucified with Christ. *Paul the Apostle* is in the world's regard another person altogether—"the filth of the world," "the offscouring of all things" (1 Cor. 4: 13), no better than his crucified Lord and worthy to share his punishment. He is dead—crucified to it. Faith in Jesus Christ placed a chasm, wide as that which separates the dead and the living, between the apostle and the church of God on the one side and the wicked world on the other. The cross parted two worlds wholly different. He who wants to go back into that other world, the world of self-pleasing and fleshly idolatry, must trample under his feet the cross of Christ to do it.]

15 For neither is circumcision anything, nor uncircumcision, —Being a Jew or Gentile does not affect a man's relationship to Christ. [With the Judaizers circumcision was everything. "The circumcision" and "the people of God" were synonymous terms with them. The Mosaic polity made the status of its subjects, their relation to the divine covenant, to depend on the rite. In virtue of this mark stamped upon their bodies they were members of the congregation of the Lord, bound to all its duties, and partakers in all its privileges. The constitution of the Mosaic system—its ordinances of worship, its discipline, its methods of administration, and the type of character which it formed—rested on circumcision and took its complexion therefrom. The Judaizers therefore made it their first object to enforce circumcision. If they secured this, they could carry everything; and the complete Judaizing of the Gentile Christians was only a question of time. This foundation laid, the entire system of legal obligation could be built upon it. (5: 3.) To resist the imposition of this yoke was for the churches a matter of life and death. They could not afford to yield "in the way of subjection, no, not for an hour." (2: 3-5.) Paul stands forth as the champion of their freedom and casts the pretensions of the Judaizers to "the moles and to the bats," when he says: "Neither is circumcision anything."]

them, and mercy, and upon the Israel of God.

---

but a new creature.—Every man, whether Jew or Gentile, having died to sin, and been raised in Christ, is a new creature. He is changed in faith, in heart, and in life. He has new ends and new purposes. His whole being is consecrated to the life in Christ Jesus. Paul says: "We who died to sin, how shall we any longer live therein? Or are ye ignorant that all we who were baptized into Christ Jesus were baptized into his death? We were buried therefore with him through baptism into death: that like as Christ was raised from the dead through the glory of the Father, so we also might walk in newness of life." "Even so reckon ye also yourselves to be dead unto sin, but alive unto God in Christ Jesus." (Rom. 6: 2-4, 11.) "If then ye were raised together with Christ, seek the things that are above, where Christ is, seated on the right hand of God. Set your mind on the things that are above, not on the things that are upon the earth. For ye died, and your life is hid with Christ in God." (Col. 3: 1-3.) This is all effected by obedience to the gospel of Christ.

16 And as many as shall walk by this rule,—This rule is the rule that is to govern the new creature in Christ. [This rule is the principle just stated (verse 15) that everything depends on a new creation in Christ Jesus; and the necessity of abiding in the truth and acting in harmony with it, and continue to the end in such a course.]

peace be upon them,—Peace with God and with themselves, the precious fruit of being in Christ, which the world can neither give nor take away. (John 14: 27.)

and mercy, and upon the Israel of God.—This expression sums up "as many as" in a phrase which is closely identified with the whole argument of the epistle: If ye be Christ's, then are ye Abraham's seed, and heirs according to the promise. These are the Israel of God, whether Jews or Gentiles, for "he is a Jew who is one inwardly; and circumcision is that of the heart, in the spirit not in the letter; whose praise is not of men, but of God." (Rom. 2: 29.) So that the blessing is invoked on all who walked according to the rule enunciated, and

17 Henceforth let no man trouble me, for I bear branded on my body the marks of Jesus.
18 The grace of our Lord Jesus Christ be with your spirit, brethren. Amen.

---

so, in fact, on the true Israel, not on Israel after the flesh, but the Israel of the promise and of God.

17 Henceforth let no man trouble me;—The Judaizers had troubled him by calling in question his apostolic authority, and by perverting his teaching. He had vindicated these, and set forth the true teaching of God. [He was often oppressed by the care of all the churches, and especially when any of them were rent by factions, or were in danger of being led away from the truth by false teachers. Such conditions imposed heavy burdens upon him, filled his spirit with anxiety, and would have been insuperable but for the strength which Christ imparted to him. (Phil. 4: 13.)]

for I bear branded on my body the marks of Jesus.—Marks made upon his body when he was scourged, stoned, and drawn out of the city for dead. (Acts 14: 19.) Of himself he says: "Are they ministers of Christ? (I speak as one beside himself) I more; in labors more abundantly, in prisons more abundantly, in stripes above measure, in details oft. Of the Jews five times received I forty stripes save one. Thrice was I beaten with rods, once was I stoned, thrice I suffered shipwreck, a night and a day have I been in the deep; in journeyings often, in perils of rivers, in perils of robbers, in perils from my countrymen, in perils from the Gentiles, in perils in the city, in perils in the wilderness, in perils in the sea, in perils among false brethren; in labor and travail, in watchings often, in hunger and thirst, in fastings often, in cold and nakedness." (2 Cor. 11: 23-27.) No doubt he had marks and brands upon him made because of his fidelity to Christ.

18 The grace of our Lord Jesus Christ be with your spirit, —He has exalted the spirit as above the body, the flesh, and emphasizes that he prays that God's favor may be with their spirit. [The grace of our Lord Jesus Christ is the distinctive blessing of the new covenant. It is to the Christian the supreme good of life, including or carrying with it every other spiritual gift. What this grace of God in Christ designs, what it accomplishes in believing hearts, what are the things that contradict it and make it void, Paul has clearly taught in this epistle. Of this life-giving stream the Galatians had already tasted. From this grace they were "removing" (1: 6); he hopes and prays that it may abide with them.]

brethren.—[This takes the sting out of the severity of the epistle. With all their faults, he loved them still, and the very rebuke was dictated by his deep concern and anxiety for their welfare.]

Amen.—So be it, may it be fulfilled. [It was a custom, which passed from the synagogues into the Christian assemblies, that when he who had read or had offered up a solemn prayer to God, the others in the assembly responded, Amen, thus making the substance of what was uttered their own. (1 Cor. 14: 16.)]

INDEX TO COMMENTARY ON SECOND CORINTHIANS.

Indignation, a, under a sense of wrong, 133.

Iniquity, what fellowship has righteousness with? 94.

Ink, written not with, 48.

Institution, every, that is not God's planting is a means through which Satan exerts his influence to wean man from God, 138.

Israelites, are they? 147.

J

Jealousy, a godly, 137, 167.

Jesus, the life of, manifested in the body, 64; teaching another, 139.

Journeyings, in, often, 150.

Joy, the, of the Holy Spirit, 28; Paul's, enhanced by the coming of Titus, 105.

Judæa, directions for raising the collection for the saints in, 107.

Judged, we shall be, by the deeds done in the body, 73.

K

Kindness, in, 88.

Kiss, salute one another with a holy, 174.

Knowledge, in, 88, 111.

L

Laws, does God violate his, to bless his children? 123; whatever is done by God's, is done by God, 124.

Letter, Paul's, of commendation to the church at Corinth, 47; the, killeth, 50.

Letters, that he might not seem to profit by, 132.

Liberality, the, of the Macedonians, 109; a proof of earnestness, 111.

Liberty, where the Spirit of the Lord is there is, 56.

Light, what communion has, with darkness? 94.

Long-suffering, in, 88.

Lord, they first gave themselves to the, 109; the, became poor that we might become rich, 112.

Love, true, makes one seek to deliver the one loved from wrong, 37; confirm, to penitent, 38; was

the motive that actuated Paul in his preaching, 61; unfeigned, 88; in your, 111; of God, 176.

Luke, did, accompany Titus to Corinth? 116.

M

Macedonian, to the, churches this grace involved more than an opportunity to do good, 107.

Macedonians, poverty of the, arose from persecutions, 108; gave beyond their ability, 109; the readiness of those of Achaia used to stir the, 119.

"Many," does the, refer to the majority? 37.

Marry, should a Christian, an unbeliever? 93.

Measuring themselves by themselves, 134.

Men, God controls the acts of faithful, 115.

Mercy, Paul felt that God was especially full of, to him at this time, 22.

Messenger, a, of Satan, 159.

Messengers of the churches, 117; the, had no authority as delegates, 118; receive, in the face of the churches, 119.

Ministers of Christ, are they? 148.

Ministers of Satan, 144.

Ministry, the, of the new covenant, 57; the, of reconciliation, 79.

Modernists, the reasonings of the, are puffed up against the revelations of God, 130.

Money, in handling, it is best to be on the safe side, 117.

Moses, the law of, called the ministration of death; 51, the moral laws of, were transferred to the new covenant, 53; veiled face of, 54.

Mouth, our, is open, 92.

N

Nakedness, in cold and, 152.

Necessities, in, 86.

Nothing, as having, and yet possessing all things; 91, though I am, 162.

"Now," there is a, running through the ages, 85.

O

Obedience, our, to the gospel was accompanied by rejoicing, 71; bring every thought into, to Christ, 130; when your, is made full, 131.

Old, the, things are passed away, 78.

Opportunity, the, to give a matter of grace, 107.

Overmeasures himself, 135.

P

Peace, live in, 174.

Paradise, caught up to, 157.

Parents ought to lay up for children, 164.

Parts beyond, so as to preach the gospel in the, 136.

Patience, in, 86.

Paul, the sufferings which, endured were in the cause of Christ, 23; hostility of Demetrius against, 25; the Corinthians helped, by their prayers, 26; no one ever had more of the spirit of gratitude than, 27; wherever, went there was a diffusion of the knowledge of Christ, 42; was accused of commending himself, 46; needed no epistle of commendation, 47; owed his confidence entirely to Christ, 49; preached not himself, 60; was persecuted everywhere, 63; the Corinthians longed to see, 101; was careful in handling money that no blame of dishonesty could be charged against him, 116; was not willing to handle means, save under safeguards, 117; and Barnabas were sent as messengers to Jerusalem, 118; I, myself, 127; his enemies charged him with cowardice, 128; his enemies said his bodily presence is weak, 133; forced to vindicate himself, 137.

Paul's letter of commendation is his life, 86.

Peace rests on the assurance of the forgiveness of sins, 21.

Perfected, be, 174.

Perils, in, of rivers, 150; of robbers, 150; from my countrymen, 151; from the Gentiles, 151; in the city, 151; in the wilderness, 151; in the sea, 151; among false brethren, 151.

Perplexed, he was often, 63.

Persecuted, he was often, of men, 63.

Pervert, man may preach many of the truths of the gospel and so, it as to make it another gospel, 139.

Poor, as, yet making many rich, 91; the, thoroughly in earnest can do much, 108; Jesus Christ became, to make those who accept him rich, 112.

Poverty, joy and, poured out a rich stream of liberality, 108.

Power, in the, of God, 89; is made known in weakness, 160; Christ lives through the, of God, 170; we shall live with Christ through the, of God, 171.

Powers, the, were given for their good, 173.

Prayers, the, of God's children enter into working of God's laws, 26; Paul asks for his deliverance, 29.

Preachers, the sense of responsibility is not shared by all, 44.

Prepared, the brethren went to urge them to be, 120.

Prisons, in, more abundantly, 149.

Pureness, in, 87.

Q

Qualified, who can feel, for a work of such tremendous issues? 44.

R

Readiness, if there is a, there must be a completion to be acceptable, 113.

Reason, Paul's, for taking no assistance from the Corinthians, 143.

Recompense, not for a, 92.

Reconciles, in Christ God, men unto himself, 79.

Reconciliation, the ministry of, 79; must be completed, 82.

INDEX TO COMMENTARY ON GALATIANS.